The Real Garden Road Trip

Elspeth Bradbury & Judy Maddocks

THE REAL GARDEN ROAD TRIP

ELSPETH BRADBURY
& JUDY MADDOCKS

POLESTAR

BOOK PUBLISHERS

Polestar Book Publishers acknowledges the ongoing support of
The Canada Council, the British Columbia Ministry of Small
Business, Tourism and Culture, and the Department of Canadian
Heritage.

Editing by Suzanne Bastedo.
Cover design by Jim Brennan.
Author photographs by Sophia Bella (front cover and page 215).
Cover photographs and all interior photographs by Elspeth Bradbury,
    unless otherwise indicated.
Printed and bound in Canada by Jasper Printing.

CANADIAN CATALOGUING IN PUBLICATION DATA
Bradbury, Elspeth.
        The real garden road trip
        ISBN 1-896095-35-6
        1. Gardens — Canada. 2. Gardeners — Canada. 3. Canada —
 Description and travel. I. Maddocks, Judy. II. Title.
SB451.36.C3B72 1997 635'.0971   C97-910817-9

LIBRARY OF CONGRESS CARD CATALOG NUMBER: 97-80426

POLESTAR BOOK PUBLISHERS
P.O. Box 5238, Station B
Victoria, British Columbia
Canada   V8R 6N4
http://mypage.direct.ca/p/polestar/

In the United States:
POLESTAR BOOK PUBLISHERS
P.O. Box 468
Custer, WA
USA   98240-0468

5 4 3 2 1

For
Magnus Flood
November 1965 – April 1997

We thank family and friends for their support,
and all our real gardeners across the country
for their generosity in welcoming us, at such
short notice, into their gardens.

The Real Garden Road Trip

Elspeth's Prologue

I first thought of a road trip when I received a postcard from friends on a touring holiday in Ireland. They were driving through the countryside, stopping to visit points of interest — castles, churches, whatever took their fancy — and I was envious. Quite suddenly, I knew exactly what I wanted to do. I wanted to tour Canada and visit gardens. Real Canadian gardens. Most of all, I wanted to meet the gardeners themselves, and discover why they do what they do.

If you believed what you saw in magazines, you'd think all gardens were effortless Edens. There are no signs of struggle in the lovely flower beds, no burned out lawns, no rusting tools, no slug holes in the hostas, no unstaked asters. Where are the weeds and the weather? Where are March and November?

My garden doesn't look like a magazine picture. It can't, I keep telling myself, because the pictures aren't real; they're only photographs taken from cunning angles, probably in the sweet light of a summer morning. Professionals have been paid to iron out the wrinkles. They've made the lawns look as smooth as a cover girl's complexion, and they've banished the blemishes from borders. They also seem to have banished the gardener. It's true that, sometimes, someone poses on a bench, but this confident person is dressed too well, and smiles too serenely to be true. Real gardeners are apt to fidget and frown. Yet, to my mind, the gardener is an essential — probably the only essential — ingredient in a real garden.

I'm not in the same class as one man I know whose favourite bedtime reading is an atlas, but I do love maps, and a map of Canada is a wonderful thing. I began to spend hours staring at mine. Imagine, a country with most of its population strung out along a few lines of longitude for more than five thousand kilometres as the crow flies! Where to begin? The adage is: *Go west, young man!* Being neither young nor man I thought it better to go east — to start at home in British Columbia, then gallop off into the rising sun. Besides, spring is almost over in Vancouver before the frost is out of the ground in the Atlantic provinces; it made sense to see the West Coast gardens first.

The longer I looked at the map, the more I became aware of the country's real shape. What of that vast northern hinterland, spreading up into realms of continual whiteness? Who gardens there? Someone, I was sure, but how could I reach them? I couldn't. Not without air fares, and these weren't forthcoming. Sadly, the North would have to wait for another day.

The Real Garden Road Trip

My husband, Ray, liked the road trip idea, but couldn't abandon his work to traipse about in gardens for weeks on end. I certainly didn't want to go alone. My thoughts turned promptly to Judy, my long-time friend and fellow gardener who lives on the other side of the country in New Brunswick. But I hesitated. Two years ago, we collaborated on a book called *The Garden Letters*, and the whole process was a joy. Then, just as the manuscript was going to press, Judy's husband, Tom, died suddenly, and her life was thrown into turmoil. Although she'd been coping marvellously through her grief, I wasn't sure whether she'd even consider a new venture. For a long time I dithered. Then, early in May, I took a deep breath and picked up the phone.

Judy's Prologue

"But you'll love it," Elspeth says. "We'll just drive across Canada, and talk to gardeners. Nice ordinary gardeners. We'll rent a car, stay in cheap motels. We can take a tape recorder and a couple of cameras. It'll be a breeze."

I ask how long the breeze will take. "A few weeks. Three months at the most." Three months! And who's going to pay? And how do we find all these *nice gardeners?* And who'll look after my place while I'm away?

"Kate will," she says. Kate is her daughter, the one we hold hostage on our side of the country.

So I drive to Toronto in mid-May, leave my car at my son David's house, then fly to Vancouver. I'm not sure why I'm here, but at least it's green and flowery and warm; when I left New Brunswick the leaves were still not out.

Land of Contrasts: British Columbia

Judy arrived in West Vancouver looking jet-lagged and apprehensive. I took her for a walk through the forest in Lighthouse Park, and we sat on the rocks looking out to sea. The waves and big trees were wonderfully soothing.

On the way home, more or less by chance, we met Don Graham, the lighthouse keeper, and stopped for a chat. He was pottering in his vegetable garden, a little suntrap on the rocks behind the lighthouse. Don gardened in raised beds he'd built using boards from old picnic tables. He trucked in topsoil and was now growing fine crops of squash and aubergines and peppers.

Lighthouse keeper Don Graham in his vegetable garden, a little suntrap on the rocks.

Most of the keepers canned and dried enough produce to last the winter, and as mail deliveries were few and unpredictable, they usually harvested their own seed for replanting. It was a lot of work but, as Don explained, the government employed married men — and the labour of their wives came for free. Don told us that the keeper on Trial Island, off the southern tip of Vancouver Island, spent twenty-five years terracing his rocky home and ferrying soil over by rowboat in buckets and sacks. All this with one leg. He'd lost the other in an accident at sea. The Trial Island light was now demanned (and dewomanned) and the terraces long since abandoned.

I asked Don about the future of his own light, Point Atkinson. Did he know if plans for automation were going ahead? He shrugged. It seemed almost certain. Judy was horrified. What would become of his job, his house, his garden?

What indeed?

Back home, I said, "I think we just visited our first real gardener. Not too hard, was it?"

"I'd like to sleep now," said Judy, "if it's all right with you."

For Don, gardening was a hobby. In the past, for isolated keepers up and down the rugged west coast, growing fresh produce was more a matter of life and death, and it wasn't always as simple as ordering in a load of earth. Don was full of stories about lighthouse keepers and their struggles with wicked winds, perpetual salt spray, and shortages of fresh water. He told us how they hauled up kelp for fertilizer, and composted everything they could lay their hands on.

So, our road trip didn't begin on a road; it began on foot and continued at sea — in the harbour of Horseshoe Bay. The picturesque cove scooped out of British Columbia's mountainous flank was always packed with fishing boats and pleasure craft. The village bustled with tourists; on previous visits, I'd enjoyed ambling along the sea wall, licking ice cream and watching the ferries shuttle back and forth to Vancouver Island and the Sunshine Coast.

There was no ambling this time. Armed with notebooks, cameras and tapes, we were about to conduct our first proper interview. Judy was anxious about handling her new cassette recorder. I was anxious because I'd promised Judy an interesting visit and I didn't know if the gardener would still be there. I didn't even know if the garden would be there. I'd spotted it the year before — a glimpse of yellow through the hefty underpinnings of a dock. Surely not marigolds, I'd thought — not out there, bobbing about on the water?

Speedy walkers at the worst of times, today we fairly flew along Bay Street, past the cafés and bars and through the children's playground. I was breathless when we stepped onto the long dock that reached into the middle of the harbour. We leaned over the rail and there it lay — thank goodness — a neat rectangle of flowers and vegetables, moored beside a houseboat.

The tide was low and the

The harbour of Horseshoe Bay, with William Lord's garden moored beside his boat.

A closer view of William's garden.

gangplank sloped steeply down to the far end of the houseboat. We descended gingerly, feeling awkward and out of our element among the fishy odours, the dock pilings crusty with barnacles, and the nautical trappings on the deck. The door to the cabin was open. We knocked and asked timidly if anyone was home. William Lord, harbour master, marine-construction worker and salvage operator, stuck out his head and grinned. He recognized me from last year's visit, and ushered us cheerfully through the houseboat, warning us to watch our step as we crossed the watery gap between boat and barge. Still grinning, he welcomed us aboard his garden.

He'd started it the previous year. An old barge — a float, he called it — had been gathering junk, and finally he cleaned it off, built a raised edge and ordered a truckload of topsoil. The soil was dumped on the dock above and, with his brother's help, he simply shovelled it over the side.

At first it was disconcerting, wallowing on the subdued swell of the harbour, but I soon found my sea legs. The clouds cleared, gulls swooped overhead and I started to enjoy myself. I asked if he'd been a gardener on land, and William told us he'd never done any serious gardening until now. Then he pointed to the tiny mulch path down the middle of the plot and said, with a smile, he'd put it there so he could take a walk in his garden now and then. A walk of about ten paces! This didn't sound like very serious gardening to me.

Last year, William admitted, he'd made a few mistakes.

Such as?

Mixing sweet peas with the real ones. The sweet peas had engulfed the others. It was a sunny spot and maybe he hadn't watered enough at first. Now he watered plenty. Not with sea water, of course; fresh water was piped along the dock. But the sunflower had been a bit stunted and the iceberg lettuce hadn't headed up because he'd pulled off too many outer leaves. This year the young lettuce still looked pale, and so did the chives and onions. He'd limed the soil in case it was too acidic, so he thought cold weather was to blame.

"If the chives don't come along," I said, "I'll drop some off for you." I liked the idea of dropping them straight off the dock, like the topsoil.

Marigolds featured in the garden again this year and I asked if he'd planted any other flowers. He pointed to a smattering of seedlings. Forget-me-nots, he told us. The seed had come in the mail from the

William Lord on his boat
Free Winds.

Alzheimer's Society and he'd appreciated their choice of flower. Judy was admiring the healthy tomatoes and the large crop of radishes. He pulled up some radish thinnings, rubbed off the earth and chewed on them thoughtfully. Radishes were his favourite crop, he told us. They grew in about three days and he'd seriously considered a career in radish farming. Seriously, William?

"No problems with root worm?" I asked.

"Not yet."

"Must be nice, at sea like this; no pests flying in from the neighbours' gardens."

"The Canada geese fly in," he said.

"They're a problem?"

"They trample on things. And then there's an octopus lives under the float. A real big fellow."

"Octopus?" We were startled. Well, it *was* startling to be told that a large creature lurked directly underfoot. Judy reached forward eagerly and shook her recorder to make sure it had properly noted this exciting nugget of information.

"Arms this long." William stretched out his arms. "Reaches right out of the water." He was warming to his tale. We were round-eyed and gullible.

"Good heavens!" we gabbled. "Amazing!"

"Reaches right up and grabs the tomatoes off the vines."

We stared hard at the gently rocking tomatoes, then we turned and stared hard at William.

He grinned.

And we were still laughing five minutes later, when we clambered back up the gangplank and waved our farewells.

A few days later, Judy and I were back in Horseshoe Bay, this time to take the ferry north to Langdale and drive up the Sunshine Coast to Sechelt. This small town hosted an ambitious writers' festival, and the organizers had invited us to read from *The Garden Letters*. When we arrived, we found we had time to spare between the ferry and the reading, so we decided to make a trial run to see if we could spot a likely-looking garden simply by driving around. Since we wanted to find a waterfront garden, we turned onto a narrow road that looked as if it might run down to the beach. Apart from the seaside position, we were watching for significant signs:

A general air of work in progress.

A wheelbarrow, spade or hose left out.

Some kind of greenhouse, shed or cold frame.

Compost.

Piles of rocks, gravel, sand, bark mulch, topsoil, grass clippings …

Ornaments — anything from works of art to pink flamingoes.

Window boxes, hanging baskets or plants in pots.

Climbing plants.

Ingenious methods of protecting vegetables.

Bird feeders or bird houses.

Any one of these, we felt, might indicate the presence of a real gardener, and several would mean we were definitely on to something. We didn't expect to find them all in one place, but no sooner had we turned off the main road than we stumbled on it — a perfect ten.

The cottage was unpretentious. Its garden opened onto a quiet, dead-end road, and was bright with flowers and shrubs. Yellow broom and rugosa roses, still in bud, sheltered the garden from the sea. Potentilla and variegated weigela were in their prime and a spectacular laburnum dripped with gold.

Somebody gardened the place with intensive care. They'd used beach stones to make a small patio and to edge the neatly kept lawn. They'd draped freshly dug tulips over the wheelbarrow. The door of the shed stood open, and more tulips hung drying on the outside wall. They'd piled compost and clippings behind the shed and arranged interesting driftwood pieces in front of it. Plants in pots stood on the patio, and this industrious gardener had even tucked potted begonias into the perennial border for extra colour. They'd trained sweet peas up strings at the back of the deck, and tied a climbing rose tidily against a lattice panel. Tires and plastic shelters protected young tomatoes and, to cap it all, we counted eleven bird houses and a bird feeder.

The only thing missing was the gardener himself. For no particular reason, we both assumed this garden belonged to a man.

We knocked on the door, peeped into the shed, and guiltily looked round the back of the house. No sign of him. Or rather, plenty of signs, but no him. We left, disappointed.

Frieda Matthies — a real gardener caught in the act.

After our reading, we had a few minutes to spare before the next ferry home. We decided to try again. This time, the gardener was out on the patio — a smiling, grey-haired woman.

Frieda Matthies had retired ten years earlier from an office job in Vancouver, and had worked ever since to turn a patch of stones into a garden. The stones were there because the area lay at the mouth of Chapman Creek, which emptied into the sea nearby. Frieda had spent years creating a layer of topsoil over the stony outwash. If high tides coincided with winds off the sea, she told us, the creek backed up, the water table rose, and water oozed up through the ground and flooded the garden. One year, the water had risen so high, she hadn't been able to leave her house. Driftwood logs had floated in from the beach and she'd kept one to use as a chopping block.

What a shock to think of this tidy garden under water and bobbing with flotsam! We knew that gardening by the sea had its own problems — salt, wind, and poor soil — but flooding was one we hadn't expected. Frieda seemed to take the whole thing in her stride. In summer, ironically, the garden often suffered from a shortage of water, as the stony ground dried out quickly. In her neighbourhood, they were allowed to water the gardens from 7:00 a.m. to 10:00 a.m. so she was often out early, watering. She didn't mind. "It's peaceful then," she told us. We found it hard to imagine this pretty spot anything but peaceful.

Frieda had a heart condition and said she was trying to cut down on her gardening activities. She also said that the only time she *wasn't* out working in the garden was when it rained, and then she stayed indoors and worked at her quilting instead. Her lawn looked pampered, and when we commented on it she told us, "If you're going to have a lawn you should have it nice. But my garden isn't what you'd call … well it's not like these gardens in magazines." Perhaps she was wondering why we'd picked on her. "It's really a hit-and-miss garden," she explained, "but I like it like that."

We liked it like that as well.

Judy's Journal

I'm staying with my friend Ellen in Maple Bay on Vancouver Island. Elspeth is finishing up some work at home in Vancouver and will come over tomorrow to join us. The renovations to Ellen's revamped church look great and, as usual, her cooking is superb. At dinner this evening — a fantastic meal of stuffed chicken breasts, anchovies, and slivered garlic with red pepper salad and wild rice, wine and a group of friends — one of the friends comments that a good meal is hard to find, and this is one big find.

"Not as hard to find as a good man!" replies Ellen.

Everyone wants to know how we're going to find our gardens across Canada. It's a good question. I'm not sure, really. I tell them how easily we found Frieda's place in Sechelt. Ellen wonders if we'll use a tape recorder and says she has no faith in them. I have no faith in myself. In Sechelt, I asked Frieda if she minded me taping the interview and she said, "Not if you can figure out a way to record words with a camera." I had my camera thrust into her face.

Ellen also wants to know about photographs, and I tell her they'll generally be of the gardeners — what they used to call "snaps," and probably out of focus with peoples' heads cut off. I have even less faith in my photographic abilities than I have in my taping abilities, so the photographs are mostly Elspeth's department. I remember, when I was growing up in Wales, one of the miners in the village died. His family thought he looked so peaceful in his coffin, they

wanted a picture of him, and they brought in a firm called "Happy Snaps." I hope ours will be happy snaps, too.

After dinner, one of Ellen's friends, Alice, mentions a nice garden that she cycles past each day. We arrange to go there in the morning — I think Alice wants to see me in action.

The next morning, Ellen, Alice, and I set off early to see the garden Alice spoke of. I knock on the door and explain what I'm about. The gardener, Noreen Butt, says she's just going out but agrees to give me a few minutes. "And you can walk around the garden when I've gone if you like," she adds generously. She shows me around and then leaves.

Back at the car I tell them that the owner didn't turn the hose on me and ask if they want to see the garden. Feeling like an official guide I point out a large Japanese maple that's over fifty years old. Noreen's mother-in-law, who originally lived in the house, bought it from a Japanese man during the war, just before he was about to be moved to an internment camp in the interior of B.C.

"What's that?" Ellen asks, staring up at an unusual tree growing in the middle of a circular flower bed.

"I'm glad you asked," I say, "because I have it written down here. It's a *Paulownia tomentosa* and it's growing in what was a compost heap for thirty-five years. Noreen said that one year it grew over eleven feet and some of the leaves are twenty-seven inches across."

"Strange place for a compost, in the middle of the lawn," says Alice. I explain that a swimming pool had been started there, but on the same day a small girl was drowned in a local pool. Noreen's mother-in-law said to her husband, "Don, we're not having one," and they used the hole for compost instead.

Alice has to leave. Ellen and I drive to Nanaimo to meet Elspeth at the ferry, then the three of us go a bit further up the coast to Lantzville. The plan is to find another seaside garden, and once again it's easy. We simply cruise the streets, and there it is: an extensive spread running right down to the beach, curved rose beds set in a manicured lawn, and raised vegetable plots. We're excited. We stop the car and all three of us peer out. A woman backs her car out of the driveway and drives off, smiling at us as if she's used to people admiring her garden.

"She's the gardener, I bet," says Elspeth, "and we've missed her."

I hear the sound of an electric saw so I get out of the car and walk down a well-laid brick path to a work area where a man is sawing boards. The other two follow.

"Excuse me," I say.

"Excuse me," I repeat, clearing my throat. I don't want to startle him in case he saws his fingers off. He

Joe Samarin, handyman gardener.

looks up, sees three women and immediately switches off the power. We introduce ourselves and ask about the garden, but he seems reluctant to talk about it. He tells us his wife, Barbara, is the gardener and insists that he, Joe, knows nothing. Barbara has gone to have her hair done and he's not sure when she'll be back.

I ask who makes the neat wooden edges that curve around the flowerbeds and he says he does. We admire the huge compost bin brimming with friable earth. I'd die for a compost pile like that. We ask how big it is and he whips out a steel tape.

"Fifteen foot by ten foot," he says. "She wanted it big, so that's how I did it."

Looking through the glass screen that Joe built to protect the work area from sea breezes, we see a new greenhouse surrounded by freshly dug beds. We ask who does the digging.

"I do the digging," he says, and tells us that the plants Barbara is planning to put around the greenhouse will be low-growing so they won't block the view. The view out across the Strait of Georgia to the mainland is beautiful. Beyond the rocky beach, bald eagles hunt for fish. They feed their young in the tall conifers along the shore. Joe says the locals gather seaweed from the beach, usually in November or December when it's most abundant. Some people wash it off before using it, others shred it. Barbara and Joe use it as it comes, for top dressing or compost.

To our left, there are cascade berries, which are a

Mary Bowman

Barbara Samarin planting her rockery.

Driftwood doubled as planters in the Samarins' garden.

cross between a loganberry and a blackberry, and es-paliered fruit trees. Joe helps with the pruning. In a bed to our right, there's a mixture of shrubs: weigela, eucalyptus and sumac. When Barbara decides they should be moved, he digs them up and puts them where she wants them. Walking around the front of the house, we pass a peach tree trained against the car port and Joe says he's supposed to pull off any leaves affected by peach leaf curl.

He still insists that Barbara is the gardener, and wishes we could come back to meet her. "She reads and reads gardening books," he says. "She was a school teacher but now she spends all day out here. It's her garden. I'm glad to work out here because, since I retired, I've not much else to do. She'll be re-ally upset about those weeds," he says, pointing to the only two weeds in the place.

Ellen is making faces of wonderment, and murmur-ing things like, "Perfect! He's the ultimate — the absolutely perfect — gardener's mate."

I smile at Joe. "Want to come to New Brunswick?"

"No!" says Ellen. "I get first dibs. I live closer."

He grins and asks us in for a cup of tea but we de-cline, having already taken up so much of his time.

As we drive off, I say, "I can't believe such a man exists, but he does and we've met him. See, Ellen, a good man isn't so hard to find!"

Tomorrow, Elspeth and I are off to another island.

Elspeth's Travelogue

Larry and Peggy Wick lived in North Vancouver, but for forty years they'd spent most of their weekends on Keats Island — gardening. I'd heard about them from my son, Rob, who met Larry at a bonsai society meeting.

Keats was one of those wonderfully appealing islands lying in the mouth of Howe Sound. To me, they were almost too good to be true, with their backdrop of snowcapped mountains and their forested slopes that hid rocky coves strewn with huge driftwood logs. Even their names sounded like make-believe: Hermit Island,

Anvil, Gambier, and Passage. You expected to come across a Smugglers Cove and you did, with a Snug Cove thrown in for good measure. They seemed to be straight from a story book, these islands — though not the Robinson Crusoe kind. There was little chance of finding castaways languishing on sun-baked beaches here. Palm trees, however, were a different matter.

Palms in Canada seemed as unlikely as igloos in the South Seas, and yet I was sure I'd seen palms in the photographs Rob had shown me of the Wicks' place — palms, and bananas, too. I thought you'd have to be

Peggy Wick, Elspeth and Judy walking past a stunning hedge of rhododendrons on the way to the Wicks' cottage.

slightly crazy to attempt bananas out of doors in Canada, but Larry and Peggy didn't look crazy. They looked like retired social workers, neatly dressed, energetic, bright-eyed, friendly, and fun. Which is exactly what they were.

With Larry and Peggy as our guides, we caught the ferry once again, north to Langdale. This time, we transferred to the small Dogwood Princess , and, in a gusty wind with sun sparkling and spray flying, we bounced across the sound to Keats pier. The Wicks' cottage lay on the other side of the island, near Hard-To-Come-By-Cove. Good name! There was one truck on this end of Keats but no cars, so we set off on foot up a gravel track bordered by a stunningly colourful hedge of rhododendrons. A smaller trail led past the cabins of a summer camp into the forest, where it dwindled to a rough path. I was glad our hosts were on hand to show us the way. Eventually we came to a gate in a high deer fence. More forest lay beyond, but now, through the trees, we caught glimpses of the sea again.

Among the native cedars and sword ferns, Larry had planted daphnes, hostas, and rhododendrons. He'd dug out a pool and started a grotto. It was all deep shade and mossy greens — a startling contrast to the garden that lay ahead.

The house stood on sloping rock that fell away steeply then plunged sheer to the water. The slope was terraced with six or seven stone walls, and densely planted with an astonishing assortment of exotic species. Their unfamiliar shapes stood out dramatically against the dazzle of sea and sky. The islands of Big and Little Popham lay just offshore and, beyond them, we

Larry Wick in his "republic."

could make out the hazy outline of Vancouver Island. Lantzville lay across the water; I wondered if Joe was still out there, working in Barbara's garden.

I felt as if we'd stumbled on a tiny foreign country, perhaps the Republic of Larry Land. This was obviously his realm, and as soon as we set foot in it, we were caught up in his passion for the place. There was hardly time to take in the wonderful view across the water before we were off on a tour of the territory. Peggy protested that perhaps a cup of tea … Too late! We were already up to our eyes and ears in horticulture. Apart from one flight of steps down the middle of the slope, there were no stairs between the levels. Instead, Larry used a shovel to descend — a kind of downhill pole vault. We scrambled to keep pace as he manoeuvred nimbly from terrace to terrace — and from continent to continent. He kept up a lively running commentary.

Close-up of the fronds, fruit, and flower of Larry's banana plants.

"These are eucalyptus, cordylines, and a tree fern from Australia. Those are bamboos and fatsias, osmanthus and a fir from Asia, *Crypto*-something. It colours up in the fall. *Cryptomeria japonica*? That's it! These are acanthus, olives and figs from the Mediterrranean. 'Desert King' figs do better than 'Brown Turkey.' When the fruit hangs down they're purple inside and juicy ripe. Those are angels' trumpets from South America. I winter them over in the greenhouse but it isn't heated. They're pink, white, and orange, and there were forty-nine blooms on one last year. These succulents and the cactus are also from the Americas and so is the monkey puzzle tree. It's dead. It didn't die of cold; the soil washed out from under and it dried out. I have a replacement coming along. The abutilon and the gunnera are South American too."

The gunnera was like a giant, prickly rhubarb, with leaves a metre across. And here, as we'd hoped, were the palms, large as life: fan palm, windmill palm, and a needle palm with graceful foliage. A Washingtonian palm was growing in a pot (it didn't like the rain so it went inside for the winter), and, finally — I hadn't been mistaken — there were the bananas.

Larry's enthusiasm was irresistible. By this time, I was well into the spirit of the place, and growing bananas in Canada seemed a perfectly reasonable occupation, especially if you owned a south-facing site on a sheltered bay just above sea level on Keats Island.

Larry grew a Japanese banana with the lovely name of *Musa basjoo*. Although it was one of the hardiest types, he wrapped his plants in fencing wire stuffed with leaves to overwinter them. It was hard to imagine how he accomplished this precarious feat — the trunks were at least three metres high. He was planning to experiment with other forms of insulation. I found it even harder to imagine how the garden would look with its bananas bundled up in plastic bubble wrap. During the past winter, some of the flowers and fruit had emerged before he'd removed their wire cages, so he hoped they'd mature successfully for the first time. Imagine, mature Canadian bananas! We gazed up through the ragged fronds at a hand of baby fruit and a flower that looked like a lampshade, and we were just as thrilled as he was.

Half an hour later, we were back up at the house, still tossing about Latin names and wondering if fig trees flowered. We were also drinking tea, eating Eccles cakes (an unexpected touch of British nostalgia for Judy and me), and hearing about Larry's Norwegian parents and his Prairie upbringing. An eclectic feast!

We asked about the pretty teahouse on the promontory. Had they built it themselves? Of driftwood. The various sheds built into the terraces? More driftwood. And the winch for the boat? Yes, driftwood.

"I'm a beachcomber," said Larry.

"He's a scrounger," said Peggy. "Have another Eccles cake."

"I'll spend hours with the row boat, going into the little coves, y'know," said Larry.

Larry and Peggy Wick at their teahouse on Keats Island.

This was no surprise. The garden was liberally decorated with glass floats, life belts, and cable spools.

"The boat was my best find. I informed the R.C.M.P. and, when it wasn't claimed after a year, they said I could keep it."

Scroungers ourselves, we envied the Wicks. How lucky they'd been, we thought, to land on such an idyllic location. Then we heard more about the creation of this little paradise. Their story reminded us of Trial Island's one-legged lighthouse keeper.

To build their terraces, the couple brought bags of cement by ferry from Horseshoe Bay and lugged them all the way across the island. They found stone and sand in the coves around about, manhandled it into their boat, and hauled it up from the sea. After many years of hauling, Peggy said to Larry, "We're getting too old for this," and they had a truckload of sand delivered to the pier. Of course, they still had to carry it across the island. The lack of soil was an ongoing challenge. Some they scraped out of the woods, and some they brought to the island in sacks. At first they backpacked it from the ferrry, then they improved the trail and wheelbarrowed it over until further improvements allowed them to use a small tractor with a trailer. For years, they'd hauled up seaweed and added it directly to the soil. Sometimes, they soaked it in water and applied it as seaweed tea. Water had always been in short supply and irrigation was strictly limited,

Larry catches Elspeth taking a photo.

Larry amongst his exotics — from left to right: gunnera, dracaena, fig, and banana.

especially as more and more cottagers tapped into the island's central well. Keeping deer out of the garden was a constant battle. The agile creatures sometimes outwitted the defences, and they'd even eaten rhubarb.

This garden, like most real gardens, had little to do with luck, and a lot to do with persistence and plain hard slog.

"Oh, it's Larry's doing," Peggy told us modestly. "I'm just the helper."

Quite a coincidence — meeting two perfect gardener's mates in two days!

Before we left, Larry told us that the Pacific North West Palm and Exotic Plant Society was planning to visit the island.

"I'm going to build more steps between the terraces before they come," he said.

I tried to estimate the number of steps required, the number of man-hours needed to assemble the materials and the number of woman-hours needed to help, and I felt exhausted before I'd even reached the building part. I asked when the Exotic Plant Society's visit was due.

"In three weeks," said Larry.

Three cheers, I thought, for the world's great optimists!

It as time to move inland. We'd been asked to do another reading, this time for a group in Whistler, north of Vancouver. Verity, a friend who'd just built a new house there, invited us to stay the night. By this time, we'd seen several seaside gardens and we were ready for mountains. What better place to look for mountain gardeners than in a famous ski resort?

Judy's Journal

There's been a landslide and the road to Whistler is blocked but may be open by mid-afternoon. We decide to risk it. The two-hour drive will be more like three with Elspeth at the wheel, so I drive. This is my first experience of the Sea to Sky Highway. On one side, massive rock faces look as if they could let go at any minute; on the other side, islands float in the mirrored sea of Howe Sound and, between the sea and the mountains, a road turns and twists like a line drawn in black marker.

"You'll get carsick?" Elspeth asks.

"Probably," I say.

"Try not to … "

I explain it's only when I'm hot that I get really dizzy (and to think I used to play tennis in Texas in the blistering heat). Elspeth says the sun makes her feel faint. We'll be a fine pair looking at gardens in the heat of the Prairies, Elspeth flat on her face in the petunias and me going around like a chicken with the staggers. What a disaster!

Road signs jump out at us saying: SLIDE AREA, ROCK FALLS, or DEBRIS TORRENT HAZARD. I am comforted by a sign announcing Furry Creek, named for a Mr. Furry, a pioneer whom I know I would have loved.

After Squamish we see the slide. The whole rock face has fallen across the road, and men in hard hats are using massive machinery to fashion a new road around the rubble. The new road seems to hang precariously over the side of the canyon.

"There are boulders up there as big as houses," Elspeth says, craning her neck. "Just look! No, no! Don't look! Not you! Keep your eyes on the road!"

At last we make it to Whistler. I find it is a strange place; everything's new. Is it trying to be a Swiss ski resort? Enormous log houses sit cheek-by-jowl. Gardening seems only a way to enhance property values.

Our audience at the reading is great and suggests a few gardens we might like to visit. By the time we get back to Verity's, we're both bushed and grateful for the beautiful guest suite that is ours for the night. I admire the bed linen — dusty-rose cut-work pillow slips, sheets with satin inserts and matching dusty-rose duvets.

"What's that little red light over in the corner?" I ask, getting into bed.

"It's flashing on and off," says Elspeth. We both stare up at the flashing light. "Sit still," she says. The light stops. "Now see if you can get out of bed without it flashing." I slither across the bed like a snake over a bank. "It's flashing," she nods. "Try again, more slowly." I try a few times and feel like a limbo dancer but never limbo enough. I can never foil it. When I stand in the middle of the room and do the Highland fling, the light flashes frantically. By now, Elspeth is choking with laughter. "It's a motion sensor," she manages to say.

"Why would they have that?"

"For burglars?" she suggests.

"What if I have to get up in the night? Will everyone in the world know?" I ask, beginning to laugh as well.

"Careful! It probably picks up sound," warns Elspeth. The more we try to muffle our laughter the harder we laugh.

I crawl across the floor looking for other devices. Near the door is a panel with buttons. "Yes, it's a security system," I mouth. I add that I hope there's no armed response during the night because my only nightdress, the one I've loved for ten years, is in shreds.

"You'd better wear your coat," Elspeth tells me, "to be on the safe side."

Writing this, I'm trying to move only my fingertips.

Shirley Thompson gardening on rock in Whistler.

Verity thinks we should see Shirley Thompson's garden, and offers to drive us there. Most of Whistler's gardeners are beginners, but Shirley is an experienced gardener who retired to the area seven years ago from Vancouver.

The house is chalet style and sits on an outcrop of rock. Shirley has, sensibly, planted the front garden with low-growing plants, like bearberry, that survive in exposed positions with little soil. Going through her gate into the small, fenced back garden is quite a surprise. I get an overwhelming impression of deep, green forest. Here there are large pine, hemlock, Douglas fir, and silver fir.

We wake to the sound of Canada geese flying by and the news of another landslide. Scalers are climbing up the rock face and setting charges to bring unsafe areas of mountain down. So once more the road is closed, this time for an indefinite period. The only other way back to Vancouver is through the mountains — an eight-hour drive. But first we have gardens to visit.

"The silver fir," Shirley tells us, "is the true fir. See, it has the upright cones." She speaks in a gentle, modulated way, telling us that most of the gardening she does here is experimental because the climate is unpredictable. Light falls through gaps in the trees, on narrow paths, and on small beds that contain a mixture of native and introduced plants, all shade-tolerant. The smell of damp pine needles is pungent as we scuff our way through primula, anemone, pipsissewa, bunchberry, and lily-of-the-valley.

"It's not what I'm used to," she says. "The winters

are cold and I sometimes wonder if spring will ever come."

I ask if she covers the rhododendrons during the winter.

"Oh, yes, my husband built shelters for them, plywood A-frames that we store at the back of the garden. They're heavy, so we try to take them off before the thaw because then we can slide them over the snow."

The snow in Whistler is good for skiing, but heavy dumps of it falling from big trees can rip small trees or shrubs in half. Shirley shows us the remaining fifty percent of her Japanese maple.

"We're up against a number of things here as well as climate," she says. "There's not much soil and it's very acidic. We've trucked in topsoil and we have to add lime for introduced plants such as the lilac. Then there are the raccoons, cats, squirrels, and bears."

"Bears!"

"Oh yes. They're often around."

"By the way," says Elspeth casually, peering into the dark recesses of the garden, "what do we do if we meet one?"

"Don't look it in the eye," Shirley says. "Just quietly go on your way."

"Look it in the eye!" I say.

Dee Harvey points out the berm on her property to Judy.

"I'd be too scared to look at it at all! By the way, what do they go for at this time of the year, when there's so little about?"

"People," says Elspeth.

"Well, thank you for the reassurance," I say, sidling out of the garden, seeing bears behind every tree.

We hear more about bears in the garden of Dee Harvey, a young woman who, with her husband, built their house ten years ago in an older part of Whistler known as Tapley's Farm. The land was once an ancient lake bed and the soil seems much better here than where Shirley lives.

"I saw this huge bear," Dee tells us. "He was rolling around in my husband's strawberries and having a heyday. I didn't know how to get him out of there. It was very frustrating."

Dee is one of the beginner gardeners Verity told us about, but what she lacks in experience, she makes up in enthusiasm. Excitedly, she shows us a lattice arch she bought on sale; she isn't sure what to put on either side of it.

"Look at this," she says, pointing to a stick at the foot of

Dee and Judy admire the forsythia beside Dee's fire pit.

Dee pulling winter debris from her vegetable garden.

the arch. "D'you think it's dead?" We peer down at what looks to be a rose and prod and poke at it.

"It looks dead," Elspeth says, "but it may come."

"I think it's dead," says Verity. "Look at it."

"Maybe it's just resting," I add. Elspeth suggests shrubs around the arbour but Dee says she has trouble with the snow-shed. I immediately think of a shed for storing snow, but no, a snow-shed is a site where a great deal of snow slides off a roof and crushes anything in its path.

"You could put a little fence along here," Elspeth tells her, "in line with the deck. Then you'd have a definite boundary, so this part of the garden would be more enclosed. You're lucky to have those big trees at the end there."

"When a friend came to excavate for the foundation he transplanted those to the edge of the property."

"And that berm there?" asks Elspeth, looking at a long mound of earth dividing Dee's property from the neighbour's.

"My husband brought in fill. He's a truck driver and can bring it in free, and hey, it's the trucking costs that add up! A friend brought in a back-hoe and we built it up," Dee says. She looks around. "The garden looks atrocious. I haven't been out here — it's been too cold. In summer this is full of perennials. You must come back in the summer, when everything is out."

We'd love to, but right now it's time to leave. We have that eight-hour drive ahead of us. Verity takes us back to her house to pick up our car. We thank her for her hospitality and Elspeth climbs into the driver's seat. A twelve-hour drive ahead?

On the way to Lillooet, it starts to rain, but what we can see of the mountain scenery is magnificent. At one point, through a gap in a fence, I see a flock of shorn sheep looking very surprised. It is the stark white of the naked sheep against the lush green meadow that catches my attention.

We keep coming across a painted VW van reminiscent of the sixties. It accommodates three young women and a loud radio. We pass it on the uphill stretches; it passes us on the downhill stretches. In Lillooet, in a bakery, where there is help-yourself coffee, we come across the girls again and they introduce themselves: "I'm Mattie, this is Tamara, and that's Tamara too."

Elspeth gets the coffee and calls to me: "One lump or two?"

"I can't believe it. I can't believe I heard it," shrieks one of the Tamaras. "I can't believe she said it. 'One lump or two!'"

"What's wrong with that?" I ask.

"I've read English books and seen a lot of English movies, but I can't believe you really say it." She brushes her forehead with the heel of her hand and goes out still exclaiming, "One lump or two!"

Outside the bakery, two old men with canes stop to admire a tiny garden full of tall blue and yellow iris; the flowers look stately and serene, and one of the men says, "They don't deserve 'um." He jabs the earth with his cane. "They don't look after 'um and they come back better each year. They're flags, that's what they are. Flags."

"Flags are they, then?" says the other. "Flags?"

"Yup, they're flags all right."

"I thought they were iris."

I say to Elspeth, "I wonder if that will happen to my garden — that it'll be better this year, because I'm not there to look after it."

"I bet you'll be mad if it is," she says.

After Lillooet we see an unusual crop growing under canopies of black plastic. If Verity hadn't mentioned it, we would never have known it was ginseng. She had told us that it's grown for export to the Far East.

As we drive through the small town of Lytton, Elspeth screeches to a halt in front of a "No Parking" sign, jumps out and dashes across the street in the rain. She chases after a small spry figure pushing a large lawnmower along a sidewalk.

"Italian lady," she reports back breathlessly. "Elderly. She'll talk to us. Magnificent clumps of columbine and trollius. Lawn like a bowling green."

Angela Greto, who was born in southern Italy, has lived in this same house for forty-five years and has the most perfectly manicured front lawn I've ever seen.

"D'you use nail scissors for the edges?" I ask.

"I was cutting the lawn in the rain," she laughs, "because I'm going to visit my family in Kamloops

Clumps of columbine and a trim grass path in Angela Greto's side garden.

tomorrow." Between the side of the house and the street runs another strip of perfect lawn, no more than a pathway really, bordered on each side by flower beds. Angela points to the outer bed, which is dotted with small sticks. "Dahlias," she explains. "They're so slow this year, because of the cold weather." Alongside the house there are well-established rose bushes, very healthy. It must look glorious in summer, this corner lot in Lytton. At the back of the house, skirting a pear tree and a peach, is a vegetable garden with chard, endive, and green beans, but mostly rows and rows of tomatoes protected by rusty cans.

"I do a lot of tomatoes," she tells us, adding that she usually buys plants from a nursery called The Fountain of Youth, which trucks the seedlings into town every spring.

"I reckon she buys a couple of pounds of 'youth' from them too," I say, as we run back across the street in the rain. "I hope we're like Angela when we're her age."

"We're not like Angela now," says Elspeth, dampening my spirits no end.

We follow the Fraser River along narrow winding roads. Yellow daisies and blue delphiniums grow among the sparse ponderosa pines, and purple penstemon cling to steep scree slopes. The terrain grows wilder, and on our right — on my side of the car — the land drops sheer into a canyon. At one point, the road shrivels to a single lane and the yellow line leads right over the cliff, with just a few measly white sticks between us and a plunge into the mighty Fraser.

A helicopter whirs down-river at our level. I tell Elspeth the pilot has blue eyes.

Then it's onto a regular highway again, and, a few hours later, we're safely back in Vancouver.

Elspeth's Travelogue

We felt we should visit a garden in Vancouver before setting out across the country. This presented a dilemma. The city is a hotbed of gardeners; how could we pick one? We couldn't. We decided to let chance do the choosing, and chance appeared in the guise of my friend Doreen, who said we should talk to her letter carrier.

"You mean talk to your mailman?"

"I mean talk to Susan," she said. "She's a real gardener."

So we did.

We phoned ahead and set out under cloudy skies with thunder rumbling over the city. Susan's directions led us through an industrial part of East Vancouver, to a long, briskly modern building. A rectangle of land, about as wide as a carpet runner, lay between the building and the concrete sidewalk, and another, even narrower, strip divided the sidewalk from the road. There was grass on both strips — in front of all but the last unit. Here there were shrubs and flowers, pots and climbers crammed in around the doorway, flagstones surrounded by creeping plants, and, on the sidewalk itself, a chair and a table decorated with a wine glass. A young woman got up.

Susan Giardin was energetic, pretty, and camera-shy. In every photograph I took of her, she was looking modestly away. Fortunately, she forgot her shyness as soon as she started to tell us about her garden.

"Bart and I bought the condominium before it was built, and we chose this one because it was on the ground floor at the end. When we looked at the plans, I thought all I had was a little piece outside, so when I saw all this I thought, 'Wow!'"

All this? We looked at the tiny rectangles of earth and tried not to smile.

"At first there was only temporary cement along here, so I broke it up with a pickaxe and put in bags of topsoil, then the city came and dug everything up again to put in the concrete sidewalks, so I had to start over. I asked them please not to plant grass but they came back and put grass seed everywhere — in my pots — everywhere. As a kid I hated gardening, but then I got this land and now … "

She stopped in mid-sentence, bent down and patted a clump of woolly thyme. We waited. The thunder growled.

"I don't like to talk about it," she mumbled. "It's scary."

Scary, talking to us? Had we upset her? It took us a moment to realize it was the gardening, not the talking, that bothered her. She was bewildered by her newfound passion.

"I have to get my hands in the earth," she burst out. "I even come out in the rain." On cue, a few large drops of rain plopped onto the sidewalk. "Sunday morning, I crawl out of bed, put on sweats, and come right out here. People think I'm weird. Bart calls me Mole, but I can't help it; I love it. I'm learning. I'm finding out which are weed seedlings. Doreen gave me this cleome seedling and this plant over here was great. A delphinium? Is that what it is? I'm working on the boulevard now and I've been looking at books so I'm planting boxwood hedges. Looking at the gardens on my mail round helps with ideas too."

I asked how long her mail run took.

She laughed. "Depends how long I talk to Doreen. Usually I start at 7:00 a.m. and finish in the afternoon. In one garden — the owner doesn't know this — I crawl around on my hands and knees to read the labels. I like it when people leave the little tags out. Then I know what the plants are. I copy them down. There's a black spaniel called Shadow who follows me on the route and, when I'm talking to customers about their gardens, he sits there patiently until he gets chased by their cats. At the end of the round I take him home in the car. I spent twenty minutes in a yard once — deadheading. No, they didn't know.

"Bart and I went to a restaurant one night and we were sitting inside, and outside there were planters getting rained on. After about two minutes I said, 'I

Susan Giardin enjoying a good book and a glass of wine in her sidewalk garden.

can't handle it,' and I asked the waitress if I could deadhead the planters, and she said, 'You want to what?' and Bart said, 'Oh no, this is embarrassing.' And there I was, out in the rain, deadheading."

The tiny beds in Susan's garden were planted with a colourful mix of perennials and annuals. Clematis 'Etoile Violette' was climbing up the side of the door. She'd bought a blue poppy at a plant sale and I was afraid she'd be disappointed if it didn't last.

"Oh, I'm used to that. A few nights ago someone cut a bunch of flowers. They couldn't have waited till after your visit? The worst thing is to come out and find your planters gone. There are two pubs down here and

the 'detox' centre is right behind us. One night, about two o'clock, I heard something and got up. They'd taken eight planters. I chased after them in my car and was honking the horn at them — six guys, all drunk. They started to run but the planters were heavy and they kept dropping them, and in the end I got everything back. Frightened? No, these plants are my children! I have to bring this hose in every night; I string it into the house, through the living room and up the stairs to the kitchen tap at the back, but it's better than carrying twelve buckets of water every day. I had a cement cat to hold the door open, and someone stole that too. They'll take anything but usually the worst stuff. They don't seem to bother with tomatoes and peppers — I think they're afraid to eat them — but a ten-cent parsley went. If I put out something bright and cheap like plastic pots with a marigold in each, they'll take those and leave my good things."

"Decoy marigolds," said Judy.

"Yes, and I've started loading rocks into the planters so they can't lift them, and I was thinking of hanging little bells on the plants. This chair is chained down, but I bring the other chair and the table out onto the sidewalk to sit. You see that big pot with the day lily? Well, it

Susan's small neighbour checks out the sidewalk garden.

went missing, and then one of my neighbours found it lying up the road when she was walking her dog. She was pregnant and it weighs a ton, but there she was, carrying it back for me. I said, 'Don't carry that thing!' Most of the neighbours like what we're doing; you hear people saying, 'Isn't this nice!' We had a pool party out here — a kid's paddling pool — and we strung tacky lanterns across to the boulevard tree and had Hawaiian torches."

While we'd been standing around, a number of cats had been checking us out. They took themselves off as the drops of rain began to patter in earnest on the concrete. Susan told us she was owned by four cats, three of them strays. The latest one, XL (but usually known as Big Guy), thought it was fun to dig in the garden. Dogs were also a problem until Susan "got nasty" and told people to take their animals somewhere else.

The vacant lot beside the condominium building used to be overgrown, and was a hangout for prostitutes and their clients. Eventually the owners cleared out the blackberries and kept the grass mown. Susan was trying to get up the nerve to ask if she might garden some of it.

"Do you think I could plant dahlias along the fence?" she asked us.

The fence was chain-link with barbed wire along the top. Dahlias, we agreed, would be a great improvement. This lively young letter carrier was affecting the whole neighbourhood. She'd already planted up containers for her next-door neighbour, and had her eye on the rest of the boulevard. She wanted to put up hanging baskets, and said she had to have a grape vine and a wisteria. She was telling us more about her plans for the future when the heavens opened, and, as we finally drove off, she was still standing out on the sidewalk — out in her garden.

Doreen had been right. Susan was our perfect real Vancouver gardener. Even her name, Giardin, seemed appropriate. We'd asked her if she came from a family of Italian gardeners. Not that she knew of, she'd told us, but her grandfather on her mother's side came from about nine generations of farmers on P.E.I.

Judy insisted there was a gene for gardening. On the way home, she said, "That red P.E.I. soil is strong stuff when it gets in your veins." Maybe she was right. The Island, we were to discover, bred great gardeners as readily as it bred great potatoes.

But P.E.I. was still thousands of miles away, and months of driving lay ahead of us. The month of May had come and gone, and it was time to head east.

Judy's Journal

No more procrastinating. It's the beginning of June, and today is the actual start of our trip. The pockets of my skirt are still damp from a last-minute wash, but it's hot, so they'll soon dry. We pick up the rental car in Vancouver. We wanted to drive it all the way to the Maritimes, but rental companies here think there is no Canada east of Toronto. As it is, there'll be a huge drop-off charge. We thought of buying a cheap car and selling it, but were afraid the drive would be a litany of: "Can you hear that funny noise?" and "What d'you mean by 'seized-up?'"

Our rental car is a white Pontiac Grand Am. Bang up-to-date. It's the first time I've driven a car in the year of its birth. I'm thrilled. I drive because Elspeth has always driven standard shift and is nervous about switching to automatic.

Back at Elspeth's, we load in two suitcases, cameras, tape recorders, file boxes, and a styrofoam cooler packed with cold drinks, sardines, crackers, granola, and Elspeth's three bottles of sunscreen. She gives her garden one last worried look. We say goodbye to Elspeth's husband Ray, son Rob, and Moses the cat, and we're off. We're both rather quiet, wondering what we've forgotten and what lies ahead.

Our immediate destination is Aldergrove, about an hour's drive out of Vancouver, where we've arranged to meet Gail Barwick — a friend of our friends Emi and Francis, who will be at Gail's to meet us. Elspeth's navigation takes us close to the U.S. border, through lush green fields where horses seem to be the main crop. "Left," she says, "left again, now right," and there we are, at Merrimack Farm. I don't know how she does it; I'm totally without any sense of direction.

A blast from an ancient hunting horn greets us. Dogs bark and horses whinny. Never have I had such a welcome in my life. Francis, still blowing the horn, comes down the path followed by a woman with long shiny hair tied back. Dalmatians dance around excitedly and a Jack Russell pursues his own agenda.

"What a welcome!" I say, as we get out of the car. Emi and Francis greet us and introduce us to Gail — the woman with the long shiny hair — who says, "We like to put on a good show."

We walk by the stables where an enormous Clydesdale shakes his mane and snorts at us. He is introduced as Clyde. Gail tells us how much she loves horses and drag hunting.

Drag hunting? I think of drag queens. I think of horses in drag, and drag queens on horses, but I'm completely on the wrong tack. Drag hunting is a chase with horses and hounds but no fox. The scent is laid down by a rider who goes ahead, dragging a rag saturated with fox urine. The reward for the hounds at the end of the hunt is a piece of tripe. You'd think the dogs would catch on, take a leisurely stroll and loll around in the grass, but no, they run like the wind. On one memorable occasion, they lost the scent and, with the horses in hot pursuit, ran into a farmyard full of pot-bellied pigs. That must have been another good show.

Gail bought her farm eight years ago and lives there with her three children. Her son, Cameron, is in his twenties and is severely brain damaged. Her daughters, Rosemerri and Lauren, are away. As Gail shows us round the garden, it's easy to see this is a well-used piece of land. No manicured lawns or weed-free flower beds — this garden accommodates children, horses, dogs, and wheelchairs. Somehow, amongst it all, Gail grows roses — especially the roses developed by David Austin in England. Her passion for them started with a variety called 'Mary Rose,' which she planted for

Gail Barwick with plants and the Jack Russell.

Rosemerri. Gail says she wanted the girl to have her own garden, "to give her a centre of life," too.

"I like to plant roses in threes, but they come at a hefty price," she tells us. "Get out of there, Clyde!" she yells. The horse is cropping the grass too close to a rose bed. "When I ordered more, I didn't have my glasses on and, well, the bill came to over five hundred dollars with shipping. But I was so happy …

"This garden here," she says, as we come around to the front of the house, "is for Cameron. He can just see it from his window." There are tough shrubs — mock orange and honeysuckle — and more big beds of roses. It's hard for us to imagine that a month from now, it will be a flood of colour, and the fragrance … This rose is 'Fisherman's Friend,' that one is the 'Countryman.' Gail throws off the names as if they were old friends. She also points out 'Martin Frobisher,' a rose of the Explorer series developed in Ottawa. She thinks it should be named after a sea nymph instead; she's sure the human explorer never smelt that good.

Elspeth asks about Cameron. Gail explains that he had an injury when he was a week old. His heart and kidneys stopped and he was in a coma for six months. She brought him home and did everything possible to stimulate him. "Now he has two attendants and although he is still totally 'unable,' I consider him my silent partner," she says. "Never assume he doesn't hear or under-stand. Rosemerri thinks the world revolves around Cameron and we both feel enormously blessed to have him." Later, at lunch,

Judy, Emi, Francis, Gail, and Cameron in Cameron's garden, during the ceremony to christen the birdbath.

Cameron's face lights up as he listens to music, and he appears to enjoy his mother's stories.

A ceremony is planned for the afternoon. Gail has bought a birdbath and three new roses, and we are to help with the planting. We hope it won't involve anything too strenuous. Lunch is excellent and plentiful and I already feel a bit tired. Yesterday I shifted a large pile of topsoil from Elspeth's driveway. The soil was so wet and heavy it felt like cement. Gail wheels Cameron out in his chair, Emi calms the excited Dalmatians, and the Jack Russell chews on the barn.

"How about here? ... no, further over ... here? ... no, Cameron can't see it there ... here then?" We push Clyde out of the way and the digging begins. We stand the birdbath in its place. "It's tipped ... this way ... no ... that way ... that's better." We plant the roses round it and finally it's christened. Amid much laughter and the clicking of cameras, holding his antique hunting horn high, Francis pours water onto the birdbath. The water spills out, catching the late afternoon sun. The dogs smile, the horse smiles, we all smile for the photographs.

We're still smiling as we drive away, but then we're

quiet again, thinking about Gail in particular and the marvellous strength of women in general.

Elspeth wonders if I ever rode a horse. I did. I went fox hunting once. I was dolled up in all the proper gear and my mount was a sort of cart horse. I couldn't do a thing with him. We were soon up ahead of the Master of the Hunt. A big mistake. They can behead you for something like that in England. I fell off many times and a red-faced old guy kept offering me brandy from a silver hip flask. The best part of the day was the journey home. I bought fish-and-chips wrapped in newspaper, drenched them with salt and vinegar, and ate them out of my riding hat — all the way home on the upper level of a double-decker bus.

Elspeth notices the words "Westminster Abbey" on her map. This one is in the town of Mission, on the other side of the Fraser river, and we'd like to see it. We cross the river, but never reach the abbey because, on our way up the hill, Elspeth shouts, "Stop! Back up! There's a real garden!"

The fence is pink with *Clematis montana*, and a wisteria trails over the porch. The planting is generous and soft, a mix of flowering shrubs and herbaceous perennials. A sign says Hazelton Pottery. We have no doubts they're British.

They're not. Jack Hazelton was born in Canada and Haruyo is Japanese. Like Joe in Lantzville, Jack insists his wife is the gardener. They're adventurous horticulturalists, starting trees from seed and making cuttings from cast-off plants that the neighbours chuck

Jack and Haruyo Hazelton with their 'Sappho' rhododendron in the foreground.

into a ravine. Their greenhouse is unusual. Roses, a daphne, spinach, parsley, two budgerigars, and a nest of singing birds all flourish together.

Elspeth is fascinated by the variety of plants they grow and asks a lot of questions. They're excited by her knowledge. I, too, am always impressed by her knowledge. Jack points to a large-leaved tree that Haruyo started from seed.

"*Paulownia tomentosa*," says Elspeth. I saw a tree like this in Noreen Butt's garden on Vancouver Island, but the name has already left my mind. Elspeth can always remember botanical names. She says she likes the way they sound: *Paulownia tomentosa* and *Magnolia soulangiana*. The only Latin I can remember is *e pluribus unum* and that doesn't count.

We exchange one of our books for a butter dish and a coffee mug decorated with a white fern. I hope Haruyo and Jack enjoy the book as much as I'll enjoy drinking coffee from the mug.

Elspeth's Traveloque

After we left the Hazeltons, we decided to spend the night in Hope. This brought on a rash of puns. We were still singing a pompous version of "Land of Hope and Glory" as we approached the town.

"We're past hope," cried Judy suddenly, and I thought for a moment I'd missed the turning. I was taking my role as navigator seriously.

"Gotcha!" she said.

At the beginning of the trip, we'd resolved to get some exercise every day, so early next morning, we set off on foot to see the town centre and check out the local gardens. A brilliant splash of red and purple drew us immediately to a corner lot on a pleasant residential street. It was too late for bulbs and too early for annuals. What was the source of such high-powered colour? Japanese azaleas. They were massed on either side of a path which started at the front door of a single-storey house, and stopped short in the middle of the lawn. Paths like this, truncated at the property line, were disconcerting but not uncommon in British Columbia. A spade hung from a nail driven into a large tree and, among the azaleas, we noticed junipers clipped into pompoms.

The house appeared to be sleeping, so we walked on through the quiet streets to the town centre. The morning air was sparkling fresh, the mountains rose clear above the roof tops, and the sky was pearly and promising blue. We bought coffee and fruit buns at a bake shop and were looking forward to a peaceful breakfast on a bench, when suddenly a tidal wave of tourists engulfed us. They poured out of coaches and spilled down the main street, shouting and laughing. I felt like telling them to shush! The sleepy town seemed unprepared for such a racket — Judy and I certainly were.

We retreated with our goodies to a small park, where we ate in blissful solitude beside a waterfall. The park also featured stone lanterns, a simple shelter, and a plaque explaining that the garden had been built in memory of Japanese Canadians interned in camps near Hope during World War II. We remarked that Judy had already stumbled on this heart-breaking episode of Canadian history when she'd visited Noreen Butt's garden on Vancouver Island. We had no idea,

Sandra and Edward Keyes on their porch. Sandra is demonstrating how to pan for gold.

then, how often it would crop up on our journey.

We headed back towards the motel by a different route and, on the way, noticed a front porch well-furnished with potted plants, comfortable chairs, and a table covered with a cloth. It's rare, nowadays, to see a front poch looking so lived in; sadly they've been supplanted by private back patios and decks. We stopped to chat with the owner, who was pottering about with a hose, and it wasn't long before her husband emerged from the garage.

Sandra and Edward Keyes were as sociable as their porch. They told us about their move from the suburbs of Vancouver, how much they enjoyed the slower pace of life in Hope, and how at weekends they went camping and panned for gold in the Fraser River. Edward said he'd heard that, if the Fraser were dammed between Hope and Yale, it would yield enough gold to pay off the national debt three times over. Then he brought out some grit and showed us how to swirl it in a shallow plastic pan of water so that miniscule flecks of gold appeared. He picked out a few larger grains of grit and gave them to us. They were garnets, he explained, semi-precious stones. Gold and garnets, just for the taking! This mountain country must have seemed like Aladdin's Cave to flocks of early fortune-hunters — at least, to a lucky few.

We asked Sandra about the azalea garden, which was only a minute's walk

Ayako Kanayama on the stepping stones that lead to her greenhouse.

away. She knew — this was small-town Canada after all — that an elderly Japanese couple lived there. She'd heard the man was unwell, and she wasn't sure if they spoke much English, but she'd often seen the woman working among the vegetables.

Vegetables? Off we went. We'd been so intent on the azaleas we hadn't noticed the large fenced plot on the other side of the house. As soon as we saw it, we knew the garden would be worth a visit. As the official front door didn't seem to be in use, we knocked rather tentatively at the back. My first impression of Mrs. Kanayama was of a tiny, frail woman with a shy, refined manner. She apologized for her hesitant English, but had no trouble understanding us as we explained our interest in her garden. She said her husband was sick and she had to attend to his meal. We were sorry we'd disturbed them, and were on the point of leaving when we finally grasped that she was asking us to come back later.

When we returned, she was waiting for us. Her household duties seen to, she was freshly dressed in a pretty blouse, and was happy to show us around. At first, we were slow to understand her accent, but gradually, with the help of gestures and plenty of smiles, we pieced together a sketch of her life.

Ayako Kanayama was eighty years old and her husband, Shoichi, eighty-six. Her parents had emigrated to Canada, and, when Ayako was three, they had

Ayako's eye-catching azalea garden.

the distant peaks, and I had a vision of her keeping house in a tiny log cabin perched on a mountain top. Their children were now scattered around British Columbia. She didn't mention her experiences during World War II, and we didn't ask, although we thought she was probably one of the internees commemorated in the memorial park we had just visited.

Now she looked after Shoichi, and cared for their garden single-handedly. I had thought her frail; she wasn't. She was wiry and astonishingly agile in both body and mind. She was also great company, and as she led us through her garden we began to appreciate her bubbling sense of fun and a deeper sense that I can only describe as knowing.

Her vegetable garden was a textbook demonstration of devices for protecting and propping plants: poles of various heights for beans, plastic shelters wrapped around canes, and plastic sheeting used as temporary cloches or as row covers for the young corn. Everything was given individual care. The entire ground surface was cultivated. She had laid stepping stones to the door of her small greenhouse and had put down boards, in place of paths, to get around without compacting the soil — though it seemed impossible that such a slight person would compact anything. She trotted nimbly along the narrow planks while Judy and I shuffled cautiously behind, determined not to overbalance and leave giant footprints in the soft earth.

We recognized most of the crops: asparagus, raspberries, cucumbers, and peas. The spring had been so cold and wet, Ayako had planted many seeds a second time. Almost every gardener we talked to complained

sent her back to Japan to live with an uncle and attend school. She had married (if we understood her correctly) after her return to Canada. Shoichi had worked for the Canadian Pacific Railway and when he retired they moved to their present house "from the mountains." Whereabouts in the mountains? She indicated

Judy and Ayako discussing the height of the beans in the vegetable garden.

of the poor weather, but Ayako wasn't complaining. She was simply stating fact.

Other crops were new to us. Japanese radish, azuki beans, and what was this? Yama … ? Yamawhat? Yamayemo?

She giggled, and repeated, "*Yama-imo.*" Then she took us to her potting shed at the back of the garage, and showed us a seed package. It was written entirely in Japanese and there was no picture. I wasn't sure whether these were the seeds of *yama-imo*, so I copied down the characters to check later.

金町小口ぶ

Although vegetables occupied most of the property, Ayako seemed to be just as interested in ornamental gardening, and her decorative plants also received one-on-one attention. The azalea beds were carefully edged with rocks the couple had brought to the gar-den, a few at a time, in their car. A mound of earth was home to a variety of low-growing plants including hens-and-chicks, some of which were planted in pots sunk into the earth. Haruyo, the woman we'd met in Mission, had also been fond of hens-and-chicks, and had grown them through holes in a barrel full of earth. We wondered if they were a particular favourite in Japan.

Ayako had tucked lilies, peonies, and Chinese lanterns alongside the house, trained a winter-flowering jasmine against her back porch, and clipped a shrub with fragrant leaves — she called it *sansho* — into a sort of bonsai. We asked about a delicate fern we didn't recognize, and this one turned out to be a native Canadian; she had found it up in the mountains. Once again, she pointed to the skyline.

Those mountains! They kept beckoning.

We could have stayed much longer, chatting with this admirable octogenarian, but the lovely morning was slipping by. She had plenty of work to do, and we had many miles to go. We thanked her and bowed our respectful farewells — though I really wanted to give her a hug.

I offered to take a turn at the wheel but Judy seemed content to drive and was handling the car like a pro. Besides, it was better if I navigated. I'd always known that Judy's sense of direction was shaky, but I only came to appreciate her inspired sense of misdirection when I once watched her walk out of a Ladies room and march straight into the Gents.

A few minutes out of Hope, we stopped at the site of the Hope Slide, where a major rock fall had occurred in 1965. I read the information plaques while Judy tinkered with her tape recorder. Just practising, she said.

The slide had been triggered by an earthquake, and forty-six million cubic metres of rock and snow had fallen away, burying a lake and the old road. Four people were killed. Above us, the mountainside was one vast scar. I thought about the road to Whistler and about the many Falling Rock signs we'd already passed along the way, and suddenly these mountains — such symbols of permanence — didn't look so solid after all. Our human span was simply too brief to appreciate the mutability of mountains. These large thoughts were interrupted by a very small voice. I could just make out the words of Larry Wick, telling us about his palm trees. Apparently, the tape recorder was acting up.

We stopped later in Manning Park, at the rhododendron flats. Unlikely as it seemed, rhododendrons grew wild there. We were early and the spring was late, so we didn't see the shrubs in flower, but the short trail through Douglas fir forest was sweetly resinous, and we drove on refreshed. We sped over a pass, where snow still lay among the slender spruce, then down through mining towns, through a landscape showing more and more signs of summer drought, and into the Okanagan valley.

Judy's Journal

It's hot. We stop for a cold drink in Keremeos, a small town slung between steep mountains. It's ranch country, like a hilly Texas. In the café, they sell prints of cowboys and most of the men wear Western gear. Later, while we're buying cheese and fruit, I ask the woman at the checkout if many people garden in the area. Another woman waiting in line shows us her earthy hands and says, "Do we ever!" The whole store is getting in on the act.

"How about xeriscaping?" Elspeth asks, and everybody (including me) stares at her. For a minute, I think she has gone crazy with the heat and is babbling on about xeroxing. I am relieved when she explains it means gardening with drought-tolerant plants.

"Never thought of it," someone says. "Everything's irrigated. If we didn't irrigate, it'd all be desert."

As we drive off, Elspeth unrolls what looks to be a strip of felt, tears off a piece and offers it to me.

"Eat!" she says.

"What!"

"Fruit leather. You'll like it."

I do. Pretty soon I'm addicted to it.

In Penticton, we find a motel at the kind of price we appreciate. The air conditioner sounds like a chain saw, and I have to rescue Elspeth from the bathroom when the door knob comes off in her hand. Still, there's a bed (for me because I'm the driver), a sofa bed (for Elspeth), and a tea maker, but no tea. Elspeth drinks hers so weak she probably wouldn't notice the tea bags are missing, but I like a cup with some colour to it. On the way into town, I'd noticed a convenience store with a sign saying "Under New Management," so I set off on foot. I cross a bridge where swallows nest. They skim the river for insects and a grebe floats by haughtily.

The smell of hamburger from Under New Management is overpowering, but the shelves are half empty. When I ask for the tea, the girl, whose face is framed with wild, blonde hair, looks up as if I've asked for a banned substance and says she doesn't have anything like that. A group of teenagers gyrate around quite madly and others slump in easy chairs watching TV. I feel like I've wandered into a living room.

Back at the motel I start a shopping list headed: teabags. We open a can of sardines, which we eat with flat bread. We drink, alas, not tea but juice.

After this sumptuous meal, we go for a walk. At a home in a mobile-home park ("pre-manufactured home park," according to Elspeth), we see splashes of pink soapwort and purple clematis, roses, fruit trees, a small greenhouse, a wheelbarrow, and a spade dug into the earth — all good signs.

"I bet it's a woman living on her own," I tell Elspeth.

George Kobold outside his colourful garden on a corner lot in Penticton.

A neighbour comes out of his front door, carrying a poodle and chattering cheerfully. When he sees us, he stops in his tracks, looks abashed, says, "Can you believe I'm talking to a dog!" and retreats. It's too late to disturb anyone else. We'll try again tomorrow.

I have a great night's sleep. I ask Elspeth how she liked the sofa bed. "Please don't feel guilty," she says, hobbling across the room. "Really, the springs were quite a bit more springy than a bed of nails."

After breakfast of granola with juice poured over it (and no tea), we walk back to the pre-manufactured home park and knock at the door of the home with the intriguing garden. A middle-aged man answers. Not a woman on her own — wrong again. George Kobold is friendly and willing to show us around, but says we should really be talking to his wife, Sue, who's at work.

In an uncertain voice, I ask whether he'd mind my using the tape recorder. "No problem," he says. I wish! I want to give the impression of efficiency but I simply can't get the little wheels to keep going round. I look at it, turn it over and stare at it, shake it, turn it upside down, and like a gorilla inspecting a new toy, I knock it against my head. George looks at it, flicks something, speaks into it, and lo and behold, the wheels start rolling.

The Kobolds' pond, tucked into a corner of the garden.

George says Sue does everything, including the garden next door. As he shows us around, he keeps up a running commentary: "Neighbour's a retired mechanic and looks after our car in return … little pond there, we put in four years ago … Sue mixes vegetables in among her flowers to fool the bugs … she works at the garden centre and knows the proper names for all the plants … has influenced a lot of people round here … always asking her for advice … very alkaline soil here … passion vine in the pot there, we take it indoors for the winter … I put in the irrigation system because watering was my job and I was always forgetting … water table here is only about four feet down … this patch of grass is getting smaller … it's going … going … but it still hasn't gone as far as she wants."

George finishes by giving us directions to the garden centre where Sue works. Elspeth listens intently and I don't listen at all. We drive straight to it, and pick Sue out right away — a short woman with a Tilley hat and

an English accent. By a stroke of luck, she's read *The Garden Letters*, so we hardly have to introduce ourselves.

"My father was a professional gardener in Yorkshire," she says, "and I helped him in his garden … his allotment really — but didn't realize I was absorbing gardening information. My brother is a tree surgeon and my son is with the parks department."

There must be gardening genes in Sue's family, little green thorns on the chromosomes.

"I'm planning a trip back to England on my own, and am looking forward to visiting gardens," Sue says. "This time with nobody to say 'Haven't you seen enough yet?' I love gardening so much, I daren't go into the garden before I leave in the morning or I'd never get to work." She says they have two thousand hours of sunshine each year in Penticton and it's semi-desert, although water is plentiful from the snow melt in the mountains. The soil is extremely alkaline. She and Elspeth talk about xeriscaping — which I now know the meaning of — and then she takes us across the road to show us a demonstration plot of drought-tolerant native plants put in by the Okanagan University College. An interesting variety of species has been planted between boulders and gravel paths. From a distance, it looks a bit weedy, but close up I like the effect.

Sue has to get back to work and suggests we visit Penticton's rose garden, down by the lake.

The garden's traditional rose beds surrounded by lawn are quite a contrast to the xeriscaped area we've just seen. On one side, the garden is sheltered by a dredge shed that housed equipment for the sternwheelers plying the Okanagan Lake. Elspeth is in designing mode again, waving her arms around and talking about enclosing the rest of the garden with more shrub roses and a fence. The gardener, Elizabeth, appears with a wheelbarrow. Her eyeliner and large, intricate silver earrings are a surprise.

Sue Kobold in a demonstration plot of drought-tolerant plants (xeriphytes) at Okanagan College.

She tells us she's been having trouble with two beavers in the garden. One of them took down her *Prunus triloba*.

"Flowering cherry," Elspeth whispers to me. I'm disappointed. It sounded more exotic than that.

Sue points to a blue stick poking out of a hole in the lawn some distance away. "That's so you won't catch your foot in their air vent," she says. "Here, in the corner, you're standing on top of their lodge. A local radio station ran a contest to name the beavers, so now they're called Bud and Rosie Rosenblum. And d'you know, the Rosenblums put in an appearance on open day at the garden."

The name Penticton comes from "Pen-Tak-Tin", a Native word for "A place to stay forever" — but we can't. We leave the cherry-chomping beavers and drive on through Oliver towards Osoyoos. Acres and acres of orchards line the road, with fruit stands, mostly closed, at every corner. Pity it's too early for the peaches, pears, apples, and plums. It's even too early for the cherries. Thank goodness for fruit leather.

Osoyoos is a surprise. Its red pantile roofs give it a Mediterranean air. Motels line one side of a strip of land between two lakes. On the other side there's a landscaped walkway. It's prohibited to skateboarders and dogs — which must take care of much of the population. The landscaped bank is attractively planted with juniper, yucca, sedum, cactus, and sage. At one end, a gazebo is surrounded by blue flowering catnip and pink shrub roses. Eager to flaunt my new knowledge I say to Elspeth, "Xeriscaping?" All she says is, "Sort of."

"But d'you know where the word 'gazebo' comes from?" I ask. Without waiting for an answer, I tell her, "Gaze about."

"How did you know that?" she asks suspiciously.

"I just do," I say, and we both burst out laughing.

We're happy. The temperature is thirty degrees centigrade and we're still standing.

"Adios Amigos," says a sign as we drive up the bone-dry mountainside from the town. When we stop to look back at the panoramic view of tile roofs and dusty hills, the air is buzzing with the song of crickets. This is Canada?

The countryside in B.C. is in constant contrast to itself. A parched mountain landscape like an elephant's hide is followed by treed valleys and shining lakes, then lush slopes leading into deep green bowls where cattle graze. And then another surprise — around a bend, craggy peaks sparkling with snow against a denim sky. I never know what to expect next.

But I know what to expect for supper. Cheese and flatbread. "Oh good," says Elspeth. "Cardboard sandwiches again."

We stop at Greenwood and eat standing up. This is mining country. Across the road rise the dramatic ruins of a smelter. Behind us, in the distance, two more buildings are also falling into ruin. They're a matched pair of large square houses, and we wonder if they were built as dormitories for miners. A plaque gives a short history of the area. It doesn't mention the block houses, but we're interested to read that during World War II over a thousand Japanese internees were settled in Greenwood, and many of them stayed on in the area. This is apparent when we drive through the town itself and see gardens that we think have a distinct Japanese flavour to them — though, as Elspeth points out, we could be wrong again.

It's well after six when we arrive in Grand Forks, a town spread out along a flat valley floor. It's Saturday evening and there's no one about as we stroll through the streets. Quite by accident, we come across a hidden garden in a narrow alley, slotted between high brick walls. Someone has built a small pond outlined with mossy stones, and planted it cleverly with ferns and yellow iris. A tree reaches to the light. Beds raised with boards contain begonias and roses. Elspeth wonders if there's enough sun for the roses, but she thinks the *Clematis macropetala*, twining up a trellis against the wall, will do fine.

It's a nice surprise in a dark alley. You don't usually get nice surprises in such places. We sit and drink coffee at one of the small tables provided by the adjoining coffee shop, and enquire about the garden.

"Yes," we're told, "the owner did it. She's American."

"Has she been gardening in the alley for long?" I ask.

"She started last month."

Last month? It looks so established! I'm impressed, especially with the pond. I loved the one in Sue Kobold's garden too. The first thing I'm going to do when I get home — if I ever get home — is dig a pond.

Elspeth's Travelogue

Judy and the Grand Am were the best of buddies by this time. I couldn't have pried her from the wheel even if I'd wanted to. I saw wonderful gardens in Oliver and at Vaseux Lake, but my cries of "Stop!" went unheeded. I resolved to return to Oliver one day, and visit every single garden in the area. Even a "Hedgehogs for Sale" sign didn't slow us down. "I won't have hedgehogs running about in *my* car," said Judy, accelerating. At this rate, I thought, we'll be in Newfoundland by early next week.

In Grand Forks and Castlegar, we noticed that borsch was a popular local dish. We also saw a Slav seniors' centre and came across a number of posters advertising a fundraiser for the children of Chernobyl. Anyone could see that the Russian connection was strong, but we didn't know why until we visited the Doukhobor museum outside Castlegar.

"If you don't stop," I threatened, "the fruit leather goes out of the window." Apart from anything else, I wanted to stretch my legs. I was still suffering from sofa bed.

The museum was a restored settlement, and the simple layout was typical of Doukhobor villages. I recognized the communal houses immediately. They

Nina Koodrin and Mabel Koodrin's shared orchard and beehives.

were clones of the twin blocks we'd seen back in Greenwood — not miners' quarters, as we'd thought, but Doukhobors'.

Our guide, Christine, explained that Doukhobor meant spirit wrestler. Persecuted for their unorthodox Christian beliefs — they were pacifists and didn't believe in individual ownership of land or property — seventy-five hundred Doukhobors, with the help of Tolstoy and the Quakers of England, emigrated to the Canadian Prairies at the turn of the century. When they were pressed to take oaths of allegiance, and to file for individual homesteads, many of them moved on again, to settle in this part of British Columbia. Russian was still being taught in schools of the area.

When Christine told us that Doukhobors were also vegetarian, we realized they must be expert gardeners, and asked if she knew any local gardeners who might talk to us. She hesitated — and with good reason. Journalists, she explained, tended to write sensational stories about small extreme factions, and the whole community suffered. We let the matter drop and enjoyed the rest of our tour, which showed us immigrants more colourful, given their strict beliefs, than we'd ex-

Nina and Mabel in their adjoining gardens by the Kootenay River.

pected. They'd worn bright clothing, loved flowers and had woven floral motifs into their rugs and table cloths.

As we were browsing through the gift shop on our way out, Christine mentioned to the volunteer behind the counter that local Doukhobors, on a recent visit to communities in Russia, had brought back the seed of unusual tomatoes. She'd been given several of the seedling plants, didn't have room for them all, and wondered if Dar, the volunteer, was interested. Dar was delighted.

I pricked up my ears at the mention of seeds. I'd always loved seeds — everything about them — their colours and shapes, their potency, everything! I asked if anyone in the area was taking an interest in saving heritage seed. Christine said that Nina Koodrin, a local Doukhobor woman, had started a project but had become ill with cancer. We went on browsing, and a few minutes later, Christine, who'd been looking thoughtful, took herself off to make a mysterious phone call. She came back with wonderful news. Nina

Koodrin was feeling much better and would be happy to talk to us.

Dar told us that the area round Robson and Thrums was known locally as the "Banana Belt" because the mountain climate was modified by the Kootenay River. The Koodrin farm lay right on the river bank and, although this wasn't exactly Keats Island, we weren't surprised to see that the Koodrins were managing to grow high-bush blueberries on the alluvial soil.

Nina was waiting to greet us as we drove into her yard. I liked her immediately — a straightforward woman and, I guessed, a hard worker. She looked pale, however, and was wearing a head scarf. We asked about her illness. "I wasn't expecting it," she said, "but I'm OK." Judy knew first-hand the effects of cancer treatments, and we'd resolved beforehand to keep our visit brief. We'd reckoned without Doukhobor hospitality.

Nina invited us to sit in the shade, offered us cold drinks, and filled us in on her family history. Nina's grandfather was one of the original group who came over from Russia, and her grandmother was born in Saskatchewan. Nina told us how she grew up with them in Grand Forks, and how collecting seeds had been a big thing in the old days.

"Seeds were the key," she said. She meant the key to survival. "You'd store some in jars in a cool pantry or in the cellar, and you'd put things like beet and carrot top seed, dillweed, and sunflower seed in paper bags. Peas and beans went into cotton bags. In February every year, you'd take them all out to see what you had; things like peppers had to be started early. Dur-ing the winter, the women didn't get out to see each other much and the first big social event of the spring was the seed exchange. The ladies would come from all around, and grandma would make tea and *pyrahi* and sweets, and everyone would exchange seeds and recipes. They have a seed exchange in Nelson and I want to start one here."

Judy and her tape recorder began another dispute. I fished a notebook from my bag, just in case …

"You always did things by the moon," Nina went on. "You'd make a list of things to plant, and soak whichever seeds needed soaking. You started most things in the house; they'd be all through your windowsills and bedrooms, and as time went on, of course, they'd get more and more crowded, and eventually you couldn't crawl through the jungle. Sometime in March, before the plants grew lanky, they'd come out of the house onto the back porch. There'd be heat from the house — the stove would be on in the kitchen — and if it was getting too cold, the door to the porch would be left open."

At this point, Judy and her tape recorder parted company. I hurriedly started taking notes.

Nina continued, "My grandma died fifteen years ago and recently my father, who still lives in the family house in Grand Forks, was digging round among some old stuff and he found this trunk full of beans."

"You mean it was full of your grandmother's beans she'd saved from year to year?" I could hardly believe my ears. Chances were, those beans were direct descendants of the precious seed brought over from Russia almost a century earlier. This was thrilling stuff — a story after my own heart. I began scribbling like mad.

"Bags and bags of all these different kinds."

"Oh my! Did they look all right? Were they mouldy? Did he plant them? Did they germinate?" I was probably squeaking with excitement. My handwriting was certainly growing erratic.

"I don't know. He only found them a few weeks ago."

"A few weeks!" What a scoop!

"Would you like to see them?" she asked. "They're here."

Would I!

Nina went into the house and returned with her arms full of drawstring cotton bags. I tried to be patient as she opened the first bag and drew out a handful of creamy white beans. They were plump and smooth and beautiful — possibly still viable. Nina gave us a handful of each kind, five in all, and I couldn't have been more delighted if she'd handed us jewels. We stowed them carefully in a plastic bag, and I asked her if she knew their names. She didn't, but thought her mother-in-law might recognize them.

Nina and her husband Paul had built their house next door to his parents' place, which was only a short way across the field. The blueberries lay below us, close to the river, and beside the parents' house, below the road, were three large cultivated plots and an orchard with beehives. After they'd started the blueberry business, and especially after Nina's illness, the two couples had combined their gardening efforts.

My first impression of Nina's mother-in-law, Mabel Koodrin, was completely false. I thought she was se-vere; she turned out to be warm, generous, and funny. Her Slavic accent was charming. We talked about the beans and she suggested a few names. We talked about preserving fruit and vegetables through the winter, and she told us how she made fruit leather. It was simple. She blended the fruit, added rolled oats and dried the mixture like a pancake in the sun. This led to more talk about food — *vareniki* (boiled dumplings with sweet or savoury fillings) and *pyrahi*. She made the *pyrahi* with wheat flour and whey or potato water. Before we knew it, we were sitting at her dining table eating a delicious lunch of Russian loaf cheese (a kind of curd cheese) and *pyrahi* with fillings of cheese, beans, and peas, served with herb tea, strawberries, and melon. So much for our quick visit!

We talked about the variety of birds in the area, the redwing blackbirds and the yellow-headed kind. We'd never seen yellow-headed blackbirds, and at the Doukhobor museum we'd spotted our first bluebirds. Nina told us that their blueberries attracted so many different kinds of bumblebees, students from Selkirk College had come to study them.

After lunch we enjoyed the flowers Mabel grew on her porch, then strolled round the vegetable plots. We admired the sturdy structures built for climbing beans (put up by Mabel's husband Mike, who, because of his efficiency with a scythe, was known as the silent weed eater), and we sympathized with Mabel's distress when she discovered that crows had pulled up some of her young corn and peas.

"Our crows," she said, shaking her head at two of the culprits perched in a tree, "they know ve are

Doukhobors and ve don't shoot. They take advantage. I talk to them and I ask them please, don't destroy! I vork so hard and the beggars just come in — you hear them caw, caw, caw! — they just come in and go after the corn again."

She shrugged. "So I plant it again. It's just the vay it vorks out. Ve don't have everything under control as ve'd like. That's how it goes."

That's how it goes.

I wasn't expecting it, but I'm OK.

If we could all be so sensibly philosophical! I hope I learned something from Nina and Mabel. They certainly gave us a lot — even more than recipes, lunch, and a bag of precious beans.

Judy's Journal

From Grand Forks we make our way to Nelson, which seems to be a nice place. Elspeth likes the restored buildings in the downtown and I like walking in the park along the Kootenay Lake. What strikes us about the park is that families and groups play together so amicably and everyone seems concerned for each other, as though they're in a scene put on by the tourist bureau especially for us.

Back in our motel, we try to transcribe a few tapes. A sort of gulp eats up the start of every sentence. Sometimes the voices sound like Mickey Mouse and sometimes as though they're suffering from terminal fatigue. Worst is when there's no sound at all, a bit like the Watergate tapes. I prefer anything over the silence. Anything.

"Did you have it switched on?" asks Elspeth after a particularly silent spell.

"Of course I did!" I sound doubtful, even to myself. Once again, I shake it, knock it against my head, and hold it to my ear. I hear a faint whirring.

"It's still alive," I say. "I can hear its little heart beating. It just doesn't want to talk, that's all."

"When you talk into it, it's OK?" Elspeth asks.

"That's because it knows me."

Elspeth asks if I'd rather take the photographs. Photographs? Headless and footless as well as speechless — no thank you! At least I can drive a car.

The next morning, from Balfour, we catch the longest free ferry ride in Canada — a thirty-minute trip across Kootenay Lake, through diamond-clear water and high mountain peaks glinting with snow. At Cranbrook, we choose our motel on the strength of its hanging baskets. Forty-two of them according to the proprietor, who truly makes an effort to welcome his guests. Our room is spotless. To celebrate, we treat ourselves to a supper of flatbread and salmon — instead of sardines — then cruise the streets of Cranbrook. At first, it doesn't look promising. We see foundation planting, white gravel, junipers mulched with landscape fabric, and birches clipped within an inch of their lives, but not much in the way of real gardening. Not much passion. Has our luck run out at last?

"Go around this block again," says Elspeth. "I think I saw something."

What she sees is a wishing well, a cement deer, and a whirligig goose. We've seen them all before. Fairly often.

"Don't you see?" she asks.

I see a wishing well, a cement deer, and a whirligig goose.

"No, no!" she insists. "This is different. It's not the things themselves, it's the way they're arranged. It's done with love. Real love. Quick — someone's in the carport — let me out!"

I stay in the car and fiddle with the tape recorder. I talk to it. I say, "Whirligigs and deer. Whirligigs and deer," and it repeats my words back to me. Have I made a breakthrough?

Elspeth rushes back to the car, beaming. "It's wonderful," she says. "It's an aspect of gardens I'd never even thought of. Winter. The wife does the garden in summer and he does it in winter."

"Winter?"

"Christmas decorations. Christmas lights. He's done it for forty-five years. More than five thousand people come each year to see them."

Jim Werden ushers us into the house, introduces us to his wife, Anne, and tells us he and Anne can't go to Arizona for Christmas because they can't disappoint the neighbours. They have ten thousand lights out there — ten thousand — and it takes three weeks to put them all up. Jim is retired from the construction business; he built their house.

Elspeth nudges me. "Are you recording?"

Oh God — I'm not turned on! The Werdens bring out photo albums of Christmas pictures and I quickly switch into action.

"In March we're going to Texas for our golden wedding. See this barn … " Jim says, pointing to one of the photographs. "It's all animated … hammer there goes up and down, up and down … Cinderella, carousel, Rudolph, Santa's workshop … like fairyland … look at the church here … lights in the windows, music, taped music … singing … one year it was thick frost … lights all shinning through … gee, it was good! … see the train … lights come on in sequence, so it looks as if the wheels go around … "

Then I notice the wheels in the recorder have stopped going around.

"Elspeth, it's not working." We all look at it, turn it over and shake it.

"The pause button's on," Elspeth says. And so it is. How did that happen?

Jim continues: "People come from all over, Germany and Switzerland. A group of Japanese arrived with a baby one cold night … I mean cold … all stripped off their coats and posed for umpteen pictures in front of our sets … asked them why they took their coats off … said they wanted to show that Canada was perfect in every way — snow, but warm … Christmas Eve, when they come out of the Catholic church up the road it's like a street party here … no, no, the

Jim Werden at the controls of the Christmas light extravaganza.

crowds don't hurt the lawn ... three generations of one family have been coming ... city keeps the road clear of snow specially for us ... people ask me why don't you put out a donation box? ... I say, 'When I have to start charging, I'm going to quit' ... "

Once again the wheels have stopped — and it isn't the pause button. I take a deep breath and decide I'm simply not a recording artist. "OK. That's it, then," I whisper to the small black box. "We're through." I feel better now the relationship is finally over.

I listen calmly as Anne tells us how they make the figures. She finds pictures in magazines, borrows a projector from the school and projects them on the wall. She draws around the shapes and Jim then cuts them out of plywood or tin. Anne does all the painting. Both their sons, one locally and one in Red Deer, put up lights. The son in Red Deer may one year outdo his father — but, "Only when I croak!" says Jim.

By now it's almost dark. Before we leave, Jim shows us the complicated electrical system he's made to control the lights and moving parts. Then, on the front lawn, he shows us the owl whose eyes light up after dark. I think of donating the tape recorder to him. If anyone can animate it, he can.

"The enthusiasm — after forty-five years!" says Elspeth as we drive off. "And here we were, thinking Cranbrook was short on passion."

Against All Odds: The Prairies

I could see that Judy's tape recorder had finally pushed her to the brink. Back at the motel in Cranbrook, I offered to take The Thing outside and quietly drop a rock on it. Then I fished out the spare recorder I'd brought along as backup. She took it gingerly and tried pressing a few buttons. Soon they were conversing like old friends and from then on we had no trouble with tape recorders. My cameras started acting up instead.

In Cranbrook, the northern horizon was rimmed with jagged peaks, and although we'd meant to go east to Lethbridge, we found ourselves driving north to Banff instead. Somehow, we couldn't let go of the mountains. Not yet.

The drive was spectacular, but even in early June Banff contained too many elk and tourists to make for good garden hunting. We bought cups of tea, the obligatory postcards, and left. Judy had been driving all day, and I volunteered to take a turn at the wheel. She wasn't interested. After all those mountain bends, she said, she could drive the straight prairie roads with her eyes closed, which is exactly what I was afraid of.

I'd never considered Calgary a horticultural hot spot. I didn't think that oil and gardens would mix, or that gardeners would stand a chance against the impossible winds, sizzling summers, and wildly unpredictable winters (which occur anytime between August and July). I should have known that when the growing gets tough, the real gardeners get growing.

On the edge of the city, looking for information about motels, we followed "?" signs which led us to the shiny sports complex left over from the 1988 Winter Olympics. A helpful young woman loaded us with pamphlets and explained that Calgary is divided into quadrants with roads named accordingly — 12 St. NW is not 12 St. NE and never the twain shall meet. This gem of information (which applied to many other prairie towns) saved me much confusion and I frequently heaped blessings on the head of Ms. Question Mark.

In the evening we thumbed through tourist literature in search of a botanical garden that might provide us with leads to horticulturalists lurking in the area. Calgary's Devonian Gardens sounded interesting, but their collection of twenty thousand plants was housed indoors, which only reinforced our impressions of the city's impossible climate.

"Here's one," said Judy. "Kart Gardens." It sounded promising. I imagined a German benefactor. Alas! The gardens offered go karts, kiddy karts, and karts which would travel at fifty miles per hour, but nothing green and growing.

I'd been collecting gardening articles and snippets of garden information, and I'd brought along a file of clippings. I rummaged through it and found a newspaper piece about a gardener, Don Heimbecker, who grew hardy shrub roses as well as tender roses such as hybrid teas — outdoors in Calgary. A Calgarian rosarian. Unfortunately, I'd clipped the date off the scrap of paper so we didn't know how old it was. We thanked our lucky stars the name wasn't Smith, checked the phone book, found a likely Heimbecker, plucked up our courage and called. Don could see us in the morning. What a stroke of luck!

The Heimbeckers had other visitors when we arrived, and Don suggested we look around the garden until he could join us. The house was on a large corner lot in an established residential area. The properties were well treed (possibly too well to please a rose grower), and Don's garden, like a few others in the neighbourhood, was attractively enclosed by a low, fieldstone wall. He told us later that the walls were built by Scots masons who'd come out at the turn of the century to build the city's sandstone schools. This was definitely not the glitzy modern Calgary I'd imagined.

In my notebook I wrote: *Outside the wall, big shrub roses and tulips still in flower. Inside, more shrub roses, immaculate grass, shady pool, beds of ferns, peonies, and delphiniums with stakes taller than*

Judy, fine oak by the gate and two unusual trees, maybe Swedish columnar aspen. The dominant feature of the place was the rose garden. A domed iron arbour formed the centrepiece, and narrow flagstone paths separated the beds. The roses looked wonderfully healthy and each plant was carefully labelled. Masses of buds promised great things to come, and already, early in June, a few flowers were opening.

Don had grown roses so well, for so many years, he'd long since graduated from grade-school gardener to *authority*, and Calgary was the beneficiary of his experience. He not only wrote, talked, and demonstrated rose growing, he conducted a steady stream of tours — official and impromptu — around his own garden, and distributed a largesse of blooms around the community. Teacher, administrator, cowboy, musician, farmer, and rose grower — I felt sure he'd applied the same intelligent thoroughness to every department of his life.

He came from a family of gardeners and had started gardening at an early age. In about 1937, his father had returned from a business trip in Eastern Canada with a sack of forty rose plants, all the same kind. They were 'Better Times,' a Great Depression variety still listed in the rose directory. That was the beginning. When Don was ten years old, he and a friend entered flowers and vegetables in a show at the Exhibition Grounds. They hauled the pick of their crop through pouring rain in a small wagon and arrived with everything muddy and dripping. A kindly bystander helped them to clean up and set up, and the boys won several prizes. On the way home, however, they had a

Don Heimbecker and Judy outside the rose garden, looking at a bed of well-staked gladiolus.

run-in with a gang of East Calgary kids who stole the hard-earned ribbons.

Fortunately, this incident failed to snuff out Don's enthusiasm. Admittedly we saw no sign of potatoes or carrots in his garden, but he did grow over three hundred roses. Among his favourite tender types were 'Pink Peace,' 'Pristine' (near white), 'Royal William' (red), 'Pascali' (white), and 'Mountbatten' (yellow). When Lady Mountbatten had visited Calgary some years earlier, he'd been able to pick a bouquet of more than a dozen golden blooms for a presentation to her at the Polo Club.

Don gave us many valuable tips about cold-climate rose growing. When he planted new grafted roses, he buried them at an angle with only the tops showing. This way, the bud wood developed its own roots and he felt this induced greater hardiness. Blackspot, the fungal disease so common in Vancouver, wasn't an is-sue (maybe the Calgary climate was good for something after all), and mildew wasn't a problem either — if Don found a susceptible variety, he "plucked it out." He didn't use much fertilizer and practised overhead watering on sunny mornings, once a week in dry summer weather. The sprinkler applied an inch of water in five or six hours, and the spray helped to wash off aphids and spider mites. Of course, he deadheaded first. Deadheading took him up to an hour a day.

In the middle of October, he told us, he cut off the remaining blooms and spread dry poplar leaves knee-deep around the plants, then he trimmed off the tops and covered everything with discarded nylon carpets. He had twenty carpets, and had used the same ones for ten winters. They still looked so presentable, passers-by had offered to buy them from him. Don told us Calgary had off-and-on cold through the winter, with unreliable snow cover, and when the chinook wind blew from the Rockies, temperatures could swing from minus thirty degrees Celsius at night to fifteen degrees Celsius a couple of hours later. The leafy insulation was needed to keep the roses at a steady temperature. He removed this winter protection in the middle of April, while the plants were still dormant. These ambitious arrangements for over-wintering reminded us of Larry Wick and his leaf-encased bananas. Like Larry, Don looked for a challenge, and he told us proudly that during the 1980s Butchart Gardens (Vancouver Island's pride) had lost a huge number of roses, while he had lost very few.

Like Larry, Don was a member of a specialist group. Calgary's Rose Society was, as far as he knew, one of two functioning on the Prairies. One summer, the German Rose Society had been visiting British Columbia and had planned to make a special visit to Calgary and to Don's garden. On August 26, a few days before the visit, a terrible snowstorm hit the city and the British Columbians advised the Germans to cancel. "Don't bother going to Calgary," they said. "They've been wiped out." But the forty-member party arrived undaunted, the snow melted in the nick of time, and the roses looked splendid. On another occasion, Don was amused when a delegation arrived from Siberia. It was their day off from a Canadian conference on how to get growing with capitalism.

We were curious to know if rose growers, capitalist or otherwise, were mostly men.

"Not nowadays," he told us, "but you look at old photographs of rose shows in Britain and it was all men back then."

Judy and I told him about our theory that men tend to be the gardening specialists and women the generalists. Judy thought that women have always had to do a multitude of different things at once — like feed the baby, answer the phone, and cook the supper. "Now with a man," she said, "if he feeds the baby, he just feeds the baby, and if the phone goes while he's feeding the baby, he yells for someone to answer it."

Don disagreed with us, and perhaps to prove his point, gave us the phone number of a Calgary woman who specialized in alpine plants.

Judy's Journal

All through the interview with Don, the tape recorder works perfectly and Elspeth suggests we eat lunch in a café to celebrate my new-found efficiency. I think the celebration is a bit premature, but the food makes a nice change from sardines. We eat borsch for the first time. It's delicious, but neither of us can finish our large bowls. Our stomachs have shrunk.

I ask Elspeth what a "sport" is, because Don spoke of a "climbing sport."

"A sport is some sort of a mutation," Elspeth says. "A shoot grows from the original plant and is different in some way. Petals or colour or growth patterns might be different, although the shoot comes from the same plant."

Enlightened, I find a phone booth and Elspeth calls Sheila Paulson, the alpine gardener.

Elspeth's Traveloque

Sheila was a self-confessed alpine nut and a specialist to the kernel. She was also a dab hand at growing regular garden stuff like peonies and roses, but her heart was really with those teeny-weeny treasures that hailed mostly from the mountains. She talked about alpines as enthusiastically as she grew them, and we captured it all on tape:

"I just rave about them. My husband thinks I'm totally mad, but look at that anemonella. Isn't that an absolute gem? In England, I went to agricultural college because they were hoping I'd marry a farmer, but I came to Canada instead and here I am, thirty-four years later, doing this. You just get hooked. Absolutely.

"That blue gentian and the white iberis — aren't they perfect together? Once the children grew up and moved away, I thought, I hate growing vegetables, and

I'd joined the American Rock Garden Society by then, so I made this garden. I have lousy knees and I'd al-

Sheila Paulson gives one of her tiny alpines an encouraging pat as she shows us around her garden.

ways wanted a sunken garden, so we dug this part out and built that part up and made these raised beds. I can sit on the edge and play around. I put an inch or two of pea gravel on the surface because alpines like to have their necks dry. Now things are seeding themselves, even in the gravel paths. Just look at those miniature wall flowers! And these gentians are coming up through the moss campion. The campion goes brown in winter and the first year, I thought it was dead, but it greens up.

"Usually I put down pine boughs in the winter. The trick in Calgary is to keep the ground frozen. I lose a few plants every year but that's fine — it makes room for new things. In spring it's always a race between drabas and saxifrages. The first bloom was April 9 this year. Last year it was March 20. People think you need full sun for a rock garden, but I wish I had more shade. I'm trying woodland orchids here in a special orchid growing mix.

"This dianthus — it's like a tiny fireworks explosion, isn't it? In 1991, I went to an international meeting of alpine people in Warwickshire, England, and brought back about forty plants, bare root. Dianthus 'Nywood's Cream' was one of the exquisite gems, and here at the

Cold frames at the side of Sheila's house shelter thousands of seedlings every spring, most of which are sold.

club they're all waiting to get a bit of it. I took cuttings last year but they died. I hate to disturb it but I should divide it up and share it because, if I lose mine, I want to be able to get it back.

"Rare plants should be shared around. Like this peony. I was visiting a friend I play bridge with, and I said, 'Sue, do you know what kind of peony you have here!' It was the wood peony, *Paeonia anomala*. Lovely! And she said, 'I don't know. A neighbour was giving everybody pieces but they all died except mine.' So I told her she'd better split it up and give it to her daughters and spread it about, and I supervised the division. What a job it was! It had roots going to China.

"This is *Adonis vernalis*. I've tried to start it from seed but without success. A lady of eighty-six had these yellow flowers growing all through her lawn, and when I identified them for her, she offered me some. She gave me such a small trowel, I didn't get a big enough bit, and it died. The next year I went back, and *she* had died. The house was being rented and they'd killed all the adonis except for little pieces round the outside. I left my card to let these people know what they had, and not to kill it, but when I went back the next year there was a huge bulldozer on the site and they were moving the whole house. I found out who owned the place and phoned. I talked to this surprised lady from New Zealand and she said, 'A little yellow dandelion? If you want to rescue it, please do!' I halted the bulldozer. It was November and the ground was hard, but we got it out and now it's safely distributed.

"Those primulas are from seed. Most alpine societies have seed exchanges, but the seeds don't always produce what you expect. I start two or three thousand plants every year in the basement under lights, then they go into the seed beds at the side of the house. Several of our members help me with transplanting and I donate most of those plants to the CRAGS plant sales. CRAGS stands for Calgary Rock and Alpine Garden Society. We sell plants to pay for speakers at the meetings.

"I'm president of CRAGS at the moment. One of our directors, Rod Sykes, has land near Radium in B.C. and a farmer was grumbling about rocks all over his land. Rod showed me some of them and I said, 'Rod,

you've got tufa!' He was grinning and chuckling. Quite a find! It's light and porous. We drill holes in it and plant it up. Those troughs are hypa tufa, a sort of light-weight concrete. I made one in my roasting pan but it was too much fuss. These ones were made by a gal in the group.

"My alpines do tend to expand into the rest of the garden, but my husband is keeping an eye on me and I think this is about as far as I'll get. But I did take out some roses from here to make a special bed for saxifrages. Can you see them? I've got close to one hundred encrusted saxifrages. I'm crazy on sax."

On that note, our tour of the garden ended and Sheila invited us to sit on her shady patio. We talked about the astonishing energy of gardeners, and she suggested we visit her friends, Joey and Norman Stewart. When we asked her to describe the Stewart's garden, however, she only smiled and said, "It's a rock garden with a difference. You'll see."

And we did.

Judy's Journal

We arrive at a house that looks much like the other houses on the block and are greeted by Joey, a small elf-like woman wearing a white shirt and jeans, her hair shower-damp.

Going through the front door I'm taken aback by the feeling of spaciousness; the high ceiling gives the house an airy feel, and each room flows into the next. The

house was designed to be environmentally friendly, with much of it below ground level. The hallway goes down into a tiled area known as the "garden room" that opens into a kitchen and up steps into a living room; the bedrooms have large plate glass windows that also open onto the garden room. Where will you hide when you have a row? The walls are hung with

Joey and Norm Stewart at their dining table.

"This was a dead flat lot and not much room, so we excavated right down to this level and opened up the dining room on this side. We heaped some of the earth up to make a waterfall and the rest was hauled away."

She opens a door onto a stone patio. I am once more taken aback, this time by the design of the garden. It is a real rock garden — not just piddly rocks but massive ones, rocks of substance. They're built up all around the excavated area.

"How on earth d'you get these rocks here?" I ask.

"By crane," says Joey, laughing. "By crane, didn't we, Norman?" she says to her husband, who has just arrived at the scene.

"Yes, we certainly did," he says.

"I know this great guy, Gordie White," Joey continues, "who is passionate about rocks. I call him my rock-star. Well, he and I went out into the wilds to find these boulders. I wanted something just right for the table there, so we'd go out and I'd take table mats and wine glasses and lay them out on the rocks we found. Must've done it about twelve times ... one was too small ... didn't like the surface on another and so on ... 'til I saw this one that seats fourteen."

The table is a large slab of rock with a flat surface, supported by a reinforced concrete base with a stone facing. A stone bench runs round the back of it. "We've had some great dinner parties and you can just hose down the table," says Joey.

"The guests as well," I say.

At the end of the garden, the rocks are built up to form a cascade. Columbine, ferns, and saxifrages are tucked among the crevices. Saucer-like curves in the

paintings and prints; pottery and artifacts abound. Plants, including a huge night-blooming cereus, hang from the ceiling, and in the background, a Bach sonata from CBC stereo floats over us.

Joey leads us down to the dining room, which is at basement level. "We decided we had to do something different and unusual with the landscaping," she says.

rocks catch the falling water. A cat drinks from the cool, dark pools, then hides among the grasses and sleeps. Fossilized leaves and trunks of trees inlay the boulders, and pottery spheres and smooth round stones lie scattered throughout.

"I have a passion for round things," Joey says, picking up a handful of small round pebbles. "See that piece of sculpture there, the metal piece?" She points to a steel sculpture against a rock. "The round holes represent bullet holes. It's a memorial to the women who died in Montreal. Rita Wildschut is the sculptor. She's also a gardener, and has large sculptured figures in her garden. She lives near the Badlands. You must see her place. I'll give you her number. I love her work. I don't really collect art; I collect eclectic people."

While one side of the dining room opens onto the patio, the other has a typical basement window that looks onto the narrow side-strip of their property. It is framed like a painting and through the

Joey and Norm's dramatic rock garden.

One of Joey's spherical sculptures.

glass is a miniature garden of tufa, rocks, alpines and thyme. A perfect little picture.

As we are leaving the house, Joey points to the night-blooming cereus. "It blooms in mid-August and only lasts for one evening. We have a party for it and I get up on a stepladder and try to pollinate it. The flowers are humungous. Wonderful aroma."

As we go out through the front door, Joey tells us we might just be on her list of eccentric people she likes.

Getting into the car, I tell Elspeth I've never thought of myself as eccentric. Tall, yes, but not eccentric. She says that not having a television is eccentric. "Mine is only broken," I say, and she says, "It's been broken since '79." True, but now that I'm on my own, I'm going to get a television for company during the long winter months.

Even though we are both dog-tired, we are having trouble sleeping. The three gardens we've just seen keep going through our heads. Roses ... roses ... roses ... should I take more care with my few bushes? … the alpines, a supreme speciality that I admire but can never attain … and then the rocks … how I'd like those! This evening we've been listening to some of the tapes, ones I'd not messed up, and these too keep going around in my mind along with *Adonis vernalis*. Who was that, anyway?

Elspeth's Travelogue

Joey's excavated garden was a remarkable concept carried out with tremendous flair. She told us she'd trained as a nurse and had then worked in occupational health for many years. I thought she could have taken up garden design instead.

We needn't have worried about finding gardeners in the city. The helpful Calgarians had passed us from one to another and now Joey had even given us a contact for a garden out on the prairie. The next morning, we set off to find Rita Wildschut's place, near the town of Brooks.

In Calgary, you oriented yourself by the mountains just as in Vancouver you looked towards the sea or away from it. But in the prairie flatlands, there were more than two directions, and as soon as the Rockies dipped out of sight, an infinite number of views surrounded us. The choice of directions made me feel slightly dizzy but they made Judy sing. She opened her window, stepped on the throttle, threw back her head and belted out "Home on the Range" as we hurtled, windswept, towards the unattainable horizon. Scratch a Welsh woman and, it seemed, you discovered the Wild West.

Rita Wildschut, in spite of her name, didn't seem to be wild. She was a motherly person with a warm manner and a slight Dutch accent. She invited us into a friendly family house full of plants and interesting art work, and offered us iced tea.

Rita had been a city girl in Holland but, at the age of twenty and newly wed, she came to rural Alberta and settled outside Brooks, where her husband, Collin, worked at the Crop Diversification Centre. Rita set about making a home and raising three children. There was no garden round their house — no trees, nothing — so she put in a few bedding plants. They died.

Rita and Collin Wildschut's property in the early days, when it was completely exposed to fierce prairie winds.

A neighbour pointed out that plants needed water. Initially, Rita couldn't understand this; in Holland, the sky did the job. In this part of Alberta, she soon learned, you could go for eight months without rain. Water came by truck, at great expense, and was stored in an underground cistern. Rita learned to ration the

This avenue of trees is part of the shelter belt Rita planted. Two of her sculptures lounge at its end.

precious stuff, with short showers and only full loads of laundry or dishes. It was unthinkable to use it on the garden. An irrigation canal ran past the property and, between the middle of May and the middle of October, it was fed with water. The trick was to work out a system for dipping into the canal and pumping the water out. Not as easy as it sounded. Twenty years later, their pump was still a major headache.

Even with water available, Rita's early gardening efforts were a battle. Everything she planted was sand-blasted by the wind. She read about shelter belts and began to put in ambitious numbers of shrubs and trees in a block of several acres round the house. The ground was heavy clay and she dug with a pickaxe. The wind brought in diseases, aphids, blister beetles, and tent caterpillars. The trees, mere twigs to start with, soon succumbed. Once again, she braved the mosquitoes and biting flies, and replanted. Ants plagued her lawns. She started fruit trees and mice ate the bark, so she learned to make bypass grafts. Grass and weeds competed with the young trees. She brought in goats to help eradicate the weeds and they eradicated almost everything. Their horses were no better; she'd never realized a horse could eat a whole apple tree. She replanted. She tried ducks and geese to keep the grass short but they kept the vegetables short instead. Winters were brutal. The wind swept away the snow cover and, with temperatures below forty degrees Celsius for days on end and the ground like granite, the trees simply shrivelled up. In spring, she replanted.

By sheer force of will, Rita finally established a few saplings, her first line of defence against the blast. They provided shade as well as shelter for the trees that followed and, in time, snow collected round them and their leaves mulched the ground. At long last came the year when the apple blossoms *didn't* blow away. Little by little, Rita had reshaped her whole environment.

She took us outside and we walked around the grounds together. The house was now embedded in greenery. Vegetables, berry bushes, and orchard trees lay to one side, and the shelter belts that did the trick

One of Rita Wildschut's larger than life garden sculptures.

formed impressive avenues and woods. Their shade was a blessing in the glaring heat of the mid-June afternoon. Rita told us robins, waxwings, and flycatchers nested in them and we heard the song of a meadow lark. Our conversation was punctuated by the *phut-phut-phut* of the irrigation jets that made this whole thing possible.

In Holland, Rita had always bought armloads of cut flowers along with the weekly groceries. In Alberta,

when she tried to buy flowers, the assistant laid one carnation on a sheet of paper and asked how many she wanted. How many? She wanted the whole bucketful! Then she heard the price. As she couldn't afford to buy flowers, she decided to grow them instead. Large beds of perennials and annuals now swept around the lawn behind the house.

Judy and I wondered if we'd have had the courage (defiance? insanity?) to take on a slab of Canadian

Rita Wildschut

Trees and shrubs shelter Rita's flower beds.

desert and spend twenty years turning it into a garden. We wondered what had made a young Dutch woman so determined. "Memories," she said. "The smell of damp earth in spring, sitting in the shade of a tree, the crunch of autumn leaves underfoot." On our trip, we learned a lot about the power of childhood memories.

Rita was a determined woman, and strong in every sense. As she talked, we saw behind the dedicated homemaker a fiercely independent being. We saw her, in the chill of winter and in the fever of summer, venturing away from the domestic shelter she'd created with such persistence. We caught glimpses of her prowling through the apparent desolation of the Badlands. Joey had told us Rita was a sculptor. She was also a painter and a potter. She painted the uncomfortable colours of the wilderness and modelled its strangely compelling shapes in clay. But the most remarkable thing we saw was the tangible result of a rebellion.

Like many artists, Rita was largely self-taught, although she eventually took a university degree. She

believed passionately that art must relate directly to humanity, and when the authorities threatened to drop life-drawing from the curriculum, she staged a private protest of massive proportions. As it happened, she had recently cut down a couple of large poplars at the end of her vegetable garden. Around the stumps, she built two figures — more than twice as large as life — using flexible poplar twigs to weave the forms, and stuffing them with brushy debris. Her "guys" were part tree, part compost, part human, and she loved them.

She built more figures, using sheep wire to create the shapes, some lounging on the lawn, some crouching at the focal point of an avenue, some looming against the prairie vastness. In the end, fifteen of these giants inhabited the property, possessing the place completely on Rita's behalf. They had grown out of it (as perhaps an immigrant never could) and were slowly returning — inevitably toppling, slumping, and weathering — back into it. She told us she propped them up from time to time and restuffed them with weedy garden waste in a half-hearted gesture of delay. She had no desire to halt the process. After all, she explained, it was life.

I wasn't surprised when she said, as we were leaving, "Everything here, we did ourselves. The garden is all ours, but walking around it reminds me of all the people who helped me with advice, or gave me a plant or tree or shrub. Each plant has a history, and this is why it's so special to me. When I die, I want to be sprinkled here. I don't think I could ever leave this place now."

Although Rita's gardening efforts could hardly have impressed us more, she kept telling us her garden was an amateurish effort, and the gardener we should talk to was a neighbour, George Smith. George was a recently retired horticulturist, and he knew how gardening on the prairies *should* be done. Here was one more link on the chain of gardeners that had started among Don Heimbecker's roses in Calgary. We tried to call but there was no reply. George did, however, live conveniently close to a bed-and-breakfast that Rita recommended. She also gave us directions to Dinosaur Provincial Park — a Badlands area and World Heritage Site — explaining that, if we wanted to understand this region, we must see the landscape in the raw.

Judy's Journal

We book in at the B&B. We want to see the Dinosaur Park but the twin beds look so comfortable we can hardly tear ourselves away. Another thing I can hardly tear myself away from is the decanter of sherry with its two small, blue glasses. Before leaving for the park, we phone George Smith but there's still no answer. On our way to the dinosaurs we are fascinated by the irrigation systems. Veils of fine spray "droppeth as the gentle rain from heaven upon the place beneath." It's as though large insects are moving rhythmically across

George Smith's home was hidden amongst the trees. Just visible on the other side of the highway is one Alberta's giant watering machines.

An intimate courtyard belies the existence of the vast prairie just beyond.

"I think we should be turning off pretty soon," Elspeth mutters, studying the map.

Turning off to nowhere. There isn't much around. An old woman in a battered straw hat rides a horse along the grass verge. Her dog ambles across the road right in front of the car. I jam the brakes on and the woman says, "Sorry 'bout that!" The dog stands and stares.

We finally reach Dinosaur Park an hour before the sun goes down. The park is a great rift in the earth, like a small Grand Canyon. The colours are magnificent: every shade of grey and brown in exciting shapes and structures. In the eerie silence, I watch an antelope drink from a stream at the foot of the canyon.

the land, jetting out fine patterns of mist. I imagine them unable to stop, going on and on forever, through forests and towns, through mountains and valleys, enveloping everything in a soft gossamer veil.

"Are you sure this is right?" I ask, as we seem to be getting nowhere. "We might drive off the end of the world."

Isolated houses, snug inside their hollow of trees, are sparsely dotted throughout, safe from the winds of summer and the storms of winter. I'd never heard the term shelter belt until we came to Alberta, but when I was in Arkansas someone showed me their "fraidy hole," which is where they hide when a tornado roars by. I think we could all do with "fraidy holes." I suppose you could say ours are our gardens.

After a breakfast of pancakes and coffee we set out to find George Smith. We find his house buried in a grove of trees, but George is not at home. The cat rubs against our legs in welcome, then walks away as though leading us into the garden. So how can we resist?

At the side of the driveway, rectangular beds hold dark blue lobelia and petunias in blue and white. Roses and junipers are banked against the house. Through an arch flanked by tubs of geraniums, and overgrown with clematis and virginia creeper, we enter a cool courtyard leading to the kitchen door. Outside the door, a chair is piled high with firewood, and growing next to it is a single hollyhock. The scent of lilac drifts throughout the garden.

The cat leads us to the vegetable garden, which is backed by a windbreak of caragana and enclosed by a low picket fence lined with chicken wire. It's only mid-June, but potatoes, cabbage, and lettuce are so well advanced that one lettuce has already been harvested. Still following the cat, we pass a table sheltered by an umbrella. On the table, a pair of secateurs rests on a garden glove. In here, tucked inside the shelter belt, everything is so well cared for and protected, we feel as if we're in an English garden. It's hard to believe that beyond the caragana hedge lies a windswept Canadian desert.

In spite of the cat's warm welcome, we feel uneasy about trespassing. Elspeth wonders how she'd feel if strangers followed her cat Moses around her garden. Not happy, she decides, so regretfully we say goodbye to the cat and leave.

For anyone to get around *my* garden right now, they'd probably need a machete.

From Brooks we drive on a dead-straight highway through flat range land dotted with oil wells. We pull off at Medicine Hat, and almost the first thing we see is a garden centre. Inside, decorating the walls, are photographs of the winners of a Great Garden Contest.

We've struck paydirt! We talk to the assistant and she says we should visit Marvin Albrecht, who won first prize. She gives us directions to a supermarket where he works, and Elspeth zeroes in on it as though she's always lived in Medicine Hat.

Alas, it's the wrong store; Marvin moved to another branch ten years ago. The manager, however, remembers him and redirects us. He tells us that Marvin has a marvellous garden, with grass so perfect he doesn't like people to walk on it.

We zero in on a second supermarket, and here an assistant in the bakery department pages, "Marvin Albrecht to baked goods!" A man of medium height appears. He has light greying hair, his tie is neat against his white shirt, and his grey pants are well pressed. I wonder what he thinks when he sees two slightly bedraggled middle-aged women waiting for him among the bread rolls. Elspeth explains why we are here and he agrees to meet us on his break, in a coffee shop in the mall.

We go ahead to the coffee shop and soon Elspeth is pulling apart a muffin as though we haven't eaten in days. Well, I suppose we haven't, much — apart from the pancakes and the borsch. Marvin appears, collects a cup of coffee, comes to our table and sits between us. We chat a while then ask about his garden.

"My first project," he says, "was the waterfall and fishpond. I have four ponds in my yard and it's a small yard. I did them myself — made the forms and had Ready Mix come by with a special-order cement for ponds, so I've had no cracking."

I ask him if he has plantings around his pond.

"I guess my yard is a little different that way from what you see in magazines," he says. "I have juniper around the waterfall pond but there is no room around the other ones. I've never really had a lot to do with perennials and shrubs. I like sharp colour. I plant in excess of four hundred annuals. This spring has been slow. It'll be another three weeks before they strut their colours." He sips his coffee and marshalls his thoughts when we ask him how he plans the colours of the four hundred annuals. He says that he plans carefully where to put the flowers, according to their colour. He uses toothpicks where he wants the different areas of colour. He doesn't start the plants himself.

"My mother used to start all her own flowers. I'd like a small greenhouse, six feet by eight, but I'm running out of real estate," he laughs. "I certainly get a lot of enjoyment out of it; it's mental therapy. I probably got in one-hundred-and-sixty hours of labour already this year, from day one, when I started spring cleaning, to finessing. Last night I could finally say, 'Yeah, I'm done now.' Then I go back to square one and swish through it much quicker. My wife, Alvena, enjoys seeing it. She's a decorator — cakes. That's her hobby."

He gives us directions to his garden and is sorry he can't show it to us himself. To get the full effect, he tells us, the water must be working. "It brings life to the garden," he says. He explains there are three switches, and makes us promise to turn them on.

We find his address, park in the driveway, and open a narrow lattice gate to get into the back garden.

Elspeth says, "Wow!" (twice) and I am completely bowled over by the brightness of it all — the sharp

Marvin Albrecht's immaculate garden.

clear colours, the hard clean surfaces. It is all of a piece under the glare of the hot afternoon sun. Even though Marvin told us he had few plantings around his ponds, I was still expecting what the seventeenth-century writer Andrew Marvell called, "a green thought in a green shade."

A narrow hump-backed bridge guarded by two bronze lions leads to the centrepiece of the garden, which is a brilliant green lawn, small, convoluted, and immaculate. Its precisely clipped edge is surrounded by a border of earth outlined with plastic edging and then another border of gravel. On the far side of the garden, a low curved wall of riverstones, set in cement and capped with flagstones, supports a bed of marigolds inset with rectangles of white gravel. Placed carefully on these gravel bases are garden ornaments: dwarfs, skunks, children, and toadstools, all freshly painted. Hanging baskets are attached to the brackets on the gleaming white fence behind.

The back of the garden is built up to form a steep

bank planted with the junipers Marvin told us about. Below them is the largest pond in the garden. It is planted with water lilies, and a small cement boy fishes from a dock.

"I'm going to turn on the waterworks," Elspeth announces, as though about to pull the switch for a vast hydro-development. She clicks the three switches. For a moment nothing happens, then a sheet of water pours out from high among the junipers and falls into the pond where koi dart about among the water lilies. At the same time, water fills the smaller pond, overflows, runs down a sinuous concrete stream bed, flows under a hump-backed bridge and ends up in another smaller pool. Most dramatic of all: beside the house, water begins to bubble up through tubes of various heights and shoots into the air to form a sparkling fountain as elaborate as a wedding cake. It splashes down into a circular pond which is bordered by stone, crushed brick, plastic edging, and gravel.

Now we understand why Marvin insisted that we switch the water on. The garden has come alive just as he said it would. This back yard is one man's vision of paradise. It's unique — a *real* garden if ever there was one. For a long time, we simply stand and marvel at the effort that has gone — that goes — into its creation. We turn the water off as we are about to leave. The fountain and cascade run dry and the life of the garden drains away.

I've never seen a place so well cared for and clean. Not a weed or anything out of place, everything painted and polished to perfection. I hope Marvin never visits *my* garden.

Elspeth's Travelogue

From Medicine Hat we crossed into Saskatchewan, and immediately the landscape changed. This southwest corner of the province was all gentle curves and subtle shadows, and the fuzz of sprouting crops made the land look soft enough to stroke. Judy changed her tune from "Home on the Range" to a hymn we both remembered from Sunday school in rainy Britain:

We plough the fields and scatter
The good seed on the land,
But it is fed and watered
By God's Almighty hand.

The words seemed appropriate because we saw no sign of the irrigation systems — the almighty man-made rain machines — that had impressed us so much in Alberta. I liked this undulating landscape but I still wasn't used to being landlocked. At the crest of every rise I expected to come upon the sea shimmering in the distance. All we saw were mirages shimmering on the hot asphalt of the road ahead. Early in the evening, we arrived in Swift Current.

Judy's Journal

Everyone in Swift Current is remarkably friendly but the gardens seem uninspired. Even standard foundation plantings of juniper and globe cedars look half-hearted and a bit battered. Only rhubarb thrives. We wonder if Swift Current gardeners suffer from a particularly debilitating climate, or if they believe in front garden conformity and keep their real gardening for the back.

"Why don't we cruise the back lanes," Elspeth suggests. I drive slowly, looking through hedges, peering over walls, stopping and starting, skirting trash cans and dodging cats.

"You know, we could get picked up for loitering with intent," I say.

"With intent to look at a garden?" Elspeth laughs.

Then we see a flash of colour. We leap out of the car and look through a knot-hole in the fence. There are people in the garden. They are looking back through the fence — at us.

"Quick, Elspeth," I shout, "in the car!" I drive as fast as I can down the alley, onto the street and around to the front of the house. We are giggling and breathless. We knock, and a woman comes to the door. We explain our mission and, to our relief, she laughs. There have been break-ins in the area; she was thinking of calling the police. Instead, she introduces herself as Jean Pearson, and invites us round to the back garden. Her son and his girlfriend are sunbathing on the lawn, and they don't seem at all put out by this sudden invasion of their privacy.

Elspeth's Travelogue

Jean Pearson's back garden was generously wide and welcoming. Perennial beds (the colour we'd spotted through the fence) curved around the lawn, and we noticed the sensible use of a maintenance path behind them. In spite of the grass and flowers, the impression was of trees and shade. Many of the trees had been given by friends, and were named after them. "This one is Wilma," Jean told us, "and that one is also Wilma — she was quite bent over, like the trees. The two tall ones are Harold and Harold. Those are Olive and Willis, and that evergreen is Gunter. The tree behind you is named after our son, Mark, because he brought it home from school as a seedling."

Although Jean's well-populated garden was lovely, she felt she was only a beginner, and wanted us to talk to her friend and mentor, Helma Weiner. She even offered to drive to Helma's with us and make the introductions.

Judy and I had been glad of the shade in Jean's garden, and now we were happy to sit in the wide porch at the back of Helma's house. Potted plants surrounded us, beautiful cushions padded the chairs, and the air was blissfully cool.

Helma grew up in Germany but had lived in Canada for forty-two years. When Helma was a child, her mother grew flowers and vegetables in an allotment garden some distance from their home. Everything had to be watered by hand and Helma was expected to help. One hot day in July, the little girl wanted to go to a birthday party instead and made such a fuss her mother relented. "I never forget it," Helma told us. "At the party, we had plenty of stuff to eat. This was during the war, and perhaps we weren't used to it. Anyway, I got sick. Serve me right! Yes, I never forget that, and now, of course, I can see why my mother needed the help."

Having to help with garden chores would have put many people off gardening for life. But not Helma. Like Rita Wildschut, she had come to Canada as a twenty-year-old bride, and had gardened ever since, even when she and her husband lived in rental property,

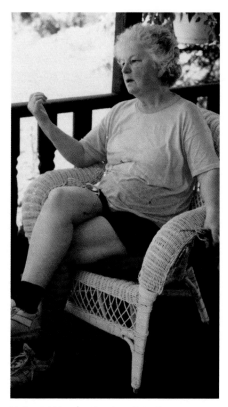

Helma Weiner with a handful of garden debris — trademark of a real gardener.

even while she worked to put him through university, and even while she raised their four children. She made her present garden from scratch and enjoyed doing all the work. Sometimes her husband offered to cut the lawn, but she really preferred to do it by herself.

We could see how the design of the garden had influenced her friend Jean. Again, a maintenance path ran around the back of perennial beds that surrounded a lawn. In this case, however, the beds were banked up to form rock gardens, so that even low-growing plants helped to hide the fence and cup the lawn in a sheltered enclosure. In some places, Helma had pounded sections of two-by-four lumber, side by side, into the ground to retain the back of the beds. She'd built up the soil with compost, peat, and manure. This black gold, she told us, had been delivered annually by a farming friend, usually as a Mother's Day present. Like Judy, Helma loved rocks and used to go rock hunting on her bicycle. She was picky. She sifted through whole rock piles until she found specimens flat enough to pass muster, then she peddled them home in her bicycle basket.

The rock garden plants were neat, colourful, and comfortably arranged. She didn't keep shifting her plants around as Judy and I did, but she replaced her tulips with annuals such as impatiens, geraniums, and asters to give colour later in the summer. I wanted to take a picture of her in the rock garden. To put her at ease, I suggested she pull a few weeds. "There are no weeds," she said. No weeds? I took a closer look, and sure enough — there were no weeds!

Helma was definite about things. She knew what she liked and what she didn't, and one of the things she liked was roses. A big bed of them grew against the porch. She over-wintered them in a deep layer of leaves, much as Don Heimbecker did, but without the carpets. She had beds for vegetables and, when her crops were harvested, she dug trenches in the soil, laid

Helma's weed-free tapestry of plants.

the taller roses down (stripped of their leaves and flowers) and covered them with newspaper, soil, and more leaves. This was a lot of work, she admitted, but then, the roses gave her a lot of pleasure.

Helma's garden was protected from the prairie winds by the other houses and fences nearby. She seemed more bothered by summer heat than by winter cold, although the previous winter had been harsh enough to scorch even junipers and cedars. The deer had also suffered, she told us, and had come into the gardens looking for food. Ah! Now we understood why so many foundation shrubs around town looked a little chewed. We talked about the mild climate of Vancouver. Helma had visited the city but had no desire to live there. "Too many people in Vancouver," she said, "and we have sunshine here even if it *is* thirty below."

Her husband liked to visit Germany, but Helma prefered to stay home. While he was away she tackled big jobs like painting the house or building the retaining wall. She also sewed and specialized in custom-made drapes and — by this time we weren't surprised to hear — she had organized two daughters' weddings in one summer. Her garden was the backdrop for their photographs, and she even grew white orchids for their bouquets.

It was a mystery to me how anyone could be so efficient and hard working, and still be so pleasantly relaxed and such good company. We found it hard to drag ourselves away from Helma's hospitality and her cool porch.

From Swift Current we headed north towards Saskatoon where we'd arranged to stay with friends Joan and Peter Flood. Their house was to become our base of operations for the next few days.

On the way, as a break from highway driving, we detoured into Rosetown, and drove, at a crawl, up and down the shady, tree-lined streets. We expected to see roses, and we did see a few, but the street trees impressed us more. Whoever planted those poplar and ash deserved a medal — or better still, a memorial tree planted in their honour.

We decided that Rosetown must be an honest place; we saw several vegetable gardens open to the street, and most of them included flowers, with iris and lilies as the season's favourites. Already on our trip we'd seen all manner of buckets and barrels, boats, bins, and barrows used as containers for plants, but here we saw our first (and last) scuttle garden — a row of coal scuttles painted grey and planted with impatiens.

After Rosetown, we continued through dead-flat wheat country. The vastness of the pale blue sky reduced us to the size of bugs. The cars were shiny beetles, a freight train wormed its way towards us, and the shelter belts were like caterpillars crawling along the horizon. Close up, these lines of trees revealed themselves as hollow blocks of spruce and lilac sheltering homesteads and goodness knows how many glorious gardens. We caught only tantalizing glimpses of trim lawns and specks of colour. Judy was still revelling in the wide open space, and was now singing: "*We'll build a sweet little nest* … Da-di-da … *in the west … And let the rest of the world go by.*" Pity she didn't know the rest of the words.

I had met Peter Flood when we both lived in the Shetland Islands. He had been the local vet. Now he was with the College of Veterinary Medicine at the University of Saskatchewan, and one of his specialties was the musk ox. Our arrival in Saskatoon coincided with great excitement in the musk ox department. Two of their animals were due to give birth at any moment, and a baby musk ox, orphaned in the wild, had just been flown in from the Arctic. Peter was as twitchy as the regulation expectant father and rushed us to the university to show off his latest acquisition.

How could I ever have thought a musk ox was a buffalo? Peter soon put me straight on that. Buffalo, he informed us, were properly called bison. Musk oxen were much smaller, had horny headbands, and were more closely related to sheep than cattle.

Tutok, the orphan, a saucy little creature quite unperturbed by his strange surroundings, was penned in a makeshift stall in one corner of a classroom. Did I want to bottle-feed him? You bet! But how to hold a baby musk ox? In my arms like a human baby? And how to coax him to take the teat? Peter laughed and handed me a plastic bottle half full of milk. Tutok saw it, lunged, and latched. I clung on with both hands while, with one enormous suck, Tutok drained the bottle dry. In fact, the plastic imploded. "I think I did that rather well," I said, as soon as I'd recovered from the shock.

The only garden we saw at the university was the one we walked through as we led the two pregnant musk oxen to their paddock. Noticing how eagerly they trimmed the bushes along the way, my growing ambition to keep a musk ox as a pet shrank fast.

Helma Weiner had impressed us with her capable productivity. Joan Flood was capable on a flamboyant scale. For years, she had co-produced an ambitious Children's Festival in Saskatoon. After handling something like that, organizing Judy and me was peanuts. What luxury for us, after days of uncertainty on the road, to be bedded, fed, and intelligently led!

It was Joan who arranged our visit to Bob, and who filled us in on his background. Bob Hinitt was a teacher. His subject was French but his real love was the stage and every year he involved himself and his pupils in ambitious theatrical productions. After his retirement, he became even more involved. He'd just spent three months staging *Private Lives*, and was currently completing a set of *Alice in Wonderland* figures and scenery to go inside the tunnel of the children's train at Kinsmen Park.

Knowing all this, we shouldn't have been surprised to find that Bob's whole garden was a stage:

Bob Hinitt (far left, in hat) gathers a crowd around his floral clock.

Judy Maddocks

Elspeth has the honour of planting the first red begonia on the clock face.

ACT I. SUMMER

SCENE I. *Front garden in a standard suburban street. Centre stage occupied, not by a patch of grass, but by a large floral clock — a genuine working timepiece with a circular clock face of earth, surrounded by stone rings and sloping towards the road. The hands and numerals are of sheet metal bent up to form shallow containers for small plants.*

Enter stage right, delivery truck. Nurseryman starts unloading fourteen hundred red and white begonias.

Enter stage left, Bob (a long, lean figure wearing a harlequin shirt, spectacles, and a small cotton sun hat). He is surrounded by a troupe of visitors — Judy and Elspeth, Joan and Peter, and a couple of complete strangers who have unaccountably joined their party. Bob attempts to orchestrate the delivery while the troupe tramples over lawn and beds, taking snapshots, offering help and generally hindering all progress in the thirty-six-hour task of covering the dial with red begonias, planting up the hands and numerals with echeveria (known in Victorian Britain as cactus rosettes) and spelling this year's chosen

Judy, Bob, and Joan Flood admire the petunia tree.

Bob shows Judy around the stage, his garden.

text (one year it was the name and dates of Bob's most recently deceased cat) around the rim of the clock face.

SCENE II. *The driveway.*

Judy. How do you get your car to the garage past these ... er ... sixteen large tubs of roses?

Bob. I drive a bicycle and as I don't drink or smoke, I can afford to have the roses over-wintered in a greenhouse. I also buy eight thousand annuals every year.

Troupe. (In chorus) Eight thousand annuals!

SCENE III. *The back garden, which contains an astonishing assembly of classical structures — a colonnade, a dome, a fountain, benches, pedestals, and statues, most items painted white and arranged apparently at random on bright green grass amid brilliantly coloured flowers, predominantly red and white. The flower beds are edged with white rocks.*

Judy and Elspeth. ! ? ! [Various sounds registering astonishment and admiration].

Bob. The rocks came from rock piles on my moth-er's farm thirty-five miles east of here; she used to pick them as a kid. It took me seven summers to bring them here and arrange them the way I wanted. The whole thing lines up if you get yourself properly placed on the axis. I love symmetry. In 1962 I went to France and saw Versailles so that when I came back home I had this wrought-iron dome made, and I made the temple, my *Temple d'Amour.* I tooled all the frieze in copper but it's falling apart now. Like me. The statues are the Four Seasons, and they came from Kitchener, Ontario. I have a replica of the Manneken-Pis from Brussels but I haven't brought him out yet.

Judy. Too cold?

Bob. No, he's been stolen twice. I have to figure out a way to fasten him down. One year at school we did a Belgian theme for graduation. The Manneken cost seventy-five dollars and they gave him to me afterwards. I have pots for the pedestals along the back; I do them in red, white, and blue, but they get stolen as well. The bridge was given to me after our production of *The Music Man*. Thirty-four students carried it over here. There used to be a full hedge along the lane, but people would poke their heads through to see the garden, so now I clip the holes into windows.

Joan. The temple would make a great set for a performance.

Bob. I *was* going to take the water out and bring a grand piano in, and ask Robin Harrison to play, but I never got round to it, and now he's retired, living in the Maritimes.

Joan. How about Robert Minden? He performed at the Kids' Festival and it's amazing what he can do on the musical saw.

Bob. Hmm …

Judy. (Standing beside an iron structure which looks like a large hat-stand holding flower pots.) Does this have a name?

Bob. It's my petunia tree. I reach up to water it with this (demonstrates with long watering wand and, throughout the rest of the scene, waves the wand to emphasize and indicate).

Judy. Is this a rickshaw?

Bob. Yes, my jinricksha. It's rotting. I have to put some legs back there (points with wand). Every year I paint it white and fill it with red, white, and blue flowers.

Judy. No prizes for guessing your favourite colours?

Bob. Well, I do love the Union Jack. See my new flags on the sun deck (waves wand towards the sun deck which is built on the garage roof). I plant eight hundred geraniums in the back garden, and fourteen dozen in the front.

Bob the magician.

Joan. Any perennials?

Bob. A lot of lilies, but perennials only last ten days. When you only have two months of summer, you want colour and instant effect.

Judy. Do you ever have time to sit in your garden?

Bob. (Laughs.)

ACT II. WINTER

Alas, we couldn't stay for the second act, which by all accounts was even more dramatic than the first.

Like the Werdens in Cranbrook, Bob put up an annual Christmas display. He'd been doing it for forty years and every year he chose a different theme, constructed a new cast of characters, and arranged them in a complete stage set in the front garden, over and around his floral clock. His latest was *The Lion King*. His version of *101 Dalmatians* really did have one hundred and one, and was still remembered in the neighbourhood.

Our visit was wonderfully entertaining, and the garden was probably the most original we saw on our whole trip. But looking back, I was puzzled; I wasn't sure who I met that day. Was it Bob, a sophisticated humourist, or Bob an enraptured child? Was it a philanthropist, an essentially private man, or a showman? I wished I'd had longer to learn about the creator of this wildly extrovert garden. Whenever I pictured him, he was still waving his wand over the petunia tree. Perhaps for me, he would always be simply Bob the magician.

It was a hard act to follow, but Joan knew exactly where to take us next. Our destination was Jane Roth Casson's garden. On the way, Joan told us not to expect a conventionally tidy suburban plot. She also told us that Jane was the granddaughter of Sybil Thorndike and Lewis Casson, and like her illustrious grandparents, had pursued a stage career.

I'd always admired a well trained stage voice, with its depth and modulations, its telling pauses and dramatic denouements. From the moment Jane said a velvety "Hello," I was her devotee.

"Ah yes, Bob!" she said fondly, after Joan had mentioned our visit to the floral clock. "I first met Bob at the Stratford Festival. He invited me to stay at his house. He had just done Hans Christian Andersen's *Little Match Girl* for his Christmas display and, come February, he took the whole thing down and, of course, he doesn't *tidy* things away, he just *puts* them somewhere else. Most of his garden was in his garage, but I came home one day from the university and I was going downstairs for something, and there, at the bottom of the stairs, behind a Spanish grille thing, was an old lady sitting in a chair — *dead*. I went, 'Waaah!' I said, 'Bob, you know, you really mustn't *do* that!' 'So sorry,' he said. Next day I came in and there was *another* body, this time under a sheet."

While she was talking, several dogs inside her house were throwing themselves against the windows in a frenzy of barking. A cat cage, well furnished with sleeping platforms and scratching poles, occupied a large chunk of her back garden. Like Bob, Jane loved animals. "This is a refugee camp for them" she said. "It breaks my heart when I think how we *objectify* creatures. When you start communicating with them you can see that their mime is simply brilliant. Their body language! They must think these humans are *so* stupid."

Now I knew why Joan had warned us that the garden might seem unconventional. Jane's interest in native and medicinal plants accounted for an unusual choice of plant material; Jane's health problems accounted for the rest.

"I know it all *looks* terrible," she said. "But next year, when my new hips are settled in, I'll get a claw thing and dig up the plants that are choking the others. I dry the nettles — they're very good for osteoporosis — and, if the cats get a scratch, the comfrey goes on that. I don't know what this is, but it's coming up like anything, and I do love things you can't *kill*. In Wolverhampton, I heard Chris Baines telling us we *have* to get some wilderness back into the cities, and I was frightfully inspired by that."

We soon heard more about the trend towards wild gardening.

Judy's Journal

On one of the walls in Peter and Joan's house is an embroidery by Margot Lindsay. I'm especially interested in it because I've done a series of somewhat similar embroideries with a group of women in New Brunswick. Joan tells us that Margot is a gardener as well as an embroiderer, and she organizes a visit for us.

Margot's garden is immaculate, and so is her workroom. Elspeth points out that the refined, tapestry style of the thread work matches Margot's planting style exactly. Margot says she hadn't realized this, but there it is, in the delicate all-over patterns of flowers and grasses. Margot is particularly interested in depicting wildflowers and she mentions Robin Smith, a landscape architect who passionately advocated the use of native plants and trees in landscaping schemes. Elspeth has read about him in landscape journals.

Margot tells us that he died recently and that his widow, Evelyn Smith, lives nearby. She explains how to get to the house.

We are hesitant about visiting and sit for some time in the car outside Evelyn Smith's house, debating whether or not to intrude. Elspeth wonders how I'd feel if some stranger came to the door and wanted to talk about Tom. I say I'd love it and wouldn't think it intrusive at all.

We look at the front garden with its tall native trees and long grasses and wonder how the lawn-cutting neighbours feel about the contrast with their own tidy front yards. Elspeth knocks at the door and a young boy answers. He goes to get his mother. Today, Evelyn tells us, she's feeling a bit shaky; it's Robin's birthday and the city has dedicated a park in his name. She shows us into the back garden, packed with ferns, daisies, and grasses, with sombre trees shadowing the house.

"I have no idea what is growing here," she says, "Robin did it all." She seems at a loss. The pond is overgrown and the goldfish have died, but meadow rue and columbine flourish. A small plaque says: *The garden of my youth was a horticultural wonder.*

"He was passionate about the environment," Evelyn tells us. "He designed all the trails along the river bank here in Saskatoon. He died of melanoma in December 1994. The day he died, he was so positive that he was

Angus, Louisa, and Dylan in Meacham, where gardening is a link between old-timers and newcomers.

going to lick it, and that this was just a setback. He was always so positive about things."

I want to stay and help her with the garden that I feel is becoming something of a shrine. We talk about death, the unfairness of it all, the big hole that it leaves, and the gradual filling up with a life of one's own.

In the afternoon we drive out to Meacham, a town reduced to just one elevator. It's about sixty-five kilometres from Saskatoon, where Joan's son Angus Ferguson and his wife Louisa live with their family. They are converting an old, two-storey school house into a home. The rooms are many and varied, the ceilings high and spacious, and the floors are of wood. On the ceiling above their bed

Angus and the bread oven he built.

is pinned a magnificent parachute of such sparkling colours, it would encourage anyone to spend all their days lazing around in bed.

The garden is part of a field that was originally prairie. The size alone would daunt most people. A heart-shaped willow arch has been built across the centre and different areas have been fenced off. The rows are neat and labelled. I ask Angus what the ground was like to dig. After all, it is original prairie.

"The ground was very difficult to dig through at first. The roots go way down, but once you've got through, it's very productive. See this tent trailer," he says, pointing to the base of a disused camper trailer, "it's the beginning of our greenhouse for tomatoes." I ask about the wind and Angus tells me that fortunately the whole field is surrounded by a windbreak. "Property in this area is cheap so we're finding more young people, generally those in the arts, are moving out here because of the low price. We bought the village hall and want to put on entertainment and Louisa, who loves to cook, would like to do some catering."

Over a dusty road, under a clear blue sky, we walk down to visit Alice, who lives near the village hall. Alice is eighty and still mows the grass around the village hall, but unfortunately she is not at home. Instead, we admire her very neat garden. Poppies flourish, sweet peas grow along the fence, and clematis are at home.

We talk with June Jacobs, who runs a

craft store. She says she's planted so many trees, she's outdone herself and will have to concentrate on growing shade-loving plants. Her vegetable plot is neatly laid out at the side of the house, away from the trees.

Meacham has a family feeling to it, but I wonder about newcomers coming into the area, with new ideas and youth on their side. Angus assures me newcomers fit in well with the older inhabitants. Maybe it's the use of the land and respect for the land that binds them together. It reminds me of the movement in the sixties to be more self-sufficient, when some of us were and some of us weren't.

Joan Flood

In Saskatoon, on a long, narrow lot beside a park, we discovered the last word in container gardens. It contained roughly: 214 buckets, 40 milk crates, 36 window-boxes, and 70 oil drums of marigolds; 180 plastic buckets of runner beans; 40 milk crates and 22 plastic half-drums of tomatoes; five more sets of plastic buckets with 55 per block, all marigolds; one bleeding heart; and one small donkey pulling a cart — of marigolds. Joan sent us the picture of the container garden in full flower.

Elspeth's Travelogue

When we arrived in Saskatoon to stay with the Floods, we had hoped to see Magnus Flood and tour his garden. My husband Ray and I had known Magnus since he was a baby and we had first become friends with his parents, Peter and Sandra (Peter's first wife). Through periodic meetings and exchanged photographs, we'd watched him grow into an athletic man with dark good looks and a great love of the outdoors. He was working with an Outward Bound program in Ontario when he noticed the first health problems. He was diagnosed shortly afterwards with a degenerative bone disease, an irreversible condition.

We'd been thunderstruck. At a distance, we went through all the stages of disbelief, fear, outrage, and grief that his family suffered on a hugely magnified scale. The senseless injustice of it! I didn't know how, or even whether, Magnus himself had come to terms with it but, in any case, he did something quite unexpected, something quite splendid. He decided to use what he thought might be his last active summer to make a garden.

This was a heroic story and it had a heroine. Sarah Lee was in her twenties, pretty and lively. She had just been accepted to the Occupational Therapy program at Edmonton when Magnus fell ill. She put her plans on hold, and became everything to him — his love, his companion, his support, and, as his condition worsened, his nurse and even his arms and legs.

We weren't sure if Magnus would be well enough to talk to us, and we were delighted when he said he'd like us to come for a visit. Delighted and apprehensive. He was in pain, and was due for another operation on his leg that very afternoon. We had no

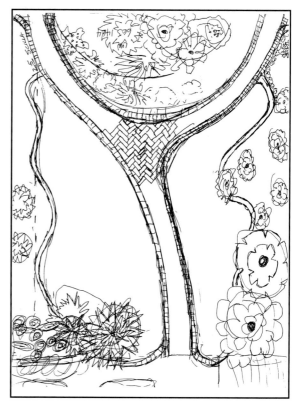

Magnus Flood's freehand sketch of his garden plan.

comfort to offer him, and in the end I felt it was he and Sarah who were comforting *us*. But share in his delight with gardening? That was something we *could* do.

The morning was cool but sunny, and Magnus was determined to show us around. Sarah lifted his wheelchair down the back steps and he managed to climb down to the garden by himself.

There wasn't much gardening in either of their backgrounds and we wanted to know what got them started. Magnus had worked briefly for a landscaper and that, he said, had encouraged him — knowing he could do it. Having a house of their own helped too, but even before then, he'd bought Sarah a set of gardening tools for Christmas. He'd designed the simple layout of the garden with freehand sketches and then on computer.

Judy with Magnus and Sarah in their garden.

A vegetable garden filled the back space alongside the garage, wide borders ran down each side of the lawn, a semicircular bed lay between the lawn and the house, and a brick path curved down the middle.

Magnus had obtained soil, peatmoss, and old sawdust from a greenhouse operation, and bricks from a demolition company. His brother, Corin, had helped to lay the bricks. The first things they'd planted were two shrubby dogwoods followed by 'Persian Yellow' and 'Hansa' roses, and a ginala maple for fall colour. Mostly they'd put in small inexpensive plants. They'd tried to avoid pink flowers, because Magnus hated them, but a few slipped past the pink police. "A bash with a tennis racquet soon got rid of them," he said. Their guide was the *Prairie Garden* series published by the University of Alberta.

"It would take about two-and-a-half hours of discussion to decide where to put anything," Sarah said, "and Magnus measured everything out. I'd never have done that. I'm his gorilla girl. He tells me what to do and I just do it. I was playing along at first but now I'm a gardener myself — hardcore!"

They started seven hundred seedlings in peat pots and grew them under glass, thanks to a local nursery that loaned them greenhouse space. Just when the seedlings were ready for planting out, the young couple were due to leave for a holiday and they ended up planting at midnight, wearing head lamps — much to the amusement of the neighbours. The vegetable garden was a huge success, producing far more lettuce than they could eat. They persuaded the neighbours to help out. Someone even gave Sarah a recipe for pickled lettuce!

Magnus Flood and Sarah Lee.

Magnus was beginning to feel chilly, so we went back into the house and looked at pictures of the garden in late summer. The borders were packed with colourful plants and gigantic sunflowers towered over everything. "Our old growth sunflower forest," they called it. The completed brick path flowed beautifully through the middle of it all. The whole thing was a remarkable achievement for one year.

I asked Magnus how he'd hit on the attractive shape for the path, which curved from the garage towards the house and then split around the semicircular bed in the shape of a Y. "Oh that," he said quietly. "That's the eternal question Y."

Oh yes, indeed, I thought, my dearest Magnus: why?

Judy's Journal

Tonight we are in Wanuskewin, a site that Northern Plains Indians visited for over six thousand years. They came for celebration, they came to hunt buffalo and to gather food and herbs, and they came to find shelter from the winter winds. It is now a Heritage Park. A magnificent storm blows up. Dark roiling clouds tumble across the sky and lightning spears around us. The earth trembles under whip-cracks of thunder and then, in a sudden lull, I see a sliver of jade drift in a purple sky.

In the bookstore at Wanuskewin Joan finds a booklet called *The Native Garden Book* by Root Woman, and buys it for us. Intrigued, we call Root Woman right away. Her answering machine says: "I have gone into the bush to collect medicines."

She returns our call and gives her address as Alvena, a village north-east of Saskatoon. We arrange to meet her tomorrow.

I imagine we are going to meet someone like Hiawatha or at least someone wearing fringed leather, but no, a jolly middle-aged woman with thick, short, greying hair greets us enthusiastically and introduces herself as Kahlee Keane. Wind chimes dance wildly on her porch. She sits us down at her kitchen table. There's a mouthwatering aroma from a pot simmering on the stove. Elspeth asks her about the name Root Woman. She laughs. "A Buddhist was visiting one day and we talked on and on for about six hours then he phoned his wife to tell her he'd be late. He said to her: 'I'm … I'm with um … um, Root Woman.' So I thought it would be fun to use it."

She makes it very clear she is not a herbalist, explaining that she wouldn't think of saying, "Come into my office. I'll give you something for that." Rather she takes people into the wild to find their own medicine and recognize it. She became interested in herbal remedies when she was cured of cancer by a Native woman, Norma Myers, in Alert Bay when she went up there to die. It wasn't just the medicine Norma gave her. Norma also gave her love, and it was this combination that cured her. "I don't think the pharmaceuticals are where it's at," Kahlee says.

"We've been trying to get the Native peoples interested in medicine again," she continues. "The grandmothers stopped telling their daughters about it forty years ago. They were told to. Now they ask us to give workshops on the reserves. I say to them, 'I'm giving you back your own knowledge.' I tend to start things and bring awareness to people, then I withdraw. Isn't that how life progresses? Somebody starts something then somebody uses it and improves it?"

Kahlee offers us apple cake fresh from the oven and makes us delicious tea from bog cranberry and, I think, licorice root.

Throughout our visit she gives us little vignettes of her life, performed with style and humour. She was born in Torquay, Devon. I tell her I too lived there.

She tells us she came to Canada with her parents. Her mother, a herbalist in England, gathered plants and her father sold baskets. When she was thirteen she met a man and went back to England with him until she was sixteen: "It was a platonic relationship — I knew I wasn't wanted in my parents' life."

She's been down-and-out in Halifax, harvested dulse on Grand Manan, and been marooned for a week on an island off Newfoundland, living on snails and whatever else she could find. She now lives in Alvena. Population: forty-nine. I ask why, and she says, "Economics." This is her first permanent home, this neat, small house in the middle of the Prairies. She tells us all this with a lot of humour. Her work she takes seriously, but not herself.

Outside, in the battering wind, she shows us where different plants are coming through and the ponds she uses for watering. She has the plastic shelter for seedlings, but repeats that she prefers to gather plants from the wild. If she could rewrite the Ten Commandments, she says, number one would be: Thou shalt not foul the earth, and another: Thou shalt not break the lovely skin of the earth.

Back in the house, Elspeth defends gardens by saying that in urban settings, gardening is the best route people have to the earth. They get their hands muddy, and even if they sometimes plant exotic and ridiculous things, it's a start.

"You may find yourself becoming a gardener, too," Elspeth says to Kahlee, "when you realize that what you find growing around you just isn't enough."

"I already have," Kahlee admits. "I've been learning how to germinate seeds and growing some non-native flowers."

As we leave, she gives us some salves she's made, and a brochure of her videos and workshops. We wave good-bye and I feel that this intriguing and entertaining woman must lead an isolated and somewhat lonely life out here on the prairies.

From Alvena we try to get to Manitoba. Along the way we stop at a restaurant where most of the men seem a bit bashed about. One has his arm in a sling, another has bandaged fingers, and a third has his leg in a cast. There are no women other than the two of us. Pinned to the wall of the restroom is a detailed description of condoms. I hadn't realized there was such a variety.

Just after Yorkton it starts to rain and the windshield wipers start to stick. The sky is black, the wind lashes at the car, and the rain comes down in sheets. I can't see a thing. We stop on the shoulder of the road so Elspeth can get out to unstick the wipers. The wind sucks the map out of the car, and I'm afraid she too will be blown like a piece of tumbleweed right across the prairies. What will I tell her family? In the pouring rain she leans across the hood, touches the wipers, and they immediately leap into a frenzy of wiping. I'm afraid she will lose her fingers, but when she complains of this very thing I tell her there have been vast improvements in microsurgery and besides, with bound-up hands she'll be right at home with the men in the restaurant.

"And Elspeth," I say, "you've always wanted to fit in."

We repeat the wiper procedure, or rather Elspeth does, many, many times until she begins to balk. By now she looks like a small drowned marsupial, but we agree that I'm the designated driver. No point in both of us getting soaked. Anyway, we can't go on much longer, stopping and hopping out, so it's back to Yorkton to a garage, where the mechanics say they can't look at the car until the morning. This is a new rented car, we moan, hoping they'll feel sorry for us, but they don't. We spend the night in Yorkton.

Elspeth's Traveloque

All signs of the storm had vanished by morning. The wipers, however, needed a new motor, and the nearest one was in Portage la Prairie. We were heading in that direction anyway, so we called ahead to a repair shop and set out once again for Manitoba.

But why was the road heading south? Judy's husband Tom had once served in the air force, and used to say that pilots never lost their way; they only misplaced their positions and attempted appropriate corrective action. My corrective actions were hindered by the lack of a map and, mysteriously, we found ourselves in Esterhazy, Saskatchewan. This little town was home to many fine vegetable gardeners and a pair of charming tree stumps, but it still wasn't Manitoba.

In the afternoon we finally crossed the border, picked up a map of Manitoba,

A pair of charming tree stumps in Esterhazy.

and headed for Shoal Lake. I'd been given the address of a nursery there, and it seemed as good a place as any to start the Manitoba ball rolling.

The nursery was a family-run operation, but when we arrived the family was away. The assistant told us we could find them at a son's house nearby. Stubbornly, we tracked them down, hoping they might give us a useful lead. They did, and they gave us something else as well — a guided tour of a splendid energy-efficient house, and a glimpse of a whole other aspect of garden design.

Wayne and Darlene Ewachewski had planned their new home and garden with sunlight and shelter in mind. They'd dug into the south slope of a natural swell in the ground, erected a retaining wall of room height against the cut, and built their single-storey house against it. The floor plan was long and narrow with all the windows facing south. They'd used the excavated material to sculpt wings of earth which projected forward in a crescent shape and sheltered the exposed front windows. The wings were planted with ornamental shrubs and, behind them, a wide lawn swept smoothly up and around the back of the house, which showed only as a roof. Finally, they'd surrounded the whole arrangement with a sturdy shelter belt, the first circular shelter belt we'd seen. The layout was beautifully simple and snug, and after my recent encounter with the prairie wind I wondered why more people didn't build this way.

The Ewachewskis also had an excellent suggestion for our next port of call. Wayne thought we should visit Dropmore.

"Dropmore as in honeysuckle?"

"Right. Frank Skinner's place." He explained that Frank had died some time before, but his wife and son, Hugh, would probably be there.

When I'd arrived in Canada about thirty years earlier, I'd read as much as I could about Canadian plants, and whenever prairie winters were mentioned, I'd noticed that the name Frank Skinner was inclined to crop up. One of his most popular introductions was the 'Dropmore Scarlet' honeysuckle, and I always felt that a Canadian garden, prairie or otherwise, was hardly complete without those orangey-flame flowers. When I first met Judy, I gave her a cutting of my own plant, and after I moved to the West Coast, she returned the favour by sending me a cutting of hers.

We wanted to see the birthplace of this wonderful plant, but there was a snag. The Skinner's nursery was near Roblin, back at the Saskatchewan border. In our wiperless state, the sensible thing to do was press on towards Portage.

"If we were sensible," said Judy, "we wouldn't be here in the first place."

It was dusk when Saskatchewan hove into sight once more and we had a hard time finding the Skinner's modest house, which was tucked into the side of dense woods. We were hoping to arrange an appointment with Hugh for the following day, but Hugh was away for the evening and it was Helen Skinner, his mother, who came to the door, graciously invited us in, and told us her late husband's story.

Who'd have thought that three years of excellent fishing off the east coast of Scotland would have a lasting effect on Canadian horticulture?

In 1885, North Sea herring catches soared and prices crashed. The Skinners, a well-to-do family in the fish curing business, gambled on better prices to come, and kept their fish in storage. The glut, however, continued, and in 1887 the warehouse charges bankrupted them. Frank Skinner's father never recovered from this downturn in the family fortunes. His mother, however, must have been an exceptionally strong woman, for it was she who held the family of ten children together and, after eight years of scrimping and saving, oversaw their emigration to Manitoba.

After Scotland, the Dropmore area where they settled would have come as a shock. It was still frontier country then, treeless and sparsely settled. At thirteen, Frank had already attended school in Aberdeen for seven years, and he found himself more knowledgable than any local teacher. The family began farming — part grain, part cattle — and Frank, although he was a sickly child, became an expert horseman. His long days on the range gradually improved his health, and also introduced him to the plants of the region. He was especially curious about the wild roses, which didn't winterkill like the roses brought in from Scotland. He began to experiment, making crosses between these hardy natives and the more fragrant and glamorous imports. As Helen said, "Plant breeding became his obsession. He just kept going and going." He spent all his spare time crossing and selecting plants for qualities such as hardiness, drought tolerance, and disease resistance as well as for good looks. By the time the Depression hit, and farming was no longer lucrative, Frank's collection of plants was so extensive he was able to start selling nursery stock.

For the rest of his life he worked tirelessly, breeding trees, shrubs, bulbs, and herbaceous plants suited to prairie conditions. He corresponded with horticulturalists around the world and obtained specimens from the Prairie States, Scandinavia, Russia, Asia — anywhere with a climate similar to Manitoba's. His interests were amazingly broad. 'Rosy O'Grady' clematis, 'Rudolph' crabapple, 'Purity' mockorange, 'Wasagaming' and 'Isabella Skinner' roses, 'Rosabella' spirea, 'Pocohontas' lilac, 'Black Prince' lily, and the 'Dropmore' linden were just a few of his introductions.

We talked about the painstaking work of breeders like Frank Skinner; how it often took decades — sometimes more than a lifetime — to breed and select a disease-resistant tree, propagate it, then introduce it to the public. Frank was given many honours for his contributions to horticulture. He became a Member of the British Empire and was awarded an honorary doctorate from the University of Manitoba. Unfortunately, plant patent laws didn't exist in Canada in his day, and for all his work, he received no financial reward. Plants like the 'Dropmore Scarlet' honeysuckle were propagated and sold in enormous numbers in Canada and overseas. A single nursery in Germany, for example, produced thousands of cuttings annually. If the Skinners had received even one cent for every plant sold, they'd have had few financial worries.

Frank was sixty-five when he married Helen, a young woman who'd just finished her nursing training. "Plants were his *first* love," she told us. "I was the other woman who came on the scene late in his life." The couple had five children. "He was wonderful with them," she said. "He spent a lot of time with them and it rubbed off." She showed us an old family photograph. "That's Heather; she works with forage crops in agricultural research. And that's Hugh — the one trying to fall out of the barn loft — he's his father all over again."

Judy's Journal

We arrange to see Hugh first thing the next morning. We find a motel, the cheapest we've stayed in, the sort you take soap *to*, not take soap away *from* — where the living room serves as the office and is chock-full of stuffed birds, dried flowers, paintings on velvet, and milk crates full of old magazines. We both sleep well, however, and are at the Frank Skinner Arboretum by eight.

Elspeth's Traveloque

The weather turned chilly overnight, and we were glad to walk briskly with Hugh through the twenty-five acres of woodland that were part of his father's legacy. The trees were a fascinating mixture of natives, species from all over the world, and various hybrids. I was especially taken with a spinney of tall Scots pine with their unmistakable reddish bark. Judy loved the clumps of spotted coral-root orchids pushing up through the leaf litter. It was hard to believe that this had once been treeless prairie.

The woods formed a unique genetic pool and Hugh was well aware of their botanical and

Hugh Skinner points out the healthy foliage of a linden species — *Tilia mandshurica.*

historical significance. In spite of a woeful lack of funding, he was determined to maintain the area and open it to the public as an educational resource. He had formed a non-profit organization called the Frank Skinner Arboretum Trail, and the group ran horticultural weekends with seminars on everything from paper making to bird watching. While we were there, a cheery group of volunteers arrived to help with a visit from a local school. There was something inspiring about the Skinner personality — in no time at all, Judy and I were volunteering to move picnic tables around, and if we'd stayed much longer I don't doubt we'd have found ourselves clearing trails and giving guided tours as well.

Even as a child, Hugh had been an early riser. As soon as he was old enough to dress himself, he was out before dawn, helping his father stoke the fires in the greenhouse. He was still up and about by 5:30 a.m., and maybe that's how he managed to run a nursery business — Skinner Garden Classics — maintain and promote the arboretum, and take an interest in plant selection as well.

Lindens were among his favourite trees and he showed us a number of promising specimens. I'd noticed young lindens as street trees in Yorkton and I'd also noticed that many were dead or dying — a far cry from these healthy specimens. I wondered if Yorkton had planted Skinner hybrids, and if not, why not.

Hugh told us he found it frustrating that many garden centres traded on the ignorance of their clients by selling inappropriate imported stock. Plants could be produced more quickly in milder climates, he explained, and for that reason were sometimes cheaper than locally grown plants. The imports, however, weren't acclimatized, and the varieties offered weren't always suited to the rigours of prairie life. We agreed that a sickly plant was a bad bargain.

Thanks to the tireless work of breeders like Frank and Hugh Skinner, wonderful plants were available for the asking. We all hoped that prairie gardeners would ask with persistence.

Judy's Journal

We're looking forward to a good hearty brunch of eggs, bacon, and pancakes — food no longer good for the body but good for the soul. We find a place to eat where you serve yourself. Nothing really tempts us but we notice that most of the people there are eating pizza. We too eat soggy, thick pizza covered with great globs of pineapple. Both it and the coffee are cold.

"I can't believe this food," Elspeth says, pushing most of it aside. "And I was so looking forward to it."

I agree that we were better off with the old sardines and hard tack. It's the most revolting pizza I've ever had; I can't eat it. Even the coffee's awful.

Elspeth's Travelogue

In Saskatoon, Joan Flood had given us the phone number of Joy and Keith Smith's bed-and-breakfast near Brandon, Manitoba. She'd told us that the house, Gwenmar, was spacious and full of character, that much of the food was home-grown (if we were lucky, the asparagus might still be in season), and that Joy was a great gardener and an expert in heritage beans. A bean expert was exactly what we needed. We thought she might be able to tell us more about our precious Doukhobor beans, and no wonky wind-shield wiper was going to deflect us from a goal like that.

Gwenmar was indeed a lovely house. Built as a summer home in 1914 for a former lieutenant-governor, its living and dining rooms opened onto a

Joy Smith and Beethoven in the garden.

wide verandah where much summertime living took place. It was a typical prairie property — embedded in a block of trees, a private island of greenery awash in an ocean of wheat, alfalfa, and canola.

In the morning, we woke to a dramatic chorus of squawks and shrieks, and looked out of our bedroom window into dense treetop foliage. From this vantage point, we found it hard to believe we were on the prairies. It felt more like a tropical jungle, except that the raucous birds were crows and magpies instead of parrots. When we mentioned them to Keith over breakfast (delicious asparagus omelettes), his reaction surprised us. Our gentle host became positively warlike. He explained with distaste that both crows and magpies were thriving at Gwenmar, where they preyed on smaller birds. Beethoven, the Smith's large golden retriever, apparently shared his master's antipathy. When we walked with Beethoven the next day, he took a flying leap at a magpie and managed to dislodge one of its tail feathers.

After breakfast, Joy found time to talk beans with us. Most of her seventy varieties of bean seed came from Seeds of Diversity, Canada, a dedicated group of gardeners striving to preserve genetic variety in Canadian vegetables and other garden plants. She also grew heritage peas, lentils, herbs, and lettuce, regrowing many kinds each year to keep the stock fresh and to have a supply on hand for distribution. She received requests from all over the country.

One, from a woman in Ontario, asked for sulphur beans; she wanted to surprise her eighty-year-old father who remembered them from the Depression when they sold for five dollars a bushel — a good price at the time. In response to such a request, Joy normally sent about twenty seeds. Successfully regrown, the yield might fill a coffee can.

We wanted to know why Joy put such huge effort into the project. "I got passionate about the beautiful seed," she said, "and I just got carried away." She certainly did. Her garden plot, which was edged by a deep flower border, was as big as a farmer's field. Keith tilled the ground for her and Joy did the rest. She had trouble with her hip, and one of her most valued posessions, a gift from her children, was a small seeding machine which saved her much painful bending.

Normally, Joy stored her seed in coffee cans or glass jars in her cool dry basement but as she sometimes gave talks to school children, she'd made a display of the different beans, using egg cartons. We showed her our precious collection and sorted through her samples to see if we could match them.

Bean heaven! There were beans like birds' eggs, beans as tempting as candy, and beans as pretty as beads. They were amber and pale green, pink and maroon, black and white, streaked, speckled, and dappled, and the names were as appealing as the beans themselves. How could anyone resist a handful of midnight black turtles, or a bowl of soup made from Canadian wild goose or from magpies? (Keith would certainly have approved!) How could anyone *not* be moved by Cherokee trail of tears, the beans saved by

In Joy and Keith Smith's vast garden, favourite deer food such as horse lentils and garbanzo beans are planted between fenced rows of Mostoller wild goose and Cherokee trail of tears.

Native bands evicted from their homelands? And how could anyone *not* want to plant a row of soldiers, and harvest an army of beans, each imprinted with the image of a tiny military man? Soldier beans were well known in New Brunswick and I often grew them when I lived there, so I was surprised to hear they were considered a rarity in other parts of Canada.

Joy's latest love was garlic. In the fall, she'd planted more than twenty different kinds, and Keith mulched them with a twenty centimetre layer of flax straw to protect them through the winter.

Agriculture Canada had noticed the valuable work being done by amateurs like Joy, and had recruited them to test existing government seed stocks. The volunteer gardeners grew up to five types of grains, pulses or tomatoes each year, and kept careful records of planting and germination dates, success rates, and problems such as pests. The same seeds were tested in different parts of the country, and the resulting information could be used in breeding programs to produce disease resistant strains suitable for various growing conditions.

Judy and I were full of admiration for Seeds of Diversity. The local strains they were keeping alive were small potent pills of our history and it would have been sad to lose them for that reason alone. But their real importance, of course, lay in their genes, which carried who knew what essential attributes into our changing world.

Keith grew up on a farm and remembered growing a type of barley called 'Vantmore'. It was replaced by cultivars that matured more quickly and now, Keith told us, 'Vantmore' barley would be hard to find. It might, however, have had assets that the newer types did not — disease resistance or weather tolerance — assets that could be bred back into barleys of the future. As Nina Koodrin said of her grandmother's day, seeds had been a matter of survival. They still were.

In Joy's egg carton display, we found a cranberry bean that resembled our pink-with-purple-streaks, and our streaky brown was something like candy. Our creamy white was a kind of broad bean and the plain brown was a kidney, but in her entire collection we couldn't find an exact match for any of them. We counted out a few of each type, left them in her expert hands, and I hoped, even more fervently now, that some of them would germinate in the spring.

Joy was one of those astonishing women who could make a gourmet meal, answer the telephone, cope with a family crisis, feed the dog, fold the laundry, and carry on an intelligent conversation all at the same time. While we were there, she helped us identify wild flowers, showed us how to avoid ironing table napkins, and even performed a miracle on Judy's trousers — all in the day's work. To my mind, such ability verged on genius, but Joy was modest and probably never gave it a second thought.

Judy's Journal

Joy and Keith suggest we visit Joe Tsukamoto who, before he retired, was a crop diversification specialist with the Manitoba Department of Agriculture. He lives in a fine old house in Brandon. When he moved there twenty years ago, the land was in bad shape and it has taken years of composting to lighten the soil.

His garden is experimental — redolent of his days with the Department of Agriculture — neat straight rows, all clearly marked. I admire his labels, which are fashioned from coat-hangers and the cardboard used in packing dahlias.

He is also engaged in a fierce battle with creeping Charlie, alias ground ivy, that I too have battled with, but my battle is tame compared to his. I confess that I think it looks quite pretty in some areas but he says, "Oh, no. No. No."

"One of the elms went from Dutch elm disease," he says, pointing to a large tree that still looks healthy. "I try and prune out the dead bits in this one, but I need a ladder, and I don't trust my wife holding a ladder."

"D'you have a lot of insurance?" I ask.

"But that won't help me."

"I was thinking about your wife," I say.

Elspeth's Travelogue

When we first met Joe Tsukamoto, we had no idea we'd stumbled on the story of Japanese internment again. He told us he was born in New Westminster, British Columbia, but went to school in Japan, and returned to Canada on the last commercial ship to make the crossing before Pearl Harbour was bombed. He might have been interned at Hope or Greenwood but chose instead to go to Alberta. He described how the internees lived there in granaries or converted chicken coops, and worked in the sugar beet fields.

"Work like a horse, I guess," he said. "Long hours too. You go out at five in the morning and you almost crawl home — can't straighten your back. Twenty-one cents per hour, or paid by the acre. Report to R.C.M.P when going more than forty miles away."

After the war, he worked for one summer as a cowboy, then went on by cattle train to Montreal where he was accepted into the horticultural program at McGill University. He worked with Agriculture Canada and then with the Manitoba Department of Agriculture until his retirement. At one point, his research took him to the North where he bred forage crops. In the Yukon, he said, the last recorded spring frost was July 15 and the first recorded fall frost was July 16. Fortunately these records hadn't yet coincided.

Joe's experience in the North had paid off in his own garden. By seeding spinach, lettuce, and carrots in the fall, he discovered he could get a jump on the spring season. This was particularly important in his garden, which turned shady as soon as the leaves came out on the trees. He thought onions and parsnips could probably be grown the same way, but his wife didn't like parsnips so he didn't plant them.

After his retirement, he was employed by CIDA (the Canadian International Development Agency) in Bangladesh, developing pulses — mostly chick peas and lentils — and he then worked as a volunteer in the Ukraine. Before he left for Bangladesh, he planted a trial patch of horseradish in his vegetable plot, and when he returned two years later his patch had become a solid mass of horseradish roots. As digging them out proved difficult, he conducted herbicide trials instead.

Large horseradish roots were awkward and expensive for farmers to plant, and Joe was now experimenting with short sections, putting them in horizontally, at an angle, right side up and upsidedown. This man was nothing if not thorough! He told us that a valuable enzyme extracted from horseradish was used in drug-use detection. By hilling up his rows and using plastic to hold moisture, he discovered that plants stressed late in the season produced more enzyme. Farmers, he felt, should be paid not by the quantity of roots, but by the quantity of enzyme the roots contained.

This scientifically minded gardener was also interested in growing mints and echinacea for their pharmaceutical possibilities, artichokes to produce fructose for diabetics, and monarda for geranial oil which, he explained, was used as a perfume base.

Joe may have retired, but his life's work was continuing apace in this miniature experimental farm that was only thinly disguised as a garden.

Judy's Journal

This evening I'm sitting on my bed wondering where I've put my pen — feeling my pockets, dumping out my purse, asking Elspeth if she's seen it. I stand up to look in my overnight bag, and behind me on the bedspread is a large blue ink stain and, in the centre, my pen. I am horrified.

"What can I do?" I cry.

"Cold water, quick," replies Elspeth.

I haul the bedspread into the bathroom. Scrub, squeeze, and rub. Then I scrub, squeeze, and rub again. The water runs blue, but not blue enough; the stain is lighter but spreading in an alarming way. I want to roll it up and hide it in my bag and pretend it never happened.

"Have you seen the back of your pants?" Elspeth says. A dark blue ink stain is spreading across the seat.

"These are new," I wail. "I'll never be able to wear them again. Look at them!" My underwear is also blue, a dark blue. I spend most of the evening in the bathroom in an agony of guilt, trying to wash out the stains.

All night I worry about the bedspread and blame myself for being so stupid. First thing next morning I show it to Joy and apologize.

"We'll look up what to do," she says calmly, and flicks through a book she keeps handy. It says hairspray and toothpaste are good for ball point pen stains. I spray the bedspread with hairspray and rub and scrub away at it, then have a go with toothpaste.

The stain comes out like magic. I put it in the washer and the results are perfect. I can't believe it. Then I work on my pants. They, too, come up clean. I can't believe that either.

In the end, we spend three days with Joy, relaxing, working on stains, walking, and getting to know some of the wildflowers in the area. When I ask for the bill it is far less than we expect, because each extra day the charge is less. Had we spent any more time, we'd have had no bill at all.

Elspeth's Travelogue

We'd been so lucky up to this point, stumbling at every turn on remarkable gardeners and on aspects of gardening we'd never thought of before, we'd begun to take serendipity for granted. As a result, we weren't even surprised when Joy mentioned that her daughter, Janet, was deeply involved with community gardening in Brandon. The gift simply fell into our laps.

In Europe, allotment gardens had been around for generations, and both Judy and I were familiar with the often ramshackle patchworks that added a human richness to the dreary outskirts of many crowded British cities. For urban workers, the allotment gardens were half food source and half country cottage. In North America, community gardens like Brandon's had evolved for other reasons. Detachment was an ailment of our times — detachment from our cultures, from nature, and from each other. Recently, people had begun to discover that community and neighbourhood gardens could break this isolation and nurture a sense of belonging.

Janet Smith was an articulate proponent of the Brandon community gardens. She'd helped start the first one three years earlier as a project of Vision Quest, a government-funded effort to promote healthier communities. A group of about twenty-five people in the neighbourhood was given permission to take over a strip of useless grass that lay between a sports field and a road. They dug up a rectangular plot and, without fences or patrols of any kind, began to plant. The Native people blessed the site and work continued in an easy-going way. In fall, they organized a clean-up and a harvest feast. In winter, they built up the sides of the plot with snow and flooded it to form a skating rink. Labour and produce were distributed in a relaxed sort of free-for-all. As Janet said, "They just let things happen — the garden was organic in every sense." Things were still just happening, and though the garden, when we saw it, wouldn't have won any awards for horticultural productivity, the real products of such a scheme were far less tangible and far more important than prize cabbages.

The second community garden was on church land. A house had been demolished next to the church, and the site was destined to become a parking lot until Janet proposed a scheme for a community garden and collective kitchen for a group of women involved in a literacy program. School for most of these women meant only bad memories but, in this new unthreatening atmosphere, they were learning to read and write, and were picking up math and basic survival skills. They were also making friends and feeling the sense of worth that came with practical achievement. Empowerment was the buzzword. The church people marvelled that the land was being put to such good use. Janet told us that the women's children were involved from the start, and this had probably helped to prevent vandalism. It was the children who told people, "Stay on the paths!" and the most telling thing Judy and I saw in the garden was a corner belonging to the children themselves. It was an imaginative layout of mud pies and flowers — definitely the work of budding gardeners.

Judy's Journal

From Brandon we head to Portage La Prairie for a new wiper motor. Nothing wrong with the motor they tell us, but there is something amiss with the switch. We ask for a new rental. Quicker to plunder a new car for a switch, they tell us, than to arrange for a new rental. So we sit in the garage, write up our notes, and go through tapes.

Argyle is the next place we look for. There, John Morgan and his wife Carol run Prairie Habitats Inc., a nursery business that supplies native plants and seeds. They are interested in conserving and bringing back tallgrass prairie to parts of Manitoba.

When we arrive, John takes us into his greenhouse, which is full of very healthy-looking plants. He and his wife have collected a hundred different species of native plants and grasses. Also displayed are publications on native plants, including booklets by Root Woman. I ask if there is a lot of interest in what they are doing. John tells us they have a core group of keen and loyal customers, but on the whole most people don't consider native plants when gardening. Only one percent of the original tallgrass prairie remains. It's a much endangered ecosystem.

"Nowadays," John says, "in Manitoba you can drive across the Red River Valley and rarely see a native plant. It's nearly all gone."

John tells us they have been in the business for nine years and have had quite a lot of publicity for what they're doing. He mentions how much he admired Robin Smith, whose widow we met in Saskatoon, for his pioneer work in native planting.

I am interested in the tallgrass prairie, and John says that big bluestem and cord grass can get to over seven feet tall. It's the bluestem that turns the prairie into a beautiful reddish purple. I can clearly imagine the vast purple prairie swaying in the wind and hear the gentle swish of the grasses.

John says that fire is an integral part of tallgrass prairie: "It gets rid of debris and weeds and stimulates plant species. The black surface left from the ash warms quicker and is good for root development."

"I thought it was dangerous when fire swept over the prairie," I say.

"No," he says, "it's essential." He goes on to tell us that, without it, the prairies would have been forest. Fire gets rid of willow and aspen and allows for an oak savanna to form. True prairie species aren't permanently damaged by fire or by summer drought because their roots go so deep. Bison sought out the tallgrass prairie because it was rich in prairie clover and legumes that they liked. Like the fires, the grazing helped maintain the prairie.

We ask if he knows anyone in the area who gardens with native plants and he tells us that the Penners in Winnipeg would likely be happy to show us their garden. Elspeth phones them and we arrange to meet early in the evening. We wish him luck and go on our way to find a place to stay for the night.

As we drive, we talk about what a fantastic sight the original prairie must have been and what the pioneers must have thought when first confronted by it. "And now it's all gone," Elspeth says. "Unbelievable, isn't it?" We agree that Carol and John Morgan, like so many of the gardeners we've met, are people with a passion.

A while later, we stop at a hotel and I try to book us in. Elspeth stays in the car as we're going to meet the Penners right away. There's a woman at the desk. I have to tell her umpteen times: "Double room, two beds, two adults." She tells me she will have to see if the room is empty and scurries off down the corridor. The lounge is thick with smoke and men. She comes back and says, "They've gone." She asks for a five-dollar key deposit. I pay up with some trepidation.

As I'm driving away and telling Elspeth about the deposit, I look up at the sign above the hotel. It advertises male and female dancers.

Randy Penner is mowing a strip of grass along the sidewalk when we arrive at his house in Winnipeg that evening. He is about six-foot-eight and towers above Elspeth. He ushers us enthusiastically into his garden.

"Actually, this garden is not labour-saving," he says,

"and before you start growing native plants you've got to prepare the ground. You've got to kill off all introduced weed and lawn grasses — dead, dead, dead. If you're going to have lawn as well, it's essential to have an edge because the lawn grass will work its way in." He says he got excited one year and rototilled the live turf up and hoped it would die, but that summer was wet and, "Did it breed!" He had to use the kiss of death … Roundup. He points out some of the flowers — deer tongue, prairie crocus, cutleaf anemone, bedstraw — all plants we'd seen on one of our walks in Brandon. Randy's wife, Janet, and their small daughter, Larissa, join us and Janet says that from their dining room window the garden is always changing: "You feel you're involved in the seasons."

"It's a lot of work, actually," Randy says, and goes on to tell us that every day in May he picked dandelions. He adds that people who've let their lawn go into dandelions and noxious weeds say it's gone wild, but that's not the same thing: "This is *contrived* to look sort of wild." If he did it another time, he would plant a lot of leafy wild flowers to choke out the dandelions. He points to some coneflowers and gaillardia, and tells us they re-seed well. "See at the back there, I have bluestem and golden alexanders. The children love it. They run through it and call it the neighbourhood jungle."

We ask whether his neighbours have shown any interest. He replies, "No, I don't think anyone else in the neighbourhood has been infected by the idea, even though I've given out seed catalogues."

We ask how it got started and he tells us they started

Janet and Randy Penner in their small urban prairie. By season's end, the grasses would be as tall as Janet.

small and got plugs from John Morgan and put them in every nine inches … half flowers and half grasses. They also salvaged some orchids from a road construction and didn't expect their survival, but last year had

Janet Penner

Randy Penner

The Penner garden in summer (top) and fall.

---

five lady slippers on each of them. He shows us some wild roses that they also dug from a road expansion. The roses are doing well. "July is really when it's at its best," Randy says. "It's not big enough. It's only fifteen feet by thirty feet. Actually, I'm thinking of burning the whole thing off in the fall."

I have visions of everything going up in smoke, house and all.

"How can you do that in such a confined space?" I ask.

"I'm thinking of doing it with a propane torch and doing a bit at a time ... a little flame shot and you just go swoosh."

"You need a bison," I say.

"Last year we had a rabbit," replies Randy.

"Oh, a *tiny* bison," I say, and we all laugh.

To escape the mosquitoes we go into the house to chat and look at photographs of their prairie at different seasons. I mention I've been looking for a lawn-free front garden and Randy suggests we go and see a front garden that is being completely taken over by flowers.

"That's what I've been looking for ever since we set out on our trip," I say. "A front garden like a cottage garden in England, with a bit of everything. A change from lawn and foundation planting."

I walk with Janet, who is pushing the stroller, and we laugh at Elspeth scooting along ahead of us beside long-limbed Randy. "I'm a teacher and just finishing up my Master's in divinity," Janet tells me, "and Randy is an electrical engineer who is longing for a career change ... maybe to divinity."

I ask how they became interested in native planting. "We did a lot of walking on the prairies and got into wildflowers. Randy saw an article in *Harrowsmith* about native plantings and said, 'I wanna do this' ... and did."

"They've stopped," I say, or rather Randy has stopped, and Elspeth has bumped into him.

The garden is at the front of a large old house shaded by mature trees. It's owned by Greg Chernish and Elynore Kendryna, who are soon outside talking to us. I ask Greg why they went ahead with digging up the lawn.

"The lawn mower broke," he says, "and neither of us likes mowing anyway. So I said to Elynore we should rip up the lawn and when I came home it was gone. The first year we planted potatoes to break up the ground but that attracted … "

"Potato beetles?" I ask.

"No," says Greg, "the neighbours. They all wanted to see what was going on."

"It's coming, but slow," says Elynore, who envies Elspeth living in Vancouver, where she too has no lawn to mow.

The garden is still in its infancy, with large clumps of different hostas, ferns, and monkshood, with lettuce and kale in among the perennials. Elynore and Greg have started a trend. The next-door neighbours are digging up their lawn too, but at a slower pace because they have children who need a place to play.

I don't know why more people don't do this. Is it because it's not traditional or because it's less private to work at the front of the house? Elspeth asks if I'm going to dig up the whole of my front garden when I get home, but I tell her I've seen so many perfect gardens I'm going to concrete the whole thing over and be done with it.

Janet takes Larissa home to bed and Randy proposes we continue on. We come across another cottage garden, though this one seems long established. It is enclosed by a black wrought-iron fence, and a path at the side leads to the front door where pots of flowers line the front steps. The garden is a mass of flowering plants such as lilies, astilbe, ferns, allium, and columbine. This is how Greg and Elynore's will look in a few years. I'm quite thrilled to see three lawn-free front gardens and hope the trend continues.

Randy shows us more of Winnipeg. We walk through an area of beautiful older homes built around an open

Greg Chernish and Elynore Kendryna survey their recently dug-up front lawn in Winnipeg.

space like a village green. We see newish houses of strange shapes constructed of turrets and pyramids. Randy teases Elspeth, saying only architects would live in places like that.

We cover miles and miles, and by the time we get back to the hotel we are quite exhausted. It is also ten-thirty, and the door to the hotel is locked. I bang and rattle many times. I see a man slowly rise up from behind the counter and, even more slowly, shuffle to unlock the door. Everyone else has vanished — there's not a soul around.

In our room, the smoke detector dangles from the ceiling, and the brown vertical blinds are tangled up like male and female dancers. There is a pristine phone book, but no phone, no TV, and the red and black shag carpeting is inching up the wall. In the bath-room, the towel rail dangles from one bracket, and the two towels have slid to the floor.

"It's so quiet," Elspeth whispers.

"You usually hear TVs and talk. But nothing," I whisper back. "I think we're the only ones here."

"No one else can afford the five-dollar key deposit," Elspeth says.

That night we sleep like logs. At about eight the next morning we wake to a terrible noise — the gunning of engines and beep-beep of trucks backing up. I leap out of bed, look through the broken blinds, and see a con-voy of trucks and cranes.

"Quick, Elspeth," I yell. "This place is slated for demolition and they're here." It turns out that heavy equipment was parked for the night right next to the hotel. The racket is the morning's start-up. We rush to get out of the place, but not before we claim our five-dollar key deposit.

Sociability & Symmetry: Ontario & Quebec

The landscape changed abruptly from the flat Manitoba prairie to the rugged granite outcrops of the Canadian Shield. It was beautiful country but more suited to geologists than gardeners. Where the road cut through rocky knolls, travellers had left their mark by balancing stone cairns on the bluffs — a great improvement on spray-painted graffiti.

At the border, Ontario welcomed us with a large sign announcing, "We'll make you feel incredible." Incredibly what? we wondered. We were reassured by an incredibly fine roadside display of wildflowers: daisies, lupines, and devil's paint brush. In Kenora, we stopped for a break by the waterfront, and watched float planes take off from the Lake of the Woods. We liked Kenora — an incredibly good cup of tea helped — but we still felt too close to Manitoba to search for our first Ontario gardener. We had set our sights and hopes on Dryden.

It took us longer to reach Dryden than we'd expected. Signs warned us constantly of moose danger, but moose were only part of the problem. The road humped and twisted endlessly — a real road sick ride. Judy hadn't brought up the topic (or anything else, I'm glad to say) since our trip to Whistler, but I couldn't help thinking she looked a little pale. Around one screecher of a bend we came upon a dramatic accident. A number of skating rinks had apparently dropped from the sky and buried the road in shattered ice — only it wasn't really ice. A huge truck had shed its entire cargo of aqua-tinted glass.

"Well, that was pretty incredible," said Judy, as the harried clean-up crew finally waved us on.

By the time we reached Dryden it was almost evening. Since we were both tired, we pulled up at the first motel we saw. No luck. Firefighters from a nearby forest blaze had taken all the rooms. The obliging desk clerk phoned another motel but it was full as well. "We'll just drive on to the next town," said Judy cheerfully. How could I tell her it was three hundred and forty kilometres to Thunder Bay? But to drive back to Kenora was unthinkable. I was starting to panic when the clerk suggested yet another motel. "It's not very … you know … " she said.

As we left to find the *you know* motel, Judy noticed a clump of bright blue wildflowers on a patch of wasteland. We couldn't identify them but didn't stop for a closer look; it hardly seemed the time to start botanizing.

The *you know* motel wasn't *very* but it did have one empty room, and for that we were truly grateful. As we hauled our cases from the trunk of the car, a girl emerged from the room next to ours. She was dressed as a pint of beer.

Later, sitting over French fries in a smoky diner, surrounded by hot asphalt and hissing transport trucks, we began to think we'd been too optimistic, expecting to find real gardens in this pulp-mill town a long way from anywhere. On the spur of the moment, I suggested we go back and check out the blue flowers Judy had spotted by the first motel. Why not? The alternative — to spend the evening in our room — was not enticing.

We were in for a surprise. The blue flowers weren't as wild as we'd thought. They were civilized veronicas and they weren't alone — a large collection of perennials surrounded them. At first they seemed to be planted at random among piles of rubble and builder's debris, but we soon realized there was a plan. Narrow paths of brick and gravel wound through the planted area and a low stone retaining wall divided it from the rough field below. Somebody had left a spade and a hose lying out. The debris that lay to one side was not scrap lumber as we'd thought, but boards nailed together to form rectangular coffers lying jumbled on sheets of thick grey material spread over the ground. They were destined, we guessed, to become raised vegetable beds.

This was obviously a garden in the making, and a well-loved garden at that. But why the mess of grit, and why here? There was no gardener in sight and the land wasn't attached to a building. It lay next to the back yard of a white house, but a high board fence divided the two properties and there was no connecting gate. Quite a mystery! Down across the field there was a man working on a car. We made our way over.

"Oh that!" he said, looking back up at the plot. "It's the lady at the little white house does that. Spends a lotta time at it, she does."

When we met our mystery gardener and asked how long she spent working on her garden, she said, "A few hours every night, and I put in about eight hours over the weekend." The car man was right. A lot of time.

Michelle Showalter was a hair stylist and had been gardening for only three years. The first thing we wanted to know, of course, was why she was putting so much effort into a scruffy piece of land when there was a perfectly good fenced yard beside her house. She and her husband owned it all, she told us, and were planning to take the back fence down soon and join the new garden to the old. That solved one mystery, but: "How about all this ... er, gravel?" We didn't like to call it "this horrible mess."

During the winter, she told us, someone had dumped a large pile of snow right on top of the garden. It was snow ploughed off the roads — rock-hard, gritty, oily, and full of salt. It had only just thawed out. She scuffed at the grimy pile with her shoe to test whether its icy heart had really melted.

"But it's nearly July!" exclaimed Judy.

Michelle Showalter in her new garden.

"Well, yes, it set me back a bit," Michelle smiled. "We let it be known we weren't too pleased. This is a small town; word gets around. I don't think it'll happen again."

If someone did that to *my* garden, I thought, I'd be more than a bit set back, I'd be apoplectic, but Michelle seemed a remarkably calm and steady young woman. I'd already noticed that the mosquitoes, which were driving me wild, didn't seem to bother her at all.

"Don't you find these mosquitoes a problem?" I asked, flailing my arms.

"After a rain they just chomp you alive," she said, looking perfectly unchomped and elegantly unruffled in her sleeveless dress. "The blue flower there is Australian speedwell and a client brought the purple bellflowers into the shop."

"You mean the mosquitoes get worse than this?" I persisted, slapping my legs.

"This?" She looked round mildly puzzled and continued calmly with her tour. "Some of the plants came from the greenhouses in town. I try to get them when they're on sale and I've been buying about two hundred and fifty new plants a year. And I bought seed and grew some in my front porch."

The bites on my ankles were itching like mad. I willed myself not to scratch and failed. Judy was tearing at her neck.

"This year I'm hoping to get the pond dug and the vegetable garden in," Michelle went on. "The fabric under the raised beds is scrap from the pulp mill; it's a sort of heavy felt the paper comes wrapped in. This part will be orchard trees." She indicated a portion of the field that lay below the vegetable garden-to-be. "It'll be the last thing I'll do here."

"Don't bank on it," we said. We'd seen enough real gardens by now to know they're never finished; they come to an end only when the gardener does.

Michelle was a determined and dedicated gardener. That was obvious. What I couldn't understand was *why*. If I'd had to contend with five months of bitter winter and an avalanche of filthy snow followed by a blazing summer and hordes of mosquitoes, I'd have

Michelle Showalter

Inside Michelle's backyard. The fence between Michelle's yard and her new garden is in the background.

been ready to opt for indoor entertainment — something painless like stamp collecting.

"Why do you bother?" I asked. Her answer surprised us.

"When all your friends are into gardening, you have to."

I'd assumed that Michelle was unique in Dryden, a sort of garden freak, a sport we'd stumbled on by chance.

"Oh, we're all gardeners," she said. "There are some *incredible* gardens around here, just *incredible*."

Ontario was evidently keeping its promise! When Michelle offered to introduce us to a few of her friends, we jumped at the chance. As she guided us through Dryden's pleasant residential streets, we quickly revised our first impressions of the town.

Barbara Rothlisberger wasn't around when we arrived but that didn't deter Michelle, who assured us we could walk right in. "We're all good friends," she explained. "We jump back and forth, in and out of each other's gardens, and trade plants all the time." She showed us round with an almost proprietary pride, and Barbara, when she arrived, didn't seem at all surprised to find two strangers wandering with Michelle among the flower beds.

Michelle's vegetable garden. Bed ends make interesting supports for her beans.

Melinda Daigneault on her newly built deck, surrounded by her larger-than-life plants.

After ten years abroad, bond trading in a Swiss bank, Barbara had felt burned out. She'd returned to Dryden and bought a small business. She'd also bought a house and it wasn't long before she was hard at work turning a barren back yard into a real garden. I'd found that most people started gardens by planting round the house, but Barbara was working her way forwards from the back of the lot, which she'd enclosed with a slab-wood fence.

"We all help each other," Michelle said. "Sometimes we'll have a fence-raising, or we'll help in other ways."

A friend had also built an arbor for her, and a yellow canary vine grew up it. The little vine still had a long way to go, and for the canary's sake I hoped Dryden would experience a long summer to make up for the slow spring. A sand cherry was also looking sad. "They sort of come and go," consoled Judy. "Mine went."

Barbara was a self-confessed scrounger. She'd picked up yellow daylilies from a roadside, where they were spreading from an abandoned homestead, and had also salvaged some fine purple iris. Whenever she went out in the car, she took a shovel with her, just in case.

Barbara, like Michelle, was obviously aided and abetted by the close-knit group of gardening buddies, but she was also inspired by her mother, a long-time gardener who lived on the edge of town. Clara Rothlisberger, it seemed, had become a kind of mentor for the younger women, and naturally we wanted to meet her as well. It was too late to go there right away, but Barbara gave us the address and we planned to call in the morning.

It was twilight when we left Barbara's place, but Michelle suggested one more visit, and we were certainly willing to go if she was willing to take us. Like

Barbara, Melinda Daigneault took our arrival in her stride, and we all peered through the gloom at the healthy plants growing against the house and around a newly built deck. Her perennial sweet peas, bergenias, bleeding hearts, and columbines all seemed twice life-size. She put it down to the sheltered location, but I thought it had more to do with the effort she'd put into building up the rich soil.

Melinda was Australian and had grown up in Melbourne, where her grandparents gardened. Like most kids, she hadn't been keen on gardening, but that had changed. "When you get interested in your own place," she said, "there are these amazing little things you remember, like popping the flower buds of fuchsia bushes."

We wondered what had brought her from Melbourne to Dryden, and she told us that she'd met her Canadian husband in Thailand. He was on his way home, having just visited Australia, and she was starting out on a world tour.

It was pitch dark by the time we said good-bye to Melinda and Michelle.

We were impressed by the three well-travelled and enterprising young women we'd just met. It made us feel warm and fuzzy, as well as slightly elderly, to think that the spades of our generation would pass into such good hands. I hoped Melinda's grandparents knew that their gardening germ had travelled half way around the world and, two generations later, was springing to life in Dryden, Ontario.

If we'd set out to investigate how the germ spreads, we could hardly have spent a more revealing evening. The next morning continued in the same vein, with our visit to Clara Rothlisberger, Barbara's mother.

The house was set well back from the road, on a large property with a friendly, rural feel to it. Linden trees and flower beds decorated the front lawn and an extensive vegetable plot lay behind the house, with open country beyond. We knew that a garden like this developed bit by bit over time. In our experience, there was seldom a master plan; common sense, practicality, and the occasional whim dictated the design.

Clara had gardened there for about forty years and her experience showed. She had an extensive composting system. She sprinkled the vegetable garden with rain water, which she collected from the garage roof in a large tank. Her greenhouse went into production so early, the family had to help her shovel a path to it through the snow.

Unlike the gardens we'd seen the night before, this one was old enough to have its own history. Clara remembered a massive plague of army worms in 1962: "We hauled them away in wheelbarrows just so we could get out of the house." They planted the lindens in 1964 and her husband used to pick the blossoms for tea. It was he who had built the large birdhouse we admired. We met one of Clara's grandchildren, Jeff, who seemed very much at home in the garden. He and the other grandchildren had a stake in the place. An intricate water feature, cut into the grass, bore their names on little signs — Jeffrey's Lake, Andrew's Stream, Cheri's Falls and Kimberley Lake.

Clara's father and her husband both came from Switzerland, and we detected a Swiss influence in her choice of plants. She was growing kohlrabi and lovage, which she called maggi, and her lettuce seed had come from the Old Country.

I noticed a yellow canary vine in much better shape than the one we'd seen the night before in her daughter's garden. Evidently Barbara still had a thing or two to learn from her mother.

Clara's garden had been an integral part of family life through three generations. No wonder her daughter had caught the gardening bug. With such exposure in her childhood, she could hardly have escaped, and I suspected young Jeff would succumb one day as well.

The European influence followed us to Kupper's Bakery and Restaurant where we treated ourselves to lunch. Mrs. Kupper was Swiss, Mr. Kupper, Austrian. We talked to Mr. Kupper about the pretty patio garden they'd made behind the restaurant, and commented on Dryden's air of prosperity. He explained that a large sum of money had just been spent on the pulp mill. Alas, it hadn't managed to eradicate the distinctive smell, nor had it found its way into a landscaping budget. The mill occupied a central position in the town, but the only attempt at landscaping we saw was a rectangle cut in a vast expanse of mown grass. The rectangular bed was planted with tiny begonias spelling out an enigmatic "A."

Jennifer Berry's gardening partner, Smarties the cat.

Michelle had insisted we visit the garden of another hair stylist, Jennifer Berry. I'm glad we took her advice. The contrast with Clara's garden was fascinating. Both were accurate reflections of their owners' lives. Real gardens — no doubt about that — but while Clara's had evolved, Jennifer's had been designed with great care and deliberation.

Because it was the end of June, Jennifer was busy with graduation students and was working with a customer when we arrived, but between applications of scissors and rollers she managed to give us a quick sketch of her gardening past. Her grandfather had been a professional gardener to one of the royal houses in England. Her father, although disabled, had also been an avid gardener, and by the time she was seven Jennifer had become his right hand. He couldn't use his own hands for jobs like pruning, but would point with a stick to the right spots, indicate the angles, and she would make the cuts. Before coming to Canada fifteen years earlier, she'd had two gardens, so she brought plenty of experience to the design of this one.

A wooden deck and steps led down from the back door to a patio wrapped around a pond. As Judy knew, I was always on the lookout for well-defined garden spaces, and here I had found one. A pergola draped with Virginia creeper, along with deep beds of shrubs and perennials, enclosed the patio area and created a comfortable garden room decorated

Judy making notes on the plants in Jennifer Berry's carefully designed garden.

planned the layout on paper first, then added the planting over the years.

Judy and I knew how tricky it was to switch from a British to a Canadian climate, and how hard it was to relinquish plants well loved but unsuited to new conditions. Jennifer had gone through her share of trial and error and said that only recently had the planting "knitted together." She avoided the one-of-everything trap by arranging golden elder, yellow iris, ferns, hostas, and astilbes in various parts of the planting to give the whole thing cohesion, and she wasn't afraid to use large clumps and groups. In choosing her plants, she paid as much attention to foliage as to flower. It certainly knitted together, and she somehow managed to make it look easy.

I wished we had time to make hair appointments with Jennifer. If she styled hair half as well as she designed gardens, Judy and I might have left Dryden looking (dare I say it?) *incredibly* glamorous.

with interesting plants. A waterfall animated the space and gave it a focal point, serving the same function as a fireplace in a living room. The outer edge of the beds curved boldly into a broad lawn which flowed around trees to the back of the property.

I wasn't at all surprised to hear that Jennifer had

Judy's Journal

On the way to Thunder Bay, we don't see much in the way of gardens, when suddenly Elspeth yells "Stop!" She has seen a garden full of ornaments. I turn, and park near a house surrounded by gnomes, pelicans, geese, mushrooms, sheep, flamingoes, chickens, and a fat, pink, reclining pig, among other familiar objects. I take a photograph of the sheep and toss the camera back into the car, but Elspeth wants more than just one close-up, she wants one of the whole setting.

About fifty yards from the house is a truck stop, and Elspeth gradually edges backwards towards it, trying for the big picture. A posse suddenly bursts out of the truck stop and marches toward her. From where I am, I can tell it's not a welcome party. They bear down on her; she has no idea what's going on behind her back.

I yell out, "Behind you, Elspeth! Run!" She doesn't and

they surround her. A young boy wearing an apron and wielding a meat cleaver protects an angry middle-aged woman. The boy narrows his eyes and looks fierce. There are others in the group — about six in all, mostly women. Feeling like John Wayne and wishing I had a pistol to twirl, I saunter over. I notice a trucker gassing up his tank and looking at the scene with a grin on his face. One of the younger women eggs on the older one: "You tell 'um mother … you don't want that … now tell 'um." One of the men, smelling the smoke of battle, deserts and scurries back to the café. I hear Elspeth trying to apologize: "But … but … I was … only … "

"We thought it all looked so nice," I say when I reach them, "so we wanted a photograph. We'd like to put it in a book."

"But people will know where they are," says the older woman, "and I don't want people knowing. I don't want them stolen. A rig came in here once with flamingoes stuck on it. I thought he'd taken all mine, but I counted, and still had seventeen."

Elspeth babbles about not taking any photographs if she doesn't want us to, and the woman becomes more friendly. Her support group melts away and she tells us that whenever she and her husband go on a trip she always brings something back for the garden.

"He doesn't mind," she says. "Got the pink pig in Roblin. I like to walk around them at night. He makes some of them." She nods in the general direction of the store.

We chat as she follows us to the car.

We phone ahead to make a reservation for a bed-and-breakfast near Thunder Bay. When we arrive, we see a house with a lawn decorated with garden gnomes. We are greeted by a landlady wearing brightly coloured harem pants in purples, reds, and greens, a puffy white blouse, white socks, and high-heeled shoes. I think she might break into the Dance of the Seven Veils. She shows us to our room, resplendent with a double bed covered by a bedspread of crushed, dark purple velvet with inserts of a fabric decorated with gold *fleurs-de-lis*. This same fabric forms a canopy above the head of bed and is the material of choice in the elaborate curtains across the windows.

"I got this," she says, running her blood-red fingernail down the *fleurs-de-lis*, "when that hotel went out of business that catered to honeymooners."

"D'you get much call for that here?" Elspeth asks.

"Well, no. That's why they went under."

"I thought I'd asked for single beds," says Elspeth, worried at the thought of us both in the one bed.

"I got some singles downstairs, but not like this," the landlady says, lovingly fluffing up the canopy.

"We'll take them," we say in unison. During the night, I get up to use the bathroom and don't realize there is an incline down to the bathroom door. In the dark, I am propelled down the slope at such an alarming speed that I crash into the washbasin, causing the mirrored door of the medicine cabinet to fly open and smash into my face. I see stars, tears come to my eyes, and my nose bleeds just a bit. The large bruise at the top of my leg is a constant reminder of the B&B of the garden gnomes.

The Real Garden Road Trip

Elspeth's Travelogue

Before Thunder Bay, we crossed into another time zone, the third since Pacific Standard Time, and we also passed the Atlantic watershed. From here on east, presumably, all waters ran to the Atlantic Ocean. Downhill all the way! In the end, we skirted Thunder Bay, not because we thought there'd be no gardens there — after our experience in Dryden, we knew better — but because we were afraid there'd be too many. I was starting to feel anxious. The rental car was due back in Toronto and, in spite of Judy's best efforts, we were barely creeping across my map of western Ontario. Ahead of us, on the back of the map, eastern Ontario occupied the entire sheet. Toronto therefore, still lay in some remote future and Quebec was no more than a distant dream. Later I discovered the map changed scale from front to back. We speeded up no end when I flipped it over.

At Marathon we stopped for gas and the attendant warned us to look out for moose and bear. "The moose are bad right now," she said, "real bad. Because of the forest fires. A big bull was jumping all over everyone's lawns last night."

And we thought mosquitoes were a problem!

Some of Marathon's gardens, in spite of the wildlife, were bright with yellow and orange poppies. The last tulips were still flowering, and crab apples were a froth of pink and white. A few minutes out of town I saw a young moose drinking at a stream and, further on, the occupants of a half-ton truck were examining a dead bull on the roadside. That slowed us down a bit.

How could we bypass a place with a name like Wawa? We had a meal in town and then visited a garden centre. This ploy had worked for us in Medicine Hat and it worked again. The owner, Brian Leverington, told us Anne Hicks' garden would be worth a visit, and gave us directions to her home on Wawa Creek.

Judy's Journal

There are two houses on the Wawa property. We see a woman gardening and assume she's Anne Hicks. We introduce ourselves and find we are talking not to Anne, but to Marie David, Anne's sister. We have found not one gardener, but two! Marie tells us their father, a Finn/Swede, bought the land way back and deeded it to his children. She adds that she has gardened for many years here. In 1997, Wawa marks its centennial, and to celebrate, Marie has plans for her husband to put in a new bridge across the stream that divides her

Sisters Marie David and Anne Hicks in their adjacent garden lots in Wawa.

property from her brother's. I wonder if Marie's husband knows about this?

Marie has a great show of Chinese lanterns — which she calls "infamous" — also campanula, veronica, foxgloves, and pansies, which she says will come back if invited. Elspeth asks her what else she is planting.

"I can never remember the name of plants. I always have to stick the tags in," replies Marie. I tell her most of us have that trouble. How embarrassing it is when you know the plant so well, and someone asks you its name and your mind goes blank!

Marie takes us over to meet her sister. Anne tells us she is comparatively new to gardening. She's only started in the last couple of years, since her retirement. Elspeth asks Anne if she is influenced by her sister. Anne quickly says she's not, but that they are the best of friends. The sisters laugh about Anne digging large holes to half bury rocks so that they look part of the landscape. "If they got too big, my sister would come and we'd roll them together," Anne laughs. Her husband died last year so she is trying to cut back. He wasn't a gardener, but she imagines him looking down and saying, "God help Anne, because I never." She is taking out all the shrubs in a bed that she says is too difficult to work: "I'm putting in another bed by the side of the garage so I'm moving into that. It's a standing joke that they're going to get me a wheelbarrow to keep shrubs in to keep them moving." She laughs again.

"Talk about moving plants," I say. " Elspeth is the prime mover. She had me shifting rhododendrons bigger than I was."

"But they have such flat shallow roots, just like a pancake, and so easy to lift," says Elspeth. "You can move them anywhere."

"Take them on holiday, even," I add.

"There was a woman here — I think she was from B.C. — who had a rhododendron. It had a fabulous mauve flower on it, just gorgeous. I wonder what happened to her rhododendron?" muses Marie.

"Took it with her," we all pipe in.

"What zone is this?" Elspeth asks.

"Zone 3," says Anne. Elspeth shivers at the thought, and I think *I'm* hard done by with living in Zones 4 to 5, though I swear some parts of my garden are in Zone 1. The season is very short here because Lake Wawa, which runs into Lake Superior, acts as a big air-conditioner.

We cross back over to Marie's garden and on the way

Marie shows us her favourite spot — a flower bed sheltered by a massive outcropping of rock, where flower pots dot the rock face, and pink bleeding heart thrives among lilies galore, with forget-me-nots flourishing along the edge. She points to the leaves of an iris she bought because the ad said: "Guaranteed To Bloom."

"That should have made me suspicious," Marie says. "It was ten to fifteen years ago, and it *is* going to bloom! They just didn't say when."

We relax in the gazebo, sip lemonade, and talk about gardening and the lives of women.

Elspeth's Travelogue

From Wawa, we drove south along the shore of Lake Superior then east along Lake Huron, skipping Sault Ste. Marie altogether. Toronto was suddenly within striking distance and we felt a kind of tension, almost as if we'd already entered the city's force field. At Old Woman Bay, we could have paused to admire the view, but a sense of urgency pushed us on. At Sand River, we might have lingered and paddled in the lake edge, but we kept moving. After Whisky Bay, I spotted an interesting formal garden but even that didn't stop us in our tracks.

We finally came to a halt at Iron Bridge. The shrub roses were in full bloom and hedges of rugosas filled the air with fragrance. We strolled; we unwound. On the spur of the moment we decided to leave the highway at Espanola, cross to Manitoulin Island and take the ferry to the Bruce Peninsula.

The peonies in Little Current were outstanding. Although we sensed fine gardens in the offing, we didn't feel like visiting. I think the roadside flowers were to blame. We were constantly exclaiming "Look at that!" as waves of blue chicory and viper's bugloss, yellow hawkweed and toadflax, pink clover and purple vetch flew past, their colours delicately blurred and blended by our speed and by the refined grace of flowering grasses. Now and then we spotted rarer combinations such as yellow sedums and blue harebells growing with junipers on rocky ledges. I kept thinking about the work of Margot Lindsay, our embroiderer from Saskatoon.

At the ferry terminal we picked up tourist literature. Surprise! We weren't the first to notice the exceptional flowers of the area. A number of hikes and courses promised the pleasures of wild gentians, pinks, cardinal flowers, and no less than forty-one orchid species.

For the time being, we were more than satisfied with nature's offerings and felt no need for gardens. Of course, this didn't last. With every mile we travelled south, the trees grew plumper, the meadows more lush, and the gardens more colourful. It was like driving headlong into summer, and by the time we reached Owen Sound we were well into garden mode again.

An acquaintance in Vancouver had given me the name and number of a gardener, Diane Greenfield, who lived near Penetanguishene, and now we had to choose whether to make a dash for Toronto (the low-budget option) or detour along the green and leafy shoreline of Georgian Bay. We detoured.

We called Diane from Collingwood, where we spent the night, and in the morning followed her directions until we came to a long driveway running between the muscular grey trunks of beech trees. It reminded me of a woodland ride in England and I half expected to see the ground carpeted with bluebells.

Diane and her husband, Jim, had moved to the property from the Ottawa Valley, and had brought their log buildings with them, dismantling and re-erecting them piece by piece. They'd fitted a large entrance deck round another fine beech and had tucked a swimming pool tactfully into its own enclosure. Diane was a spinner and weaver, so they'd kept goats and a few sheep — until coyotes began to take a toll. Jim grew vegetables, and Diane cultivated a south slope to grow perennials, mostly sun-loving, drought-tolerant foliage plants and grasses.

Diane was a knowledgeable perennial gardener and talked on the topic to local garden clubs. Someone once asked what perennial meant, and she told them, "It means the plants are on the move; it doesn't mean they'll come back." She certainly knew whereof she spoke. "Last year," she told us, as she gazed ruefully at a thin patch in the fabric of her planting, "this was a river of *Santolina,* and there was lavender and globe thistle. But it all winter-killed. Through there I had big exotic grasses and a couple of lovely climbing roses. They both died. This corner was about twelve different kinds of sages." Even junipers and a silverlace vine had succumbed to the brutal winter just past, the worst she'd known in sixteen years. Diane was dismayed but not discouraged. As she put it, she was "re-fighting the fight."

It began to rain, but none of us took much notice. We were too busy examining a dwarf silver thistle.

"I got it totally by fluke," Diane said. "You know: when you go to a garden centre and they've sold all the ordinary stuff, and there's this little aberrant thing at the end of a bench, marked down because it hasn't been watered … "

We knew.

"I have a friend who's as wacko as I am. We egg each other on. We say, 'We'll go to the garden centre, but let's not bring our wallets.' But you can't go without your driver's license, can you? So we come back with about two hundred and thirty dollars' worth of plants."

One of Diane's talks was on drift planting. "You plant in a sort of swoosh," she explained. "Like blues that run into mauves that run into pinks. People think I've actually accomplished it. I laugh. 'Well no!' I tell them. 'I'm aiming towards it. Maybe *next* year!'"

She stooped and pulled a leaf to show us. "I was giving a talk at the Pentanguishene Horticultural Society on mystery plants and plants they should get to know and, in the bouquet they gave me, was this lovely ferny-leafed flower with a spray of tiny blossoms, a mysterious find from an old abandoned homestead in the area. They called it Pentang pearls. No one could provide another name and I didn't know what it was, but finally I found it in a book: a dropwort, *Filipendula hexapetala* 'Flore Plena'."

Judy was admiring the labels. I wasn't sure why she was suddenly so keen on labels. I couldn't remember ever seeing one in her own garden. Diane used them to keep track of plants, but also because she had visitors who wanted to know the plant names. The previous summer, her garden had been on the Library Garden Tour, a project she'd started with two other friends as a fundraiser. We wanted to hear more about the tour, but as it was raining heavily by this time, we retreated to the porch.

The goal was to raise five hundred dollars for the local library. Twenty-five gardens were on view for one day in July. They kept it to a single day deliberately, to limit the number of visitors likely to descend on any one garden. The event was a huge success, not just because they raised thirty-five hundred dollars, but because, as Diane put it, "We felt a sense of community, and it really was the most incredible way to demonstrate what's happening in terms of gardening here. We had all kinds of gardens on the tour. One was a xeriphytic garden, and people kept asking to see the xeriphyte."

Judy and I exchanged self-satisfied glances. After seeing the drought-resistant plants in Penticton and Argyle we felt like old hands with this xeri-stuff.

Diane described some of the other gardens. One belonged to an artist who was trying to create the effect of water. Blue plywood ringed his trees, and fish sculptures leaped among vertical plants like iris. Some people had said, "All those blue things in the trees!" But Diane thought it was lovely — divine. The artist also had an area of tiny plants, which he called his bird's eye garden. A bird sculpture hovered high above it.

On another tour, one of the gardeners was a rock hound. He'd set out huge crystals and planted everything around them to match: pink and mauve flowers around an amethyst, weird plants and whites around something silvery and flecked. Again, some people had said it was just a few rocks and flowers. It was true, Diane felt, that not everybody could respond to everything on a garden tour. For instance, people wondered why she didn't fill in blank areas in her own beds with annuals. Well, she simply didn't grow annuals.

One woman, Diane told us, had spent ages in the garden and then, when she was reaching towards a plant, pruning shears fell out of her sleeve. This, Diane thought, was tacky, but it did say something about the passion people had for gardening. In their next tour brochure, the group was planning to add a section on garden tour courtesy.

Like Michelle in Dryden, Diane generously offered to introduce us to her gardening friends. "Di Lindblad's

Undaunted by the rain, Diane Greenfield shows us her friend Di Lindblad's water garden with its series of small pools.

my guru," she told us. "You walk round her place in a state of amazement. She lives on the 17th Concession of Tiny."

"The *what*?" We knew Ontario's system of land division involved parcels of land called Concessions, but Tiny?

"It's really Tiny township," she explained. "Tiny was one of Queen Victoria's lap dogs. She had two others,

Tay and Floss, and they're townships as well."

The legacies of colonialism!

Diane guided us to Tiny's 17th Concession. Even in a downpour, Di Lindblad's garden looked remarkable. Heaven knew how she did it all *and* still managed to raise donkeys, serve as a national horse judge, and go riding in the rain. She was out on an eight-mile jaunt when we arrived, so we didn't have a chance to meet her, but Diane made an excellent substitute guide. She walked us past the deep perennial border and pointed out a lovely combination of pink Oriental poppies with 'Palace Purple' coralbells. She showed us the Japanese garden, the staging Di had set up to display orchids and bonsai, the series of ponds complete with goldfish and a bridge, the seepage area, and the shady bed for bamboo and astilbes.

And this was just the infield. The outfield included a fifty-acre forest. Through curtains of rain, we could just make out its dark silhouette across a pasture. Since we weren't dressed for a muddy hike, we took Diane's word for it that this was no ordinary forest. Di couldn't bear to throw away plants so she loaded spares onto a trailer behind a ride-on mower and drove them to the woods. She saw nothing strange in transplanting five hundred foxgloves or three hundred lupines. She limbed up some of the trees to let in more light, and encouraged the native flowers. Diane explained, "She'd find an area with four orchids in it so she'd fence it against the rabbits because they eat the young plants. Soon she'd have fifty orchids, so she'd fence a bigger area. Once the colonies were solidly established, the fences could come down. Now she has hundreds of orchids. You walk among the trees saying 'My heavens!'"

The wildflower theme was evidently still with us. Diane took us next to see a garden of native plants created by a group of seniors at the Wye Marsh. The skillfully designed beds included native shrub and woodland gardens as well as gardens to attract butterflies, birds, and bees. There was even a transition garden, where native and introduced plants rubbed shoulders. The whole thing was done with outstanding care and painstaking research.

Now it was my turn to admire the labelling system. Instead of cluttering the beds with detailed information, these smart seniors had provided hand-out sheets referring to discreet numbers placed among the plants. Pity Judy wasn't there to admire them too! By now she was huddled in the car, trying to conserve her few remaining dry parts. Diane and I had decided we couldn't get wetter than we already were.

Photographs were out of the question, my notebook was turning to pulp, and the tape recorder was waterlogged. I'd seldom been out in such rain. I was thinking it couldn't possibly come down harder, when suddenly it did. We couldn't hear each other speak. We couldn't see. We scrambled for the cars. I yelled a hasty thanks to Diane, and whispered a prayer that her kindness wouldn't be repaid with a bout of pneumonia.

Right there in the cramped front seat, I stripped to the skin, bundled my clothes into a soggy ball, and shoved them down among the crumbs and candy wrappers floating in the puddles at my feet. My suitcase was buried under junk on the back seat, but I managed to pry it open and yank out a crumpled skirt and T-shirt. Too bad they didn't match.

That was *not* how I'd imagined our arrival in Toronto — especially since I would be meeting Felicitas, Judy's new daughter-in-law, for the first time when we arrived.

Judy's Journal

After Elspeth has walked quickly around the seniors' garden in Wye Valley in the pouring rain, we sit in the parking lot in our steamed-up car and eat dry bread and cheese. From here we spearhead our way to Toronto. The rain is coming down hard and loud; it bounces like hailstones off the road and jets from the backs of cars like huge fans. I feel we are white-water rafting on the 400 — a new sport. This is my first experience of Toronto driving and it is like a baptism. Cars are parked along the shoulder. I too would like to park along with them, but with white knuckles and tense shoulders I keep going.

Elspeth manages to find the way to where David and Felicitas live. This is where I left my car after the drive from New Brunswick to Toronto. We arrive at their place at four o'clock and can think of nothing but slamming the door on the messy rental car and having a cup of tea. We take just one sip, then someone mentions that we have to get the car back to the rental firm — unless, that is, we want to pay for yet another day. We phone. They close at five. We rush to empty the car. Who knows where our energy suddenly comes from, but in no time at all the car is cleaned out and we are again driving in the rain.

"I was so looking forward to that cup of tea," I say. "Funny, isn't it, but when you've had just one sip of something, or one mouthful, it's constantly on your mind? You feel deprived."

Elspeth assures me that as soon as I've navigated the downtown Toronto traffic, we can relax for a few days in Toronto, visit the Civic Garden Centre, eat well ... and drink plenty of tea.

We are now into July, and after a much-needed respite in Toronto, we set off once again, this time bound for Pickering and a visit with Jim and Joan McWilliams, who have been recommended to us because they specialize in dahlias and chrysanthemums.

We have heard how obsessed such specialists can become. We've imagined fierce battles between contestants sabotaging blooms and plundering display boxes, but we don't really know much about the hard work these specialists put in until we met the McWilliams.

Only Joan is at home. She says they were up at five-thirty this morning doing general gardening, and Jim also had to attend to his fields of corn, wheat, oats, and soy beans.

Walking to the wooden shelter that houses the plants, Joan tells us how they got into dahlia and chrysanthemum showing: "I wanted a garden and Jim wanted competition. Jim had shown pedigree shorthorns when he was younger and says there's not a lot of difference between preparing a cow for show, and preparing a dahlia."

Joan says her interest was really in flower arranging, although she does help with the weeding and the disbudding of the show flowers. When Jim gets a bud on a plant he puts a bud bag over it, and when the bloom fills the bag, he changes the bag for a bigger one. The bags are to protect the blooms from bugs. Jim puts screening over the shelter and in mid-August covers it with plastic to keep the rain from damaging the blooms. Everything has to be done at the right time.

Joan invites us into the house where we see several impressive flower arrangements. I ask if she uses dahlias and chrysanthemums when they're in season, and she tells us she's allowed to choose hers after Jim has had his pick for the shows. He likes the big blooms and she prefers smaller ones like the cactus dahlias, so it works out pretty well. She's also allowed to have some of the waterlily dahlias, which she thinks are out of this world. She grows most of the flowers she uses in her arrangements: larkspur, allium, lady's mantle, and miniature roses. When she makes wedding bouquets, she tapes the rose buds shut and takes the tape off just before the bride goes down the aisle.

Most of the arrangements on display are of dried materials. Joan tells us she dries some of her flowers in silica sand, and uses glycerin to preserve leaves. Some of her material is novel. She likes big seedheads of the dandelion type, and sprays them with hair spray. She also uses the curls of grape vine, and has discovered that strands of sumac root are a beautiful white.

She smiles when she tells us that the flower arrangers are treated like the lowest of the low by the chrysanthemum specialists.

"But come November for the lates show — that's the late chrysanthemums and dahlias — if they've had a bad year, they're looking to us to fill the show and make it more attractive for the viewers. Can't do enough for us then!"

Joan takes us down to the basement and shows us one of the boxes used for transporting blooms from one country to another. It's decorated with drawings of Lady Godiva, and she tells us it was made by growers in Coventry when they brought their blooms over from England for a competition. A prize is awarded for the best decorated box and one of the most beautiful is from Leicester. It has drawings of all the different Leicester cathedrals on it. The boxes are five foot by three foot, and hold forty blooms that stand individually in defective Coke bottles.

Back in the kitchen, Joan makes us a cup of tea and we meet Jim, who comes home for a few minutes before going on to a meeting. We say they work too hard. He laughs and says it's something to be doing or else they'd fight all the time.

While we wait for the tea I flick through a catalogue and see this ad: *Show off your lovelies in their bikinis and catch the judge's eye.* It turns out that a bikini, in this case, is a two-piece exhibition vase that doesn't leak, tip, fade or dent. And further along the ad says to dress the lovelies well and massage their necks. I ask Joan about the well-dressed bloom.

"Believe me," she says, "you spend a lot of time dressing blooms." She explains that they use a Q-tip or a paint brush. They start by layering underneath, and all the petals have to be turned back to lie on top of each other. To keep the tops flat, they sometimes put a hairnet or a hankie over them. In dahlia showing, the judge looks for the proper angle of the stem, no less than forty-five degrees, and contestants will massage the stem just below the neck of the bloom. "Oh, there's a lot to all this showing," says Joan.

In fall, she continues, all the tubers have to be lifted out of the ground and stored. Last fall it was so wet she was out there in hip-boots and a shower cap, with the water running down her neck into the waders. It was so wet, the ground filled up with water every time she dug out a tuber. To add to it, she couldn't see because of the mud on her glasses. "I stepped back into a hole and went right over backwards with my feet so deep in the mud I couldn't get my waders out. I was like a turtle! I tell you, that was the worst, and I thought I must be crazy doing this."

"Did you think of quitting?" I ask.

"Not really," she replies. "We get so much fun out of it."

Elspeth's Travelogue

After we left Pickering, we drove east along Highway 401, which was fast, efficient, and forgettable. By the time we reached Gananoque, we were ready for a change of pace and treated ourselves to a cruise round a few of the Thousand Islands. My excuse was that we were looking for riverfront gardens. Judy said she didn't need an excuse. Bar diving off the boat, we couldn't have done much about it if we *had* seen a garden, so we both sat back, enjoyed the scenery, and tried to ignore the guide's amplified commentary. I couldn't help hearing, however, that an island was only an island if it supported at least two trees and encompassed six square feet of ground.

Judy's Journal

We book in at a motel that has seen better days. I open the mirror above the sink and instead of seeing shelves in a medicine cabinet, I see that it opens up to the outside world — no glass, no screen, just fresh air. I feel quite disoriented by it.

We get up at six to visit Jean Marr, who lives near Mallorytown. Jean is a friend of one of Elspeth's friends.

Along a country lane, in a clearing in the trees, we see an old mellow stone house with clematis and roses growing against the wall, and large beds of poppies, peonies, and hostas. It's a scene that epitomizes a country garden at its best. Jean greets us and invites us into her kitchen where a group of people is eating breakfast around the kitchen table. She explains to us that they are friends attending a sculpture workshop at the Brockville Community College and introduces us to the instructor, Christina MacEwen. Christina says we are welcome to visit the class later. We talk and laugh about gardeners and potters, and Jean, who is both, says potters are often gardeners because they have their hands in clay all winter and in earth all summer. And besides, she says, when you have so many pots, you have to put something in them.

The other guests leave and we agree to meet them a little later at the community college. Then we stroll through Jean's extensive garden, along with her daughter Janet. When Jean says they have four hundred acres, Janet remarks: "And she will garden them all."

"I wish I'd done this pool differently," Jean says, as we stop to admire a pottery turtle that serves as the water source for a pond. Jean tells us her pond was dug out over an old dump where they found shards of glass and china and broken pieces of old knives. Her granddaughters were thrilled by this and used all the bits to build an "artifact fort."

Jean Marr's lily pond is home to many frogs, but the turtle is one of Jean's clay sculptures.

"I'd like a shelf for plants and I could have hidden the pond liner better," Jean says. "One year I was late in draining it and the frogs were already hibernating, so when I put them on the grass, the sun woke them up, poor things. I take all the fish to a friend's horse trough for the winter."

"And they survive?" we ask.

"Oh, yes. They're fine."

Jean buys a lot of things from the catalogues. Although she admits it is expensive, she also considers it therapy. She sits on the couch with her feet up surrounded by catalogues — all with colour pictures — and if she doesn't have a plant, she wants it.

"You're not alone," I say. Most gardeners are like that, curled up with a catalogue on a cold winter's day, just wishing. I notice Jean often uses phrases nearly every gardener we've met uses: "I have to get in there and weed that," and, "Next year it will be better" — the rallying calls for most of us.

Jean points out a large rock and says that it provides some protection from the icy west wind, along with the many trees they have planted.

"I'm at an age now when my friends are dying, so I plant a tree for them. They tend to get sick in the fall, which is most considerate of them, because the trees are half price then," she says, laughing. "We might as well be practical, they'd appreciate that. Frances is there, and Donnie, and over there is Sheila, but poor Marguerite ... she's that standard viburnum and of course it gets bugs. I feel so badly that she isn't doing well at all."

When Elspeth asks Jean if she ever has a quiet time, Janet chimes in: "She doesn't quit much!"

Elspeth's Travelogue

It was good of Christina MacEwen to let us barge into her well-managed class at the Brockville Community College. Her pupils were obviously having a great time using small slabs of special sculpture clay to build an impressive variety of pieces. We chatted briefly with each of them and I made notes about their creations:

Shirley's gnarled figure was called *Gnot a Gnother Gnome*.

Lynn's herb pots had a pressed cabbage-leaf decoration.

Ann's splendidly scaly devil was going to live under a birch clump.

Rita's lion would "cost less to feed than my cats."

Dixie's head with a long neck would have asparagus fern for hair.

Kathryn's bird bath doubled as a planter.

A devilish sculpture by Christina MacEwen brandishes his stick at visitors to Jean Marr's garden.

Ellen's dog stood beside a pump.

Jean's sundial/lantern/planter was in the form of a tree trunk.

Gill's musician played cello.

Bob's back-to-back faces were called *Tears of Laughter, Tears of Sadness*.

Diana's abstract female form was "just happening."

Mary Louise's *Isaac* would maybe stand in his grandfather's garden.

Roger's ... well, I wasn't sure what Roger was making, but previously he'd made a big concrete cat and a naked woman. His cat stood at his front door, he told me, but he kept his woman in the back yard because he didn't want to shock the neighbours.

It was good to know there were so many interesting alternatives to pink flamingoes.

Judy's Journal

"And now we're in Quebec!" I cry, as we drive through Lachute in the pouring rain.

"You going to find us a motel?" Elspeth asks.

I tell her I can't speak French. She points out that I come from a bilingual province, and I say that it's the province that's bilingual, not the people.

"Try it," she insists. *Une chambre avec deux lits* is about it. My French is entirely without verbs. I run in and out of three motels but there are no vacancies.

"D'you think it's because of my French?"

"Probably." In the end we have to take an expensive room, a great deal more than we'd budgeted for — luxurious even. But we enjoy it.

Elspeth's Travelogue

I wasn't looking forward to this leg of the journey. So far, we'd had no problem explaining to people why we were curious about their gardens. Miraculously they'd welcomed us, not only into their gardens, but into their lives; they'd talked to us as if we were old friends. But that was in English. Trying to explain ourselves in French — well, I simply couldn't imagine how we'd do it. Fortunately, Judy had fewer linguistic qualms. She managed the negotiations for our motel room while I was still sitting in the car trying to negotiate the verb *vouloir: Nous voulons* … No! *Voudriez-vous* … No! *Veuillez nous donner une chambre* …

My map of Quebec showed a bright green patch marked "Laurentides," which lay directly above Quebec city. When I'd heard people speak of skiing in the Laurentians, this was the area I'd envisaged. Now I discovered that just northwest of Montreal lay the popular *Région Touristique des Laurentides*. The terrain was hilly and picturesque and it was easy to understand why it had become a major winter resort.

For the pleasure of the drive, we took side roads as far as Sainte-Agathe, then turned back to Saint-Sauveur-des-Monts. This was such a charming tourist trap we ended up spending the afternoon there. The sun was warm and the young tree lilacs along the sidewalks were in full flower, adding a musky sweet scent to the tempting smells of coffee and cooking that hung around the restaurants. We were on holiday, we were having a good time, and I was more than happy to postpone the ordeal of our first Quebec garden interview.

It wasn't delayed for long.

We were browsing on Rue Principale (which sounded so much classier than Main Street) when we spotted exquisite flower beds squeezed into a strip of ground between the sidewalk and an art gallery. The garden wasn't much bigger than Susan Giardin's sidewalk garden in Vancouver. Most of the plants were annuals, but there were also mallows and pink evening primrose, shrubby dogwoods and spireas, and all were chosen to create a lovely colour scheme of pinks, blues, and purples. Tiny petunias, lobelia, purple basil, heliotrope, bachelor's buttons, and larkspur were all tucked in together, but datura was definitely the crowning glory. Although the property was commercial, it was easy to see that the hand of a real gardener was involved. Whose hand? The only way to find out was to enter the Galerie d'Art Michel Bigué and ask.

We entered. Now ask! I told myself. I stared at the art work. Ask! I tried to open my mouth. *Voudriez-vous … ?* Not that again! *Nous intéressons dans … I* mean, *nous nous intéressons dans … I* mean, *nous nous intéressons à …*

By this time, Judy was chatting merrily with Claire Bigué and Carol Paxton, who both spoke perfect English and didn't seem at all surprised that we wanted to talk about horticulture instead of the high-quality paintings on the walls.

"We get more questions about the datura than about

Balançoires are an institution in Quebec. We saw several sales outlets and stopped at one to test the wares.

the art," Claire laughed. "Every day, people ask about the garden." It was she who had started planting the previous year. "My sister has a beautiful garden and she gives me tips. She taught me how to pinch the flowers. I really enjoy it all. They say gardening is now the second-most popular pastime in Quebec, and it grows every year."

We didn't ask about the first most popular pastime, but we did ask if gardening on a busy sidewalk presented any special problems.

"It isn't a question of vandalism," she said, "but the roller-bladers sometimes end up in my flowers."

Roller-blades — an unexpected garden pest!

Carol and Claire returned to their work in the gallery, and we hung round and took photographs.

We left Saint-Sauveur-des-Monts determined to stay on quiet secondary roads and give Montreal's traffic a wide berth. The land north of the St. Lawrence River was flat, mostly arable, and the air smelled distinctly rural. The domed silos that pegged the horizon dwarfed even the silver-spired churches, and reminded me of prairie grain elevators. I wasn't surprised to see a sign to Notre Dame des Prairies.

Some of the stone farmhouses were as pretty as pictures, with masses of colourful annuals banked against their foundations, forming flowery plinths. Others had only mown grass, perhaps a tree or two and a

Clipped trees and shrubs are a Quebec tradition with roots in the aristrocratic gardens of 17th century France. These grow in front of a farm, the *Ferme des Vallons*.

balançoire, a cross between a double garden seat and a swing. Quebec's *balançoires* were a social institution. As evening came, we noticed they were used by families or neighbours relaxing together. Equally sociable were the streets of small towns, which were narrow, full of interest, and often overlooked by balconies or porches decorated with hanging baskets and

We noticed that symmetry is another feature of many French-Canadian gardens.

window boxes. As Judy commented, "Quebec seems more lived in than the rest of Canada."

I had been wondering whether Quebec's cultural history would show up in its style of gardening, and was thrilled to find it did. I knew it was a sweeping generalization, but I felt that francophones' gardens were extrovert — to be looked at — while anglo-phones' gardens are introvert — to be gone into. The great age of gardening in France was the seventeenth century, when *parterres* were designed for viewing and where the fashion for symmetry demanded tight control over nature. The formal style had been modified by time and distance, but we saw more clipped hedges and topiary bushes in Quebec than in all the other provinces put together. I was constantly begging Judy to pull over so that I could take more photographs.

In many Quebec gardens, statues of the Madonna were an important feature. They were set in a niche or on a rock, or became the centrepiece for a special plant-

M. Robillard's Madonna gardens.

ing. In a modest housing development, we spotted a particularly elaborate setting and stopped for a closer look. The Madonna stood on a mound planted with shrubs and flowers and, from her feet, a small cascade of water flowed down to a pool. The whole arrangement formed a sort of island in the grass at the side of a house. Its shoreline was lovingly bordered in marble chips and — more surprisingly — wood chips dyed in different colours and held in place by plastic edges.

We hadn't seen such care taken over edging since we'd looked in amazement at Marvin Albrecht's garden in Medicine Hat. Even the wavy outlines were similar. In Marvin's garden, however, the lawn had been an immaculate inner sanctum surrounded by concentric borders of water, stones, crushed brick, and earth. Marvin's borders seemed designed to protect. Here in the Madonna garden, the framing was intended to expand and emphasize the design.

I was trying, as usual, to sort out my cameras as well as my thoughts, and didn't even notice that the distant grind of a power mower had been growing less distant. By the time I looked up, the machine, propelled by a burly man stripped to the waist, was almost upon me. In a flash, Judy sprang to my rescue once more. She stepped into the path of the advancing blades and, fearless francophone that she was, yelled above the roar something that sounded like: "Jolly jarden! Tray jolly jarden! Votre? Votre?"

The shock loosened my tongue. From some remote burial ground in my brain, French vocabulary rose up, verbs and all, and poured forth in a mighty stream. Judy looked on amazed. The mower man switched off his power and looked on bemused.

I could speak! I could speak! No doubt the accent was ridiculous; I didn't care. I blabbered on. The mower man smiled and nodded and spoke back. He understood! That was enough for me. Well, not quite enough. I'd have liked to have understood him in return. Still, I caught enough to learn that Monsieur Robillard was retired, he gardened not only his own piece of land but his next door neighbour's (whose grass he'd been mowing when we arrived), and he'd made another Madonna garden for a neighbour a short distance across the road.

He took us over to see it. The curvy outline and elaborate borders were unmistakably his handiwork, but this time there was no water. Instead, the statue stood under a white canopy, a sort of rounded niche.

"*Bain,*" he said.

I drew a blank.

"*Bain,*" he repeated.

Bathtub? Why was he saying bathtub? I turned on taps in mime. "*Bain comme ça?*"

"*Oui! Oui!*" He sketched a tub in the air.

And suddenly it dawned on us that the statue's canopy was made from an old tub turned on end. An ingenious piece of recycling! I thought the tap end was buried, but no! M. Robillard made vigorous chopping and sawing motions. He'd cut it in half. By this time, my French had reached its limit and I never did find out exactly how he'd sliced an iron bathtub through the middle.

Because of a slight navigational error, we found ourselves boarding a ferry which carried us from the north shore of the St. Lawrence to the south shore at Sorel. I told Judy I'd chosen this route because I was fond of ferries. She said she liked ferries too.

We spent the night in Nicolet. *How neat is Nicolet!* I wrote in my notebook. We cruised a residential area and stopped to take pictures of trim hedges and spherical bushes. Whole neighbourhoods were gardened with green topiary and even the trees, such as globe Norway maples, were selected for their tidy geometric shapes.

When we booked into the motel, I spoke French with hardly a tremor. Now that I'd overcome my language block, I was thoroughly enjoying *La Belle Province.*

In the morning, our erratic course continued. When we accidentally crossed back to the north shore of the St. Lawrence by a bridge at Trois-Rivières, I told Judy I'd chosen this route because I was fond of bridges. She said she liked bridges too. Judy was the ideal travelling companion.

Judy's Journal

Gardening in Quebec seems different from gardening in the rest of Canada. Shrubs and trees are neatly shaped and clipped. One cedar hedge is planted in a wavy line and clipped to within an inch of its life. In Deschambault, the strip in the centre of the road leading up to the church is planted in perennials, large clumps of healthy-looking flowers that convey the pride of the citizens in their village. In the shadow of the church we find a restaurant with a paved and gravelled outdoor area set up with tables and chairs and coloured umbrellas. A group sits laughing and drinking coffee in the midst of a garden brimming with flowering shrubs and blossoms — a scene of pleasure and tranquillity that I wish I were part of.

On the outskirts of Quebec City, practically on the sidewalk, Elspeth sees a small cultivated plot and yells, "Stop!" I spin around the block a couple of times until I find a place to park.

We walk back and stare at the garden, which contains rows of bachelor's buttons, marigolds, dahlias, and rhubarb. A thin wire strung between posts supports a grape vine. It's all at the front of an old house that is divided into offices. A notice in a window advertises a psychotherapist. This might be a demonstration of gardening as therapy; so many people on this trip have mentioned they find gardening therapeutic and in some instances they have even said it saved their lives. I am eager to meet the psychotherapist.

Just as we climb the metal steps to the house, a middle-aged man comes up behind us and I know he's *the one*. We all three try to get through the door together, but because the door barely misses scraping the reception desk when it is opened, there is not enough room for all of us to enter at the same time. Elspeth goes first and gets trapped in the corner, behind the door. In order to close the door and set Elspeth free, I will have to press myself against the psychotherapist, an action I'm not prepared to take. The psychotherapist frantically flips through his appointment book, no doubt wondering who we are and who has screwed up his appointments.

We never do find the owner of this densely planted urban garden in Quebec City.

I hear a small voice crying in the wilderness: "*Aidez-moi. Aidez-moi.*"

It is Elspeth still stuck behind the door. The psychotherapist and I shuffle around the counter. There's a roomful of patients who are beginning to look edgy. I close the door and set Elspeth free. With much gesturing and flinging about of hands, she asks about *le jardin* at the front of the building. He looks puzzled as though he's never noticed it. Some of the patients drift over to the window and look out. He tells us it is nothing to do with him, but belongs to someone else in the building. I am disappointed. I am especially disappointed for the patients, who look as though a dig in the earth would do them a power of good. In spite of knocking on many doors, we never do find the owner of this enigmatic urban garden, and eventually we get into the car and drive into Quebec City.

In the city, a July festival is in progress. Groups of dancers, acrobats, and singers roam the streets. Many of the businesses in the narrow streets are awash with colour — tubs of flowers deck the sidewalk and blossoms spill from window boxes; trees grow tightly up against walls and clematis climb the stonework. Elspeth calls it vertical gardening. We sit outdoors enjoying onion soup and the passing crowds until lightning flashes, clouds burst, and we run helter-skelter for the car.

Elspeth's Travelogue

From Quebec city, we crossed the St. Lawrence yet again — this time intentionally — and drove along the south shore. The expanse of water was so wide here it was more like an arm of the ocean than a river, and the small windswept settlements strung out along its edge had the air of seaside villages.

A flowery sign marked the entrance to the village of Rivière-Ouelle, and an unusual vegetable garden lay close to the road. It was laid out in the shape of a sunburst with a central disk of marigolds, and rays formed by various crops. The whole design, not much bigger than a living room carpet, was both pretty and functional, and I'd have liked a closer look, but we were through the village before I'd gathered my wits. At least it put me on the alert. We'd discovered that where there was one gardener, there were usually more, and sure enough I spotted something else of interest right away. A mass of brightly coloured flowers filled the roadside ditch.

"Gaillardia!" I shouted. "Back up!"

The gold and crimson daisies spilled down from a ledge on the rocky bank, seeding themselves happily in the thin soil. Both Judy and I grew gaillardia as ordinary garden perennials, but we thought they looked

Judy Maddocks

Gardening on stony ground: Alain, Andrée and Alfred's vast rock garden.

better this way, *en masse* and growing wild. We climbed out of the car and I took some colour pictures. A house sat well back at the top of the bank, with a gravel driveway to one side. A middle-aged man had spotted us and was strolling down to see what we wanted. His approach was friendly and when I explained our interest in the flowers, he seemed pleased and asked if we'd like to see more.

It was only then that we realized the whole bank, which sloped from the house to the driveway, was one vast rock garden. The bedrock was made up of a puzzling mixture of stone but was mostly a kind of shale weathering into fine flakes. This meagre substance supported a great variety of low-growing rockery plants, all thriving on their lean diet. At a distance the plants made a pleasant, muticoloured ground cover. Close up they created an exquisite landscape as fascinating as an undersea reef. All manner of hens-and-chicks clustered together like sea anemones

and starfish in the gullies; stone crops spilled over tiny cliffs; pinks, thymes, saxifrages, and soapworts flowed together like cushions of coral, and a sprinkling of taller flowers — campions and daisies — floated over them like small coloured fish.

I thought of the trouble Sheila Paulson had taken in Calgary to create the right conditions for alpine plants. How she would have coveted a vast natural rock garden like this!

As we walked up the driveway, we grew more and more impressed. Alain Pelletier, our host, wanted us to meet his partner and fellow gardener, Andrée Gagnon, who appeared with her granddaughter in her arms. For the rest of our visit the little girl clung patiently to one or the other of her grandparents. We'd met many gardening couples on our journey, but not many of them worked with matching fervour. Alain and Andrée's garden seemed to belong to them equally. Later, we learned that this harmonious gardening partnership was not a duo but a trio — Andrée's eighty-six-year-old father, Alfred, was also very much involved.

When we mentioned the gaillardia to Andrée, she told us she encouraged plants to self-seed, and showed us a volunteer serviceberry and bulrushes that had appeared in a natural depression. Another hollow held a small bog garden complete with a pitcher plant. This was a gentle kind of gardening, a combination of encouragement and *laisser-aller,* but among the wildlings there were also varieties of rarer rock plants which, Andrée explained, had come from a local nursery specializing in alpines.

At the top of the driveway, another rock garden rose steeply to a wooded area. Nearby lay a heap of loose boulders which Alain had been collecting from their land and stockpiling to build into a cascade and water course. The technical aspects of the project would be no problem. He was a plumber by trade, and his father-in-law, Alfred, was a welder.

Just as we were thinking we should take our leave, they asked, almost shyly, if we'd like to see another part of the garden. There was *more*?

Behind the house, a lawn sloped up to a grassy plateau featuring a fine blue spruce. Andrée told us that, at night, when a spotlight from the house shone on the tree, it glowed with a kind of phosphorence. Then they led us across the lawn and there, behind the woods, lay a huge vegetable garden, a magnificent *potager*.

Like the sunburst *potager* we'd seen in the village, this

Sedum and sempervivum thrive on flakes of shale in the rock garden.

The *potager* as we saw it …

… And the *potager* in its summer glory.

one was laid out in a pattern and contained almost as many flowers as vegetables. Along the upper side, a band of perennials divided the plot from the fields and woods beyond, but the flowers within the *potager* were all annuals, mostly petunias, marigolds, and snapdragons (*gueule-de-loup*, 'wolf jaws'). As with almost every gardener we'd met, Alain complained about the cold spring weather, and wished we could have seen the flowers in their prime. Before we left, they showed us photographs taken the previous summer, and gave us one to keep. What a difference a few weeks would make to the look of the garden!

In such a rural area, we thought they'd have problems with wildlife. "Only with squirrels, chipmunks, and hares," they said.

I wondered if they meant rabbits. *"Les lapins?"*

No, they really did mean *les lièvres*. One year, the hares had nibbled the tops off the

André Gagnon

young lettuce, but the plants had kept coming and had headed up beautifully.

The original soil in the *potager* had been a mass of stones, but constant additions of compost over the years had improved it greatly. On the way back to the house they walked us past their vast composting area and this route led into the woods. They'd cleared a secret path through the cedars and were in the process of making a woodland garden.

We were astonished by the size, scope, and quality of this garden, and told them so. They admitted that two years earlier they'd won the prize of excellence in the *Concours Villes et Villages Fleuries*. I wasn't sure if this was an individual prize or an award given to the whole village. The couple was obviously much involved in village affairs. Alain had designed the sign we'd noticed earlier, based on the rugosa rose — Rivière-Ouelle's floral emblem — and they were looking forward to Fête 1997, which would celebrate the three hundred and twenty-fifth anniversary of the village's founding.

We asked if they'd set themselves limits to their gardening ambitions and they shrugged. No, they said, they just kept expanding. Would we like to see the greenhouse?

A greenhouse as well! Needless to say, it was large. Although all the bedding plants for the *potager* had originated here, the benches were still half full of impatiens, petunias, begonias, and lilies. This was plant propagation on near-commercial scale. Andrée told us that her father loved to collect seed and kept large stockpiles of it. I'm sorry we didn't meet Alfred; he sounded like a man after my own heart.

We never did manage to discover how the internal politics of this gardening trio worked. They seemed to proceed in complete harmony, each perhaps having jurisdiction in certain areas. In the greenhouse, for instance, I guessed that Alfred was prime minister, with Andrée as deputy and Alain as a mere backbencher.

Having met these three gentle and enthusiastic gardeners, I knew I'd always feel a special affection for this lovely part of Quebec. I hope we managed to tell them how much we enjoyed our visit.

Deep Roots: The East Coast

It didn't take us long to cross into New Brunswick. Judy was almost home now and it felt like a homecoming for me, too. After all, I'd lived in the province for more than twenty years and my daughter, Kate, was still living in Hampton. But we weren't quite there yet. We still had a couple of stops to make. The first was in the Woodstock area, where we hoped to catch up with a very special gardener and old friend, Murray Hubbard.

Judy's Journal

In New Brunswick, our publishers have arranged a number of promotional signings and interviews, so the first things we do in Woodstock are find the radio station where we are to be interviewed and find the bookstore where we are to sign books. Then we find the Farmers' Market. At the market I buy a baby-food size jar of rose hip syrup and we are tempted by the delicious smell of a bacon-and-eggs breakfast for $2.75. Instead of breakfast, though, we are drawn to watch the Hat Lady demonstrate Hat Magic.

"Eighteen ways to wear it," she cries, turning a sophisticated black and white fabric hat into a wide-brimmed floppy one, and then into a floral turban, and all for $70. I doubt a hat this price is a big seller in Woodstock, even though I imagine the Hat Lady can sell anything.

I listen to a salesman selling "aub-ri-*eta*" and arguing with an older man, whose high-pitched joshing voice complains he can dig fresher stuff "out the ditches." A young man selling kohlrabi has a head of thick, black, wedge-shaped hair, and I wonder what the Hat Lady could do for him.

We are nearing home, so I start to meet people I know. At the book signing we meet an ex-girlfriend of my son's, a woman I shared a hospital room with, and the mother of a young man who married a friend's daughter. We even meet a woman called Ellen who knows the gardener we are going to see, Murray Hubbard.

I remember the first time I visited Murray. He played the organ and we sang hymns. His wife, Gwen, who had a perfect peaches-and-cream complexion, always intrigued me. Gwen's family was from Wales, as was mine. My mother had often spoken in hushed tones of a beautiful cousin called Gwen, who ran away to America with the postman. I used to look at *this* Gwen in her pale pink jumpsuit and flawless skin, and wonder if she was a relative, in spite of knowing that she was not (Murray had told us many times the story of how they'd met).

Elspeth's Travelogue

I was living in New Brunswick when I first met Murray. He was in his seventies, still earning a living from farming, and his wife, Gwen, was still alive. My friend Kathy had met him several times and asked me if I'd like to go along on her next visit to the Hubbard farm. Not many New Brunswick gardeners were specializing in perennials then and I was intrigued to hear of a sheep farmer who was also a perennials enthusiast. We had set off early because his home in Carlton County was several hours by road from Hampton where we lived.

It was spring, but only just. The sky was overcast, the trees were leafless, and remnants of dirty snow still lay in the ditches. I'd always enjoyed the drive along the Saint John River between Fredericton and Woodstock, but I'd never left the wide valley before and driven into the hills to the west. As we climbed, the views became more dramatic and the farms less prosperous. Fields that had once been cleared were growing back in alders and shrubby dogwood — a sure sign that the farming population was abandoning marginal land. The area was beautiful but at that time of year it was a bleak sort of beauty, and I thought it an unlikely place to find a perennial garden.

In those days, the words *perennial garden* made me think of immaculate herbaceous borders with waves of carefully manipulated colour arranged against sturdy yew hedges. In other words, they made me think of England. This was not England. It was Speerville, New Brunswick, and when Kathy had finally pulled off the dirt road into a muddy driveway, I was disappointed. As far as I could see, there was no garden at all.

Murray's home was directly in front of us, with a large barn to one side. On our right, running along the driveway was a rickety fence built of scrap lumber — old doors and barn boards. On our left, an empty field still bleached from winter sloped away to a panoramic view of shallow hills. Hills and more hills blurred into the horizon. Looking in this direction, it seemed to me

that not a building, not a soul, not even a sheep stood between us and the infinity of grey sky.

"He calls it Wit's End," Kathy said.

Not a bad name, I thought.

We climbed out of the cozy car and stood shivering in the wind. It had already occurred to me that the human hold on the land was tenuous, and I knew I wouldn't have lasted long in this bleak spot. For two pins I'd have jumped back into the car there and then, and headed for home. But a figure appeared from the barn, a small energetic figure with a woolly cap and a patch over one eye, a figure who looked more like a friendly elf than a sheep farmer. He hurried towards us with a big welcoming smile.

"My dears!" He clasped Kathy's hand. "Here you are!"

And here we were. Some people have the extraordinary knack of making you feel as if you are exactly where you want to be. One minute, Wit's End was the back of beyond; the next, it was the very heart of New Brunswick, central and vibrant, and all because this sprightly man was with us, laughing and chatting and charming our socks off.

Kathy wanted to see the livestock, so Murray led the way to the barn and ushered us in with great courtesy. As I stepped over the threshold, it seemed as if the scene switched suddenly from black-and-white to colour — a Wizard of Oz effect. A golden light fell over the hay and the clutter of farm equipment. The air was warm and smelt of animals. We could hear their comforting snuffle and scuffle around us — the mottled sheep and white lambs, a brown milking cow and a heifer, an assortment of Technicolor hens. The hens, I suspected, were more for decoration than production. It was lovely to be out of the wind in this magical place.

Of course, most of the magic was not in the barn but in the man. I listened enthralled as he and Kathy talked. He was telling her about an aunt of his — an opinionated lady — who was in the habit of saying, "I am not a humble person but I do admire the quality in others." It crossed my mind that Murray was perhaps a kind of changeling — an elf with the mind of a scholar and the heart

Murray Hubbard examines the seed head of an ornamental onion.

of a gentleman — cast into the life of a sheep farmer by a mischievous fate. Later, when we met Gwen and drank tea with her in the house, the sense of incongruity struck me even more strongly. Although her health was already fragile, she was delicately pretty in a shell-pink housecoat, and her manner was genteel. Murray was lovingly attentive.

The house was frugally furnished but against one wall of the living room stood a small organ. Among his many interests, Murray played organ for his local church. He was also writing a local history and some time earlier had started a Credit Union. "The first truly pastoral credit union," he claimed. "Members had to walk

across a pasture to reach it."

This pair didn't match my farm-family stereotypes, and I was curious to hear more about their backgrounds. Gwen showed us a picture of her family home in Wales and told us about the lovely garden round it. Murray's mother, a school teacher, and his father, an engineer, also came from Britain. His parents had left Britain as a young couple, in search of a better life, and after various false starts in the United States, had washed up in Carlton County, New Brunswick, where they put down roots among the Speers of Speerville, who had claimed the land about a century earlier. Murray's mother loved flowers and grew pansies but, as he explained, "The chill penury of the life stifled any more ambitious flower gardening." I could understand that.

I had almost forgotten we had come to talk about gardening, and as there were still no signs of a garden, it surprised me when Murray asked if we'd like to look at his plants. I thought there must be a small cultivated plot tucked behind the house. There wasn't. A flock of geese lived there. We headed instead for the fence we had walked past earlier. I'd been in such a hurry to reach the shelter of the barn, I hadn't noticed that the makeshift barrier helped to enclose a long thin strip of land. We entered by a gate at the top end.

The view down the strip was not inspiring. The bumpy ground was partly bare, partly grown up in tufts of vegetation. Scattered here and there were cardboard boxes, carpet remnants, plastic bowls, rusting iron pots, rotting oranges, corn cobs, lettuce leaves, and a few coconuts. A path of trampled earth, barely wide enough to walk on, wound in a haphazard way among the litter, and Murray set off along it, pointing this way and that, and talking enthusiastically. We followed hot on his heels, in single file;

Murray and Snug.

when he stopped suddenly and dropped to his knees, I nearly fell over him. Murray didn't even notice. He had lifted a wooden crate and was poking about in the earth, exclaiming joyfully.

"You've made it through the winter. My little darlings!"

We peered down at a couple of tiny green shoots, admired them and were off again, Kathy and I keeping a safe distance behind as he darted from bucket to milk crate, pulling them off to reveal "Treasures! Treasures!" All the time, he was tossing botanical names over his shoulder and I was straining to catch them as the wind whipped them away. My amusement turned to admiration as we progressed from *Allium giganteum* to *Paeonia tenuifolia*. Soon I was oblivious to everything but the cultural requirements of *Adonis vernalis*. Kathy finally protested that she'd had enough Latin for one day and shouldn't we be on our way?

Before we made our farewells, I asked about the corn cobs and coconuts. Every weekend, Murray explained, he would drive his truck to the supermarket in Woodstock, pick up a load of spoiled produce, and dump it around his plants. It was a sort of open composting-cum-mulch system that the plants obviously appreciated.

I visited Wit's End often after that, in summer when coneflowers towered over the fence, and huge clumps of phlox bulged between the boards, and in fall when Michaelmas daisies toppled over the path.

Once or twice, Judy came with me, and sang Welsh hymns with Gwen while Murray played the organ.

Murray was one of the most generous people I'd ever met. We never left Wit's End without garden loot of some kind — a few precious seeds in an envelope or an earthy mass of lily bulbs in a garbage bag. We tried to return the favours, and trunkloads of plants started to move between Speerville and Hampton. As the years went by, Murray's strip of garden grew longer. One year, he rebuilt the fence with conventional materials. A shrubbery and a small plantation of unusual trees appeared on the other side of the driveway. Cardboard boxes and banana peels grew less noticeable as the treasures grew more desirable and rare. After Gwen died, Murray spent more time with his beloved plants. Word got around, and gardeners began to visit him from all over the province. He corresponded with enthusiasts in other parts of the country, and gradually became something of an authority on perennials. When I moved away to British Columbia, I missed my visits, I missed Murray's scholarship and gentle courtesy, and I even missed the coconuts.

Judy's Journal

Murray greets us at the door. He's wearing smart red suspenders and his small white poodle called Snug trots up beside him. Murray looks a little older and a little frailer. I've imagined different lives for Murray. The preferred one is seeing him as gardener at one of England's stately homes, or supervisor at a botanical garden. I don't imagine he'd be any different — he'd still be one of life's gentle men — but his life might have been easier in a softer climate.

We sit beside him on the couch and he tells us his granddaughter and her son are living with him and taking care of things. He has written a book about Speerville, the place where he lives, because the people of the town were so good to his mother when his father was away at war.

Murray and Judy in Murray's garden.

About his mother, he says that no stretch of the imagination could make her a gardener, but when he was twelve or thirteen his grandmother gave them a packet of pansy seeds. "We had the most marvellous pansies and they have a way of wrapping around your heart," he says, his face breaking into a big smile.

He is concerned about his mind because he has so few people to discuss things with. "I haven't the equipment to remember names any longer," he says. He thinks he is forgetting all the botanical names, but when Elspeth comments on his *Euphorbia polychroma,* he is quick to mention that the new name is *Euphorbia epithymoides.*

With Snug bouncing alongside him, we go out into his garden. The path down the middle is overgrown, and the beds are almost choked with weeds. Murray points to a nondescript plant in the rockery saying, "That one came from the Falklands. It should have stayed there."

He is still brimming with enthusiasm, and plans to tidy things up. He says he is going to move a crambe, a sea kale

Murray ponders his garden.

almost as big as he is, to a spot beside the barn. He looks at the weeds, then smiles and says that if his garden goes, it's not tragic because "there are bits of Wit's End all over New Brunswick."

We never leave Murray's empty-handed, but this time, instead of a plant, he gives me a chunk of marble "quarried from down there," he says, pointing to some distant hills and asking if I will build it into my new wall.

The visit with Murray is one of the high points of our trip — especially seeing him so thrilled that, with some coaxing from Elspeth, all the botanical names come flooding back.

Elspeth's Travelogue

From Murray's, it was an easy drive to Lincoln, where we stayed overnight with our friends Mollie and George Fry. Their handsome old house had a lovely garden which sloped down to the Saint John River. In the hot July evening, Mollie took us for a leisurely jaunt upstream in her houseboat, the *Olga-Polly.* On land, Mollie was a specialist in early childhood education, but when she climbed aboard the *Olga-Polly* she was Captain Cook, Columbus, and Rattie from *Wind in the Willows,* all rolled into one. She encouraged us to take turns at the tiller and we puttered contentedly up and down the quiet water, leaving a very unprofessional wake zigzagging across the reflection of the setting sun.

It was a welcome change from highway driving and next morning, with Mollie and George as guides, we set off refreshed and ready for another day of garden hunting. We weren't disappointed. In nearby Burton we found a little hot-bed of horticulture.

The gardeners in this area were exceptionally friendly and generous. No tucked-away, private retreats for them! All the gardens we visited were clearly visible from the road and the Frys had often admired them in passing.

The Esligar house stood well back, with a large front yard planted in shrubs and perennials. Jean Esligar was a calm and capable woman with a gently unassuming air. Even if she hadn't told us she was a retired nurse, I might have guessed. She seemed astonished and a little embarrassed that a carload of strangers would be interested in her gardening efforts. She wished we could have come earlier to see the poppies in their prime and, like most gardeners we'd met, she apologised for the weeds. There was no need. She obviously worked hard to keep her beds of shrubs and

Jean Esligar in her front garden.

flowers in good trim. "I'm here all day," she explained, "when I should be doing the house-work." We could relate to that.

When we asked why the garden meant so much to her, she said she'd like to show us something, hurried off into the house, and reappeared carrying a plaque inscribed with Dorothy Frances Gurney's lines:

The kiss of the sun for pardon,
The song of the birds for
*   mirth —*
One is nearer God's heart in a
*   garden*
Than anywhere else on earth.

Nursing, she explained, had taken away her faith in God. Only here, among her flowers, had she found some sort of spiritual renewal. "I garden on my knees," was how she put it. She was one of the many people who told us their gardens were important to them spiritually.

She thought of her flowers as individuals, and loved them with an intensity that made me think of Murray Hubbard and his "treasures." While Murray took a scholarly interest in botanical names and the diversity of species, Jean reserved her special affections for sweet-smelling flowers and for plants that brought back fond memories. She showed us a dahlia given to her by a dear friend, Mary, who had since died. Mary had called it her peppermint dahlia because the blooms were sometimes red and sometimes striped in red and white.

Jean bent down to examine a white lily, took a long appreciative sniff, and sighed with satisfaction. Her barberry was lemon-scented, and I wasn't surprised to hear that lilacs were another of her favourite plants. She wouldn't let anyone cut branches for the house as she preferred to see flowers growing outdoors.

Among her shrubs were three big hydrangeas. No fragrance, so I suspected they were not Jean's choice. Right. They belonged to the grounds of the original house that burned down before the Esligars bought the property. Design wasn't foremost in Jean's mind when she chose her plants, but her mix of shrubs and perennials was effective. The shrubs gave bulk and a feeling of permanence to a perennial garden that, in winter especially, would have been shapeless without them.

While we were talking, Jean's husband, Lloyd, was pottering around in the background, a cigarette dangling from his lip. According to Jean, Lloyd's philosophy was, "If you can't eat it, it's not worth growing," but when I talked to him quietly on the side, he admitted he enjoyed the flowers. I asked if he grew

Lloyd Esligar in his back garden.

anything to eat and, like Jean, he seemed surprised that anyone would take an interest is *his* garden. He took me around to the back of the house and showed me an orchard and a vegetable plot even bigger than his wife's flower garden in the front. A row of giant leaves grew alongside the usual tomatoes and carrots. I knew what they were because my thrifty Scottish grandfather once grew his own tobacco too. He mixed it with treacle (could it really have been treacle?), pressed it into blocks, and carved off slivers for his pipe. For Lloyd, growing tobacco was a new venture, and he planned to shred the leaves in a spaghetti maker. He agreed that the end product wouldn't be exactly edible but hoped it would at least save him tax money.

When we returned to the front garden, Jean and Mollie were planning an exchange of plants. I was sorry to leave. I always found it hard to say good-bye to the gardeners we met — they felt like friends so quickly — and I was beginning to think our cross-Canada journey would have to become an annual event.

A short drive from the Esligars, we pulled into another driveway. Even without the Frys' guidance, we'd have spotted this one. The flowers were at their peak and the house was set in a brilliant display of annuals

The Hollands — a family of gardeners.

and lilies. Our knock brought a whole family to the door — Gerry and Lucy Holland, their teenage son, Michael, and the dog, Max. The younger son, Robert, appeared later in baseball kit. As usual, we tried to find out who was the chief gardener. In this case it wasn't so simple.

Gerry was born in the Netherlands, grew up on a farm, and looked every inch the part: hale and healthy. We weren't surprised to hear how much he loved to grow colourful flowers. Lucy's grandmother came from England and enjoyed gardening, and her mother, she told us, was also a keen gardener. The Dutch and the British — as

Michael Holland shows Judy the vegetable plot.

Judy pointed out — tended to be great gardeners but — as *I* pointed out — that still didn't prove it was a matter of nature over nurture. The debate raged on …

As we walked round admiring the lilies and arguing about garden genes, the older son, Michael, came with us. I was impressed by his interest and knowledge. I was even more impressed when I noticed he was unconsciously, but methodically, deadheading the lilies as we went. A teenager — voluntarily — deadheading? I suddenly realized we'd stumbled on a family in a million: gardeners to the core, every one of them. Even Max the dog stayed out of the flower beds and only ate carrots when they were offered to him.

The Hollands started their annual flowers from seed and, one year, the boys sold surplus petunias at the roadside. The reward, in pocket money, was encouraging and sparked their interest in a repeat performance. Soon customers were giving them advance orders. They received commissions to plant around a church and a funeral home, and before they knew it, they were running a little business. Michael also found time to look after a vegetable garden, in addition to a flock of hens and a couple of Holstein-Hereford cattle.

How did Gerry and Lucy explain their sons' enthusiasm? "I guess it was just like going to church," said Gerry. "You do things as a family and you look up to your father and want to do what he does." Lucy told us her mother, in her eighties, still grew enough vegetables to feed the whole of Burton.

Judy and I immediately wanted to meet Lucy's mother. Where did she live? Just up the road, on the bend. As it happened, this was the very place Mollie had planned to take us next.

Lucy warned us that her mother might be picking beans at her vegetable garden, which was some distance from the house (she had only put up thirty-one quarts so far), and indeed she was out when we arrived. We were sorry to miss her but at least we didn't miss the garden. The ground fell

Michael and Max the dog in their colourful front yard.

Max the family dog.

sharply from the house to the road and every inch of the bank was crammed with flowering plants. Hollyhocks and clematis grew against the walls of the cottage, and a tendril of Virginia creeper was even sneaking across the mesh of the fly-screen door. It was one of the prettiest spots we'd seen on our whole journey, and certainly the last word in roadside gardens. A perfect end to our day.

Cautiously, as cars sped around the corner, I crossed the road to take a photograph. In the short time I was there, I noticed several drivers braking to look at the garden, and it occurred to me that the Department of Highways would be well advised to put up road signs in the Burton area: *Drive with Care: Gardens Ahead.*

Now we really were on the home stretch. I was longing to see Kate, who'd been house-sitting for Judy, and Judy was longing, rather nervously, to see her neglected garden.

It was the end of July and we'd been travelling for so long, I think we'd given up believing we'd ever *arrive*. It was a shock to find ourselves suddenly there — in Hampton — driving across the green bridge and, before we had time to gather our wits, swinging into Judy's driveway.

Oh my!

The place was a blaze of purple and yellow — masses of golden daisies, phlox, and beebalm. It was stunning. Judy turned off the ignition. In the silence, we sat and stared. I thought we were both going to burst into tears. Then Kate, all smiles and laughter, came rushing out to meet us.

We decided to stay at Judy's for a few days before heading to Prince Edward Island. We wanted to visit some local gardens, but here on home turf there were simply too many possibilities. As in Vancouver, we turned to friends for help. Ann Andrews and Kathy Hooper — sisters and both great gardeners themselves — suggested not one, but three gardens, and offered to come along with us on our visits. Our first stop was to be in the nearby city of Saint John.

Judy's Journal

The neighbours living around Elga Garnett say she is a pioneer. She started gardening on the limestone cliffs of the area and now most of her neighbours are doing it. Offspring of Elga's garden live along the street, close to home, close to their mother. Most of the gardening along this street is practically vertical. Elga's back yard was part of a lime quarry. I look up and see a tapestry of muted colours — mounds of pinks, pale yellows, and blues, and large spreads of different greens, all nestled snugly among the rocks that stretch way to the top. It is a unique way to garden, a way I've never seen before.

I ask Elga how this came about. She says she started about twenty years ago when the kids were small. "I had to do something," she laughs. A friend with a rock garden gave her bits and pieces of plants.

"Hauled buckets of soil up there," she says, pointing up the cliff. "My husband told my son he couldn't go and play until he'd lugged up so many buckets, so all the kids in the neighbourhood helped. Had a parade of buckets going up there." Rocks also had to be hauled up, to keep the soil in place, and she adds that if they come rolling down the hill, they'll have to stay put now.

"It's quite steep for you to work, isn't it?" I ask.

"Oh, I go on up there," she says, and like a mountain goat, this very nimble grandmother goes up the cliff face, followed by Elspeth.

"I'd really like to have heathers up there," Elga adds, when they get back to earth, "but they're hard to find in this area. I'll take you to see someone else's, if you'd like." As we stroll down the street, she points out other rock gardens growing on the cliff. She also tells us that some years ago, her husband and son died within eighteen months of each other.

"I couldn't do anything for years," she says, "then I started to garden again and my neighbours were some relieved to see me out there." I can empathize with her because for many of us, in times of sadness, the garden is our salvation.

The garden belonging to Elga's neighbours, Cindy and Glen, is even steeper than Elga's. Glen says, "Everything washes down — dead trees, those cedars up the top there, most likely killed by pollution from the

Elga Garnett on her limestone cliff.

pulp mill — but it all washes down. The stones move down, too." He has carved a path across it and put in beautifully constructed steps.

They started to garden when the house was raised and a basement dug out and all the earth was piled up on the hill. It seemed a shame not to continue the garden that Cindy's own mother had started.

"But it's Elga who's the pioneer," Cindy says. "All along this cliff there are bits of Elga's garden."

You wouldn't think you were practically in the centre of the city of Saint John. From their garden, looking down over the cliffs, the sun glints off the silken waters of the Saint John River, a pleasure boat glides by on the Kennebecasis, and I'm happy to know that this same river is the one I see from my windows.

Elspeth's Traveloque

To the list of gardeners compiled by our friends Kathy and Ann, we added an extra name — Sue Hooper, Kathy's daughter. Like her mother and aunt, she had a glorious garden, but she had the added distinction of gardening with — and sometimes in spite of — three very lively young children. We wanted to hear more about the art of mixing lawn mowers and manure with motherhood.

Sue Hooper talks with Judy on the sweeping lawn of the Hooper/Long property.

When Sue was in her teens she used to baby-sit for me and, even in those days, I admired her thoughtful nature and artistic abilities. She studied graphic design in Ontario, but eventually came back to Hampton and married Jack Long, a local carpenter. Many houses in Hampton (including Judy's) boasted samples of Jack's skillful handiwork. After talking to so many strangers across Canada, it felt odd to be interviewing someone we knew so well. Sue was feeling a little uncomfortable about it, too.

"How are we supposed to do this?" she asked nervously as the three of us stood in the middle of her lawn.

"You're supposed to talk about your garden," said Judy, "and we're supposed to listen."

"Yes … well … right. There was nothing here but a hayfield and I dug up a bit, and started with plants Mom gave me, then I used a seed mix of perennial wild flowers, but I didn't know what was weeds and what was flowers so that was a mess, and the next year I started again from scratch … is that the kind of thing you mean?"

"Perfect," said Judy. "Go on!" But before Sue could go on, we discovered we were standing on an ant hill, and that brought Jack over to see what all the fuss was about.

"What do you do to help in the garden, Jack?" Judy asked, brandishing the recorder at him.

"The manly stuff," he grinned.

"Such as?"

"Cut poles."

"Poles?"

"Yep."

This was the typical New Brunswick countryman's economy with words. Jack's quiet humour was liable to slip right by you, and it could slip right through you too — but only when you deserved it.

"What else?"

"Dig holes."

"Holes?"

"Yep. Holes for the poles."

Judy soldiered on.

"Anything else?"

"Build walls. Grow raspberries." He pointed to a row of short sticks just visible beside the vegetable garden. "Dwarf varieties," he said.

"Really!"

Sue and Jack, and their children Isaac, Julian, and Hannah.

Jack wandered off, perhaps to cut more poles, and Sue took up the tale, explaining that deer had eaten the raspberries down to stumps. "They didn't touch basil, onions, leeks or squash, but everything else in the veggie garden was neatly cropped. I bought a new clematis — 'Apricot Bells' — and they ate that within a week. Eventually," she glanced towards Jack's retreating figure, "the veggies will be properly fenced."

Deer were obviously a sore point, so we switched back to the early days of the garden. She told us she had worked out the design of lawn and beds by moving a hose about on the grass and then studying the shapes from an upstairs window.

Behind us lay the house and the wooded hillside; in front of us, the land fell away to the wide valley of the Kennebecasis River. The lawn sloped gently down from the house, surrounded by vast borders of perennials and shrubs that curved around to a generous gap which, Sue explained, would one day become an archway — presumably when enough poles and holes were forthcoming. Here, shallow flagstone steps, almost inundated with creeping thyme, led to the vegetable garden, fruit trees, and a row of gigantic sunflowers.

By now, Sue had forgotten to be shy about the tape recorder and was starting to muse aloud: "I'd really

Sue Hooper, garden mom, among her lilies.

---

like to cut into the lawn and make the beds bigger but Jack doesn't want me to, and you *do* have to think of the kids having a place to play and drive their wagon. I used to keep a journal, but that was before the children came, nine years ago. I've hardly touched things since then. Except the 'Jens Munk' rose, which everyone told me I should prune back, so I did and killed it. I get frustrated at times, not being able to do as much as I'd like, but I'm learning to think 'It looks beautiful' and not to get in a panic about it all."

Hardly touched in nine years? We took that with a pinch of salt. The garden was certainly beautiful. Orange butterflies danced from golden coneflowers to beebalm the colour of bubble gum. A peach daylily looked truly peachy against the grey leaves of an artemisia, and I'd never seen the purple spikes of gayfeather look as purple and spiky as they did among the white foam of *Achillea ptarmica* 'The Pearl'.

"Don't tell me," I said, "that the white lilies over there just happened to find themselves beside the blue monkshood."

"Well, no. I stick things in and then I think, 'That would be a pretty combination,' or, 'Those ones bloom at the same time,' so I move them round, but it doesn't always work out. I put the blue delphiniums, the pink peonies, and the white Siberian iris together, but this year the delphinium flowered later."

It wasn't only the colour combinations that made this garden glorious; it was the generosity of the planting, the girth of the clumps, the robust foliage. Sue put it down to compost and cow manure, but I knew it was also her vision, her ability to think big and bold. As she didn't have time to cut flowers for the house, she encouraged Hannah, who was seven years old, to pick bouquets, and Hannah's friends took bunches of flowers home as well. With such large clumps, Sue explained, she hardly noticed that bits were missing. "Hannah knows she can pick some if there are plenty of any one kind — but not the lilies. She's pretty good about it."

We asked if the children did any gardening themselves. "They started things from seed this year," Sue told us, "though Hannah's shrivelled up, and they have bits of garden they call their own, but they don't *have* to do garden chores unless it's a consequence, unless they've damaged something. The angriest I've ever been about the garden was when they climbed up the cherry tree and broke it all to pieces. Isaac loves working; he drives the wheelbarrow round and picks up weeds, and he helped Jack to get poles out of the woods to build the arbour."

We wanted to see the arbour, and Sue took us around the back of the border and through a gap be-

Wilson Studio Collection

The old Lower Norton schoolhouse, the pupils, and the daffodils.

tween large shrubby honeysuckles. The arbour was planted with grape vines that scrambled over it to form a kind of tunnel. The cat was lying in the shade, and Garf, the dog, followed close on our heels. Sue explained, "I wanted to have different areas for the children; they love to have secret places where we can go and eat popsicles."

Many of Sue's plants began life in Kathy's garden. Mother and daughter often started seeds together, but Sue was always on the lookout for new plants and had managed to salvage a few from derelict sites. Her favourite rescuees were the daffodils which had grown

outside the small local schoolhouse. When the school was closed and demolished in the seventies, the site became overgrown. Sue saved a few of the bulbs and planted them in her own garden — a memento of quieter days along the valley.

We talked about the role that gardening had once played in the school curriculum, and I mentioned that a move was afoot in Vancouver to bring nature back into the school yard. We agreed it was an idea who's time had come — again.

Sue took us over to where the daffodils were now multiplying merrily, but at this point in our visit,

Julian, Hannah, and Isaac arrived home from a friend's house, and our interview quickly fell into disarray. It didn't take me long to remember how hard it was to get anything done with small ones around, and I marvelled that Sue managed to do as much as she did.

Before we left, Sue took us indoors and showed us a photograph of the old schoolhouse complete with pupils and daffodils. We liked it so much we had a copy made. It was good to think that all those children had daffodils tucked into some corner of their grown-up minds, and it was also nice to think that, thanks to Sue, the very same daffodils were quietly planting themselves in the memories of Julian, Hannah, and Isaac.

Judy's Journal

Our friends and guides Kathy and Ann come with us to see Maureen Bourque's garden on a small city lot in Saint John. I can't believe that behind a house that looks no different from other houses in the street, we have come across such a lush and shady haven enclosed by trees and hedges and alive with dappled light. I want to put my arms around this little jewel and keep it safe.

The small oval lawn is edged with cobbles originally brought as ballast in ships from England. Curving along one side of the lawn is a heather garden that has an almost mystical quality to it. It's a lush, moist,

Newie Brown's valley of flowers.

peaty garden with a variety of heathers and heaths, along with dwarf rhododendrons, azaleas, astilbes, and Japanese maple, all flourishing under the branches of mature birches. Across the lawn, opposite the heather garden, the small yellow bells of *Clematis tangutica* spill across the garage, providing a background for old roses and perennials.

Maureen tells us that the garden grew gradually — starting at the back steps and expanding along the edge of the property. In time, the lawn shrank as the borders widened to accomodate shrubs, phlox, and daylilies.

In summer, the creek (on the left) is a mere trickle, and the valley is flooded with flowers.

During spring thaw, the creek floods the valley and dumps ice floes on the garden.

From Maureen's, we drive to Fairfield, near Saint Martin's, and see a generous rambling piece of ground ablaze with vibrant colour, shimmering in the still of the August afternoon. Into my mind floats something Proust wrote: *"Life ... that it should consist always of a series of joyous afternoons."*

In contrast to the controlled space of Maureen's garden, the one we are in now is a meandering, bountiful piece of ground. A man with a small blue and white umbrella strapped to his head comes out of the house to greet us. Ah, Mr. Umbrella Head. He says he is called Newie, but his real name is Ernest Brown.

"D'you do all this?" I ask Newie in amazement.

"Yes," he nods. Why isn't my garden like his? I ask myself. Because I'm not Newie, that's why, I answer. He tells us his father had been a farmer. "Daddy sold the soil to a chap near the airport who was a gardener in the thirties. Sold it for two dollars a load. Sure would like that soil now," he says.

We walk along a grass path that divides the garden in two. On one side are masses of monkshood, delphinium, loosestrife, and astilbe, along with a bed of volunteer cosmos through which grow tall cleomes; then there's a fence sprawling with orange-flowered honeysuckle. On the other side of the path, dug into holes in the grass, are large clumps of daylilies in yellow and orange and wine along with clusters of dark blue Japanese iris.

"I whipper-snip around these," Newie says, pointing to the clumps of iris and lilies. I imagine that in a few years' time he won't have to — all the clumps will come together and form another large bed. That's what happened to older parts of the garden.

Newie is very knowledgeable about all these plants, though reticent about his knowledge. We pass a dark purple buddleia and he says: "They call it 'Royal Red'; they're very loose with that red, aren't they!"

Elspeth asks whether there are sheltered areas or

frost pockets in his garden, and he answers that the whole area is one big frost pocket: "It's slow to get going, the soil is slow to warm up. But I love June. There's something about the flowers that's just nicer."

A stream running over a rocky bed forms the boundary on one side of Newie's garden. In it he's fixed up a sump pump that he uses for watering.

"This stream," he says, "floods the whole garden in spring when the freshet comes through. Large ice floes all over the place. They grind up against those trees there and strip some of the bark off."

"And these perennials sit under water and ice all that time, and then do so well?" I ask.

"Yes. The daffodils were all under water, too," he adds. Newie tells us that he organized a daffodil show that ran for nine years until a severe winter in 1991 destroyed most of the bulbs.

His wife comes into the garden and offers tea. She tells us Newie's arthritis is so bad that to plant his

Newie and his hat.

impatiens, he lies on a blanket, and often has to use a crutch to get around. She shows us photographs of the flooded garden with the ice crashing against the trees — a scene in absolute contrast to the one we are witnessing now. In early spring, it was a monochrome in white and greys; today, it's a scene of vibrant life and colour.

For a number of years Newie kept a store at his house and that's why the front door opens directly onto the road. On the hill across from the front door is a rhododendron which bulges onto the pavement, not an usual sight for New Brunswick. When I ask if the snowplough rips bits off it, Newie says, apparently with no bitterness, "Oh, yes, bits." There is also the most robust smoke bush I've seen in this province — bright, with a coppery glow.

"The sun goes down behind that hill," Newie says, "'round about six, and others will have another three hours of sunshine."

"Imagine what you could do, Newie," I say, "with another three hours of sunlight."

Elspeth's Travelogue

It was the beginning of August — time to set out on the last leg of our journey. We loaded up the car, and reluctantly I said good-bye to my daughter Kate.

The road between Sussex and Moncton was a corridor through cut-over forest. The terrain was neither flat nor hilly, and the highway so featureless my eyes snatched gratefully at any detail: a patch of sweet fern, a necklace of distant pylons, tiny clouds dabbed on the flat sky, a crow on a fence post — anything to relieve the monotony.

It was hot. I dozed off and didn't wake up until two bikers roared by, glossy black and welded to their wheels. We were plodding up a long incline and Judy was humming "Nearer My God to Thee." Below us, the sleepy grey-green Peticodiac River (whose tidal bore no longer does, on account of a new causeway) slid across a sleepy grey-blue panorama.

We bypassed Moncton, the hub city, and detoured into adjoining Dieppe where we hoped to discover the hub of Acadian gardening. We saw brightly coloured play equipment in many back yards, and a few home owners had erected fancy fences or decorative ironwork, but sadly we didn't have time to search out the real gardeners of Dieppe, and left, unsatisfied, to catch the ferry to Prince Edward Island.

The road to the ferry terminal at Cape Tormentine had a slightly grim air about it, and I wasn't surprised to see a sign admonishing me: *Prepare to Meet Thy God*.

Somewhere along the way, the road turned pink; the land of red roads and Green Gables was at hand, and suddenly before us lay the shining sea.

We'd travelled on a surprising number of ferries across Canada and enjoyed them all. They'd been pleasant interludes between roads and between moods. The ferry trips to and from Prince Edward Island framed our stay there and emphasized the province's distinct landscape. At first I thought the decision to build a bridge — the "fixed link" — was insanity. Only after a three-hour wait on our return journey did I begin to appreciate the pro-bridge point of view.

On the Island, I felt wide awake again. Maybe the salt air did the trick. The countryside was unabashedly pretty. The soft swirl of the land was patterned over in arable fields and the trim farms had an air of moderate prosperity, which may have explained why there were flower gardens everywhere — no feeling of Murray's "chill penury" here. The roadsides were foamy with Queen Anne's lace and dotted with baby-blue chicory. Even the tourist attractions on the road to Charlottetown, the miniature golf and antique cars, were polite in their mown grass aprons.

I found it hard to imagine anything horrible ever happening on this gentle green island — but then, I thought, perhaps one felt the same way about Ireland.

Judy's Journal

We head straight for the CBC building in Charlottetown where we are due for a radio interview. It's a relief to get out of the sun. We sit in the foyer and talk with the producer, and suddenly I have a terrible headache. Is my speech slurred? Is my vision blurred? I'm convinced of it. I suspect I have a brain tumour.

After suffering excruciating pain for about five minutes, I excuse myself and go to the restroom, where I can collapse and die out of everyone's way. Elspeth will have to do the interview herself, finish the trip on her own. In the restroom, I stare at the mirror to see if I can find signs of imminent death. I take off my Panama hat. What I see is a large dent in my forehead, above my right eye. My brain is imploding! I prepare myself for death. I am quite calm. I wait. I even fold my arms. An obituary forms in my mind. Then it dawns on me that I no longer have a headache.

My hat has a thin leather strap that passes through a wooden bead. The bead has been trapped under the brim, pressing against my forehead. As I leave the restroom, *O Death where is thy sting-a-ling-a-ling* runs through my mind.

I tell Elspeth about this after the interview is over.

"It was the best interview you ever did," she says. "You were brilliant. Put the bead back!"

Elspeth's Travelogue

A few years ago, my daughter Jean was married in Charlottetown. Because many of the guests were travelling long distances to the wedding, she and my son-in-law Charles decided to extend the celebrations over a weekend. One of the events they planned was a Sunday walking tour around the old part of the city. This was how Judy and I first met Reg Porter, a local historian and teacher. He had generously volunteered to be tour guide for the occasion, and kept us entertained on a leisurely stroll that began at Confederation Building and ended at his own home an hour or so later.

Reg lived in the ground floor apartment of a substantial house built around 1870, but it wasn't the house that had interested me so much as the garden behind it. Among the close-packed buildings of the old town, Reg had created a small green retreat. The cliché "urban oasis" sprang to mind. There were no palm trees, however, and there was no pool of water. Instead, a deep border of hardy perennials surrounded a circular brick patio. There were no camels either — only cats.

Reg's home, known to some as Neuterville, was home to four well-loved cats including the Grand Duchess Margaret Theodora. It was also headquarters of *The Neuterville News*, a journal as erudite as it was wacky. The paper, purporting to be published by the feline family, started as a joke and proved to be so popular it simply wouldn't stop.

Now that Judy and I were back in Charlottetown, we were eager to revisit Neuterville, meet Reg again, and see how the garden was progressing. It was hotter than ever, and I was looking forward to a quiet interlude in the shade. I imagined us sitting peacefully on Reg's handsome wooden bench, enjoying some light laughter and a little cultured conversation.

There was no reply at the door of the house, so we walked round to the back.

The shock! The garden we remembered was in ruins. The screech of a power tool shattered the peace. Plants were torn out and others were in

At first, Reg Porter's garden seemed to be in shocking disarray …

Soon it became apparent that a classical revival was in progress.

tatters. Cables, hammers, and broken rock lay scattered on the bricks, and Reg, looking worn-out, was kneeling in the middle of all this destruction, wiping sweat from his brow. He had lost weight. The garden also looked smaller, and in the first moments of surprise, I couldn't understand why. Then I realized that a massive board fence had been erected around the yard.

"An unspeakably horrible story," Reg groaned.

A boundary dispute with neighbours had escalated over several years and the animosity had become unbearable. Fortunately, the landlord was sympathetic and had finally arranged for a barrier to be built between the properties. His landlord, Reg said with feeling, was a compassionate man.

With the new fence — his "mighty fortress" — in place, Reg's spirits had revived. "It was probably the best thing that could have happened to the garden," he told us. "In life, there are no catastrophes, only

While Reg talked to Judy, the cat became jealous …

… and sulked.

events, and all events can be useful." This quotation from a Dutch writer, whose name I didn't catch, was his long motto. His short motto was, "Do it!"

There was no doubt that something was being done, but what?

In the middle of the fence on the far side of the garden, someone had sketched, in paint, a building with columns. Lattice panels flanked it, and the beginnings of a stone path led from the diagrammatic building to the existing brick patio. Against the adjoining fence, which ran along the back of the property, an extraordinary structure was taking shape. Sections of massive stone columns stood in a half circle round a raised pool. From the pool rose a pillar made of more stacked-up stone sections, and mounted on this was a carved Greek column cap topped by a sickle balanced on the tip of its blade.

"What *are* you doing?" we asked.

"I decided I may die here," he replied. "I have to create my paradise."

He looked so weary I was half afraid he meant to die on the spot. It was a relief when he staggered over to the bench, lowered himself down, and almost immediately turned into the enthusiastic and genial Reg I remembered.

"A fence eight feet high!" he said. "A challenge! Instantly I thought of a garden seat, two feet wide in Roman mode, and a Tucson temple to Victory. The podium will be the seat."

"And the lattice panels?"

"For various vines — of the sort that covered the palace in the story of Sleeping Beauty. Horizontal panels? Too much, I thought, so diamonds? A little bit vulgar? But vegetation will obliterate them. The path is local sandstone. I've made two trips to pick up pieces and I'll have to make two more. I've become a scrounger. It's amazing what hardware stores throw away, and I cruise industrial dump sites. That's how I found the fluted column drums; they're Nova Scotia sandstone and weigh four hundred pounds each."

I looked across at the massive chunks of stone around the pool and marvelled that Reg had managed to manoeuvre them into place.

"The sound of water is an essential element in the paradise garden," he informed us. "It's a feature borrowed by the Arabs in the seventh century from the peristyle courts of the Romans." He showed us how water would flow down the fluting of the central pillar. "At night, lights will shine on the ripples and the whole thing will shimmer beautifully."

I believed him. I was starting to catch glimpses of the vision that lay beyond the wreckage. Reg brought me back to the present.

"But I'm having trouble with the bloody liner."

Night-time effects were important to Reg because, on summer evenings, he often sat out in the garden and read until dusk. He also entertained his guests outdoors and encouraged the other tenants to use the garden whenever they wanted to.

I wondered if the jade colour of the water was deliberate, as in Chinese gardens. But no.

"Paint fell into it."

We admired the colour of the painted fence, a dark blue-green. It was Reg's special colour — Porter green — and he was planning to use it on all the garden furniture. The sickle was to be gilded and accompanied by bronzed Roman letters announcing,

"*Et in arcadia ego.*"

Reg stepped into his professorial role to explain the translation: "I, too, was in Arcadia" — not, as was commonly thought, an allusion to the good life, but a reference to death. Hence the sickle. Judy and I tried to look as if *we* knew that. The rim of the fountain basin was unfinished as Reg planned to make a coping from a copper tray. This would hold a pebble mosaic inspired by those he had seen in Greece which dated from the time of Alexander the Great. He was going to practise on a small scale first. There were also plans for the fence on the other side of the garden. Over the bench and under a cornice would stand a bust of Hadrian, Reg's favourite Roman emperor, the man responsible for the splendid gardens at Tivoli, Reg's favourite Roman place.

We weren't surprised to hear that Reg's passion for gardening grew out of his interest in art and architecture. It wouldn't have taken a genius to realize that this man was an art buff, a scholar, a classicist, and more besides. His business card read: Heritage Consultant. *The Neuterville News* revealed a wit that could be silly, sophisticated, and — why not? — catty. The interior of his apartment exposed another Reg, a collector of esoteric bric-a-brac, including geological samples, maps, and stipple engravings. Before we left, I asked him how he would describe himself.

"I am only qualified to be a school teacher," he said, "but … "

We waited. We knew by now you could depend on Reg to deliver a good punch line.

" … but in my *real* life," he went on, "I am an anachronistic creature who belongs to the 1830s or '40s, the classical revival; *that is my real life.*"

Of course! Out there in a small back yard, in a small Canadian province, safely fenced from a world that could hardly be further from classical Greece and Rome, aided and abetted by an aristocracy of cats, Reg was working like a dog to resurrect a world where he could *really live.*

An electrician arrived to attend to the outdoor lighting. The work in hand suddenly reclaimed our host. It was time to thank him and take our leave.

My daughter's high school friend, Barbara Bovaird, had invited us to stay for the night in her new house at Rice Point in the Cornwall area. It had been a long day, and we drove straight there from Charlottetown.

Barbara was now a school teacher, while her husband Chris Jette ran a busy craft business. They welcomed us with a hearty meal of P.E.I. mussels doused with warm garlic butter. Judy and I tried not to eat ravenously, and failed. By the time we'd finished the mussels it was too dark for a tour of the grounds and we settled for coffee and dessert, then staggered to our beds, too tired and well fed to be good company.

The next morning was bright, with clouds running ragged before a brisk wind. The house was light and airy and sat at the top of a sloping field with views down to the sea. Both Barbara and Chris had degrees in architecture, and they had designed the place themselves. During construction, they told us, the excavated material was pushed forward and flattened. They sculpted the edge of their new terrace into a large "S", and using flat beach rocks paved a roughly circular patio on the projecting bulge. To make things look less raw, they began planting.

Barbara explained that the wind whipped away the snow cover in winter. She wanted us to know that this made it hard on perennials and was one reason for their choice of plants. What choice? Well, marigolds. Mostly big orange marigolds. We went outside to look.

They were there all right — plenty of big orange marigolds and a good number of big yellow ones too, sprinkled about on the S-shaped bank. Among other foliage and flowers, and in the brilliantly clear island

Chris Jette and Barbara Bovaird with Judy. One of Chris and Barbara's driftwood trees is "growing" on the right.

air, they looked sturdy and cheerful and somehow just right. I hoped that Barbara and Chris, when they became experienced and sophisticated gardeners, would still enjoy a brazen blast of gold.

The beach had provided this enterprising couple

the steep, rough track from the beach. Chris told us he had run behind, supporting the projecting trunks and inhaling carbon monoxide all the way.

Later in the morning, Barbara took us to meet John and Martha Burka, who lived nearby. The Burkas were a multicultural family. John's Czechoslovakian background was Catholic and Jewish, and he had grown up in downtown Toronto. Beside a mix like that, Martha's Mennonite origins seemed almost commonplace. Their four children were more or less grown up and we didn't have the chance to meet them, but we soon

The Burkas' greenhouse and formal garden.

Chris and Barbara's cheerful seaside patio.

with more than rocks. Near the house stood two over-sized chunks of driftwood — whole tree trunks embedded upside-down in the ground. Bird feeders hung from their water-worn roots. We asked how they'd hauled these pieces into place. Barbara told us she had driven them in the back of their Dodge Caravelle up

learned that they'd played a big part in the design and construction of the garden.

In the few years they'd lived on their rambling rural property, the family had transformed the place. Apart from renovating the house, they'd surrounded it with new shrubs and perennial beds. At the side of the garage, they'd made an archway of bent saplings which lead to a large vegetable garden. On the side of the barn, they'd built a lean-to greenhouse of salvaged materials. Next to the greenhouse, and partly enclosed by a white picket fence, they'd laid out a formal garden of raised beds.

Peter, the eldest son, was the driving force behind this last scheme. He was a computer programmer with a bent for gardening. "Intensely logical and creative at the same time," his mother told us. He liked to put parameters around everything, so when his sister Martina had suggested the fence, he'd jumped at the idea.

Martha with one of her well-trained dogs.

In one corner of Peter's formal garden was a pond made from an old bathtub. Judy wanted to know how he sealed the plug hole. She had tried for years to seal an old sink, but finally gave up, filled it with gravel and planted it with hens-and-chicks. Peter used a piece of an old rubber dinghy, which he glued down and covered with rocks.

The family was also turning its attention to the edge of the woods behind the cleared land. Every winter, they banked up the house with leaves and, come spring, they spread the remainders between the trees as mulch to kill off weedy growth. The plan was to naturalize flowers there. "Next week," Martha said with a sweep of her arm, "we'll spread more leaves and wood chips in that whole area."

If Judy or I said something like that, the spreading of wood chips might or might not occur next week — or any other week — but when Martha said it, we had no doubt wood chips *would* be spread. We asked if the children had always been involved in the garden and she said, "Absolutely! From the time they were tiny. That's where I was, so that's where they were. They still have to come out in the garden if they want to find me. I'm out here before breakfast and at the end of the day till it's dark." She was starting a new career and her days were full, but her husband supported her efforts in the garden. "He'll weed and deadhead and he'll also clean the house or do the laundry so that I can garden. He knows it's something I *need* to be doing, if possible every day."

While we were talking, two handsome dogs hung round patiently. "Australian Blue Heelers," Martha told us. "They're perfectly trainable and we've taught them to respect the borders of the planting areas. They won't cross over the edges. The only snag is that, in spring, they're not quite sure where the edges are."

Martha told us that discipline and hard work were part of the Mennonite upbringing, and so was the idea that gardens were for food production. Martha had broken with tradition and was growing flowers, but she still felt there was more beauty in a good row of carrots than in daffodils.

The most notable thing in her vegetable plot was an area neatly lined out with divisions of perennials. It gave her "intense pleasure" to see them like that, she said, and she was planning to grow more of her flowers in rows instead of in borders. Having admitted flowers to the fold, perhaps she felt it was less frivolous to grow them in straight lines, more honest than in the contrived informality of conventional herbaceous beds. And I could see her point. There certainly was beauty — to say nothing of reassurance and pride — to be gleaned from a patch of clean dark earth and a healthy crop of any kind. These rows-of-flowers were a neat cultural compromise for Martha, and for us they were a first brush with a Maritime style of gardening I'd never even thought of before.

After leaving the Burkas, we began to spot other floral/vegetable gardens. They were typical farm plots — simple rectangles cut in the turf beside barns — planted in the normal rows, but the gardeners, instead of seeding beans and peas, had put in cosmos, sunflowers, dahlias, and petunias. It looked as if some farmers had simply switched from edibles to ornamentals without switching techniques.

It was a short drive from the Burkas to our next stop, the garden of Sandi and Ernie Jones. Sandi's great-great-great-grandfather had been a professional gardener in Scotland. Judy thought the gardening gene was at work again, but as usual I had a different theory.

By now we'd met people who gardened for every conceivable reason: for the challenge, for food, for therapy, for children, and for God. They were sentimental about the flowers or fascinated by the science. They were in it for a rest or for a workout. They were trying to create a setting for their house or a stage set for their lives. They gardened to get away from people or because their friends were gardeners. They were prompted by concerns for the earth's future or goaded by memories of the past.

I thought Sandi's garden was her creative act.

She told us that when she was a toddler, she found a small depression in the ground where a basin had been left out through the winter. At first she tried to dig it deeper — maybe all the way to China — but when that didn't work out, she used bits of glass and dandelions to make a garden instead. If she couldn't go to an imaginary place, then, by golly, she'd make one!

I thought this was perhaps the story of her life. I suspected she had always been an adventurer at heart. Her daughter, Kelly, certainly was — she'd just arrived back from Australia and was still jet-lagged (no need nowadays to burrow through the middle of the earth to get down under). Kelly was full of stories of life in the Antipodes, and Sandi confessed that she herself had been wondering what it would be like to start again in a new climate.

Ernie Jones, the "Rodney Dangerfield of gardening."

Sandi Jones' impeccable front garden.

Sandi, as a young woman, didn't get to China — or Australia. She started a family instead. Then a miscarriage jolted her domestic life off track and the loss aroused in her, she said, "a desperate need to create things." She turned to plants. She started growing moon flowers under lights and just never looked back.

When she and Ernie had moved to their current house eleven years earlier, her obsession with gardening had been unusual in the area. Now, in this pleasant subdivision, it seemed that non-gardeners would soon be the unusual ones. Sandi told us that a wave of gardening was sweeping the whole island. The Rural Beautification Society had held an annual competition for fifty years but the interest in the flower garden category had never been so strong. In Charlottetown a move to "Make Your Hometown Beautiful" had been underway for about five years. This was having an impact and even little Souris had a new garden club called Clayful Hands.

Although the balance was tipping in favour of gardeners, not many could hope to keep up with the Joneses. Sandi not only gardened creatively, she gardened intelligently. She was a Master Gardener until the program in P.E.I. ended for lack of funding, and her knowledge was apparent in her skillful use of plants. The perennial beds in her front garden were impeccably designed and maintained. Her back garden, though not huge, contained everything to delight a gardener's heart: a backdrop of trees, sun and shade, roses, a greenhouse, a salad garden, a fish pond, even bird and bat houses. The bats were supposed to move in and eat mosquitoes but hadn't yet cooperated. The bird houses hung like ornaments from a bird tree, which was just as dead as Chris and Barb's driftwood version but was planted the right way up.

Sandi also had an invaluable ally in her husband Ernie. While we sat on the deck drinking coffee, Ernie worked steadily in the background. A chickadee landed on the rail of the deck and informed us that the bird feeders were empty. Ernie filled them. Sandi described her husband as the Rodney Dangerfield of gardening — he did the work and didn't get the credit.

The deck was surrounded by sweet-smelling plants: heliotrope, mignonette, night phlox, and tobacco flower. The warm air was fragrant, the coffee was great. It was hard to tear ourselves away.

We were inspired by our visits to Martha and Sandi, but we were also a little daunted. Both Judy and I prided ourselves on our enthusiastic gardening efforts, but these Island

For Sandi, gardening was a creative act.

women were in a different league. Such ambition! Such energy! If we'd known what still lay ahead, we might have caught the next ferry back to the mainland and salvaged some of our self-respect. But no. Our hosts Barbara and Chris invited us to stay on for a couple of nights, and we accepted. By this time we were so enchanted with the scenery, the mussels, and the comfortable beds, we were tempted to stay on for the rest of our lives.

In the morning, Barbara packed us off with suggested destinations and a picnic lunch (I don't know which we appreciated more), and we headed north.

Judy's Journal

Barbara suggests we visit the garden at Stoneware Pottery, and we find it between two main roads at Winsloe. The pottery is owned and run by Sandy Mahon and Katherine Dagg.

"It was about three-and-a-half acres of sour soil," says Sandy. "A lot of rubble and junk from building the road was dumped here. The soil was so poor, a neighbouring farmer said to us, 'If a jack rabbit crossed this piece of ground, he'd have to take a lunch.'"

"You must have worked hard at improving the soil, then," says Elspeth, laughing. "Look at all these flowers!"

They built the house fifteen years ago; they have also had pottery in constant production since 1973,

Judy Maddocks

A guest cottage gave Sandy Mahon and Katherine Dagg a good excuse to create a garden within a garden.

Sandy and Katherine's three-acre garden — an oasis of peace between two main roads.

along with a shop where they display and sell their work.

"We started by planting three tamarack trees and the garden evolved from there," Sandy says.

"This bed here," says Kathy, pointing to a large bed of pale-coloured perennials, "is to be pulled out in fall, while we still have the lad who does our mowing. Then we'll dig in compost to raise it somewhat and then re-plant everything. All in three days."

"Three days!" we both say. I'm always amazed at the amount of work gardeners put themselves through; endlessly digging up, digging in, moving, improving, and re-doing beds.

We stroll over to the other side of the garden to see the pond. It's large and deep, with an island in the centre, forded by a wooden bridge.

"The water level is going down," Sandy tells us and wonders if it's because of the new subdivisions. Queen Anne's Lace, lupines, columbine, and poppies are abundant on the sloping bank, but the herons have been too quick for the once plentiful goldfish that no longer flash between the arrowheads and cattails. Further along, Sandy calls some tall hollyhocks, grouped together and leaning towards each other "the gossips," and goes on to show us a delightful guest-cottage with its own small garden.

Even though the property is between two busy roads, because it is fenced and landscaped it is like an island of peace in a sea of traffic, an ideal place for a business, a home — and a garden.

"Perennial Pleasures," painted on a sign, heralds our next stop. The sign stands amidst flowers at the end of Betty Lou Frizzell-Abbott's vast garden, which is a stone's throw from the farmhouse where she was born in rural P.E.I.

"Started with hundred and some rosebushes, and fifty or so died the first spring," Betty Lou laughs, "so my girlfriend and I asked if we could take some perennials from two houses they were pulling down to make room for a mall. We hauled these home and put them in. No, first it was a vegetable garden that I rushed home from my honeymoon to plant. I put in tomatoes, and marigolds bloomed. That's companion planting," she says.

I ask if her husband helps at all in the garden.

"Well, I don't keep him just for his good looks," she says. "He does some of the heavy work, like the tilling — come see the outhouse. You need one for an event like today."

The event is a family gathering; tables are lined up in the barn and the hamburger is defrosting. "My husband built this," she says, pushing open the door

Betty Lou Frizzell-Abbott and her perennial garden, with Island farmland in the background.

of an outhouse. "Isn't it great?" We peer in. "A two-holer. My five-year-old nephew sat on it for size. One of the girls picked the jug of flowers there, and the note-book is for your thoughts," she says, rearranging the flowers.

The view from here is beautiful. The cows in the distance look like wooden toys and the dark forest-like cut-outs. "And that rose," Betty Lou says, pointing to one next to the outhouse, is called 'English Elegance'. Then she shows us something else her husband built — a beautiful gazebo painted white and ringed by beds of flowers. And after that, there's a greenhouse.

"Once you grow from seed, it opens up all sorts of horizons," she says, clipping the blooms off some bright pink phlox. She says that ten years ago she grew three hundred and fifty-two dozen annuals. She also does the annuals for the church garden. "Eighty-some dozen!" She adds that she is trying to turn that around to perennials. I ask her how she keeps the flower beds so tidy and she says that she's never had children — "Never went into the kid detail." She has two nephews, Stanley and Darrel, who are a big part of her life. Their mother was killed some years ago and Betty Lou says that tomorrow they're all going on vacation together — along with two other special kids, Alanna and Timmy — "to do kids' stuff." She adds that there are always kids around, and that's why the beds are so well-edged. "I think there's a competition going on between Gill and Tim," she says.

The summer house built by Betty Lou's husband Charlie is adorned with honeysuckle, virginia creeper, and grape vines.

After we leave Betty Lou's garden, I drive down the road a short distance. I park the car at the side of the road and put my head down on the steering wheel.

"Oh, I can't believe it," I moan. "That garden! It's ruined me for life. It makes me feel totally inadequate in every way. I can't find my way anywhere, and what's more, now I've lost my lipstick. I want to go home and pour concrete all over the garden."

"I know," sympathizes Elspeth.

"That I'm totally inadequate?"

"That you can't find your way anywhere! Be-lieve me, I know. Here," she says, fishing around in a bag at her feet, "have a nectarine, it'll make you feel better."

"It'll take more than a nectarine," I say, leaning back in the driver's seat. I run my hands through my hair, "Can you imagine it? Two acres, and all under cultivation. Those flower beds. How does she do it? She even does her own sewing. She made the floral top and pants she was wearing. She's a powerhouse of energy, that one. Remember when you asked what sets her apart from others? She answered, 'A strong back and a weak mind.'"

"Her water garden was lovely, wasn't it," Elspeth says, "with no water in it, just rocks and plants imitating water. Betty Lou said she moved the stones on a dolly — 'on a dolly you can take them anywhere, even to a picnic' — so remember that. A lovely idea, the thyme flowing around the stones mimicking the wind pushing water up against rocks. And I liked the ceramic fish poking up through the thyme ... I wouldn't mind spending *my* life swimming in thyme. She doesn't pussyfoot around, does she?"

"No, she certainly doesn't," I agree.

Betty Lou absorbed in her flowers.

"'I don't allow slugs,' she said. And she doesn't have any. If I said that it would be as good as an invitation; they'd come from all over the world! And that lavender. I can still smell that lovely scent. She said she'd had all those bushes for ten years. I had a lavender bush once, for one year, and that thrilled me."

As we drive away, I think of the last question I asked Betty Lou: "What are you going to do with these huge beds when you get older?"

"Get outta here," she laughed. "I'm not getting older."

Elspeth's Travelogue

After seeing Betty Lou's magnificent garden, we felt we couldn't handle horticulture for a while. We took the rest of the day off and paddled in the sea.

Next morning, after the long wait in the ferry line-up, we drove to Truro in Nova Scotia, then turned east, heading for Wolfville where we were scheduled to read from *The Garden Letters*.

We were glad to be off the highway and enjoyed the drive. Heavy foliage of high summer draped the maples and cherries, and among all this verdure, dead and dying elms stood out starkly. Dutch elm disease had struck hard in the area. Later, we heard that Wolfville was trying to save its remaining elms. It was an expensive operation with no guarantee of success, but if the experiment failed, at least the town was blessed with other fine trees: chestnuts, lindens, maples, and locusts. Many farm sites had been sheltered by elms alone and would look forlorn for many years without them. It was sad to think that Elm Knoll Farm would soon be plain Knoll Farm.

We wanted to arrive in Wolfville in plenty of time for the reading, but the line-up for the ferry had thrown our schedule out of whack, and Judy was driving fast. Suddenly, out of the corner of my eye, I spotted a blur

The "farm garden."

Mildred's Burrow's cottage mix of hollyhocks and roses.

of brilliant colour beside a farmhouse. On the other side of the building I caught a glimpse of more flowers.

"Stop!" I squawked. We were already well past the driveway before Judy braked.

"Are you sure? Is there time? Yes? No?"

"*Yes!*"

We backed up.

Two women were unloading groceries from the trunk of their car. I'm sure they'd been looking forward to a cup of tea with their feet up, but they seemed happy to talk to us once they knew we were genuinely interested in the garden. The older woman, the garden's owner, was Mildred Burrows. The younger was her daughter, Elaine, visiting from Prince Edward Island.

Mildred could tell us exactly how long she'd lived on the farm because she'd moved in right after her honeymoon fifty years earlier. She had started gardening straight away, making flower beds beside the drive-

way — beds that were driven over so often that she finally grassed them over. Her husband hadn't been a gardener himself, but hadn't objected to Mildred's efforts, and she had gradually appropriated a large chunk of land for trees, shrubs, and flowers.

The farmhouse stood on one side of the driveway, its doorway prettily planted in a cottage garden mix of roses, hollyhocks, and annuals. On the other side of the driveway, behind a wide grass verge, beds of perennials formed a broad U with its base to the road. It was a simple and effective layout. Mildred told us it came about because she'd been trying to enclose a space for her children to play in. I suspected this was only part of the story; this gardener seemed to have an innate sense of design.

Many of the plants in the perennial garden had come from Mildred's childhood home in the village of Wittenburg, a short drive away. The Wittenburg property had been in the family since 1832 when her great-great-grandfather, Joseph Pulsifer, received a

Mildred's flowers growing in rows and rows and rows!

land grant. (Pulsifer was an unusual name and Mildred believed that someone far back in the family tree invented it to hide a shady past). Joseph had built stone retaining walls to create garden areas. These still existed and Mildred's sister still tended the planting round the old home. Their maternal forebears were gardeners as well, so the sisters came by it honestly.

Mildred had inherited more than a green thumb. Delphiniums, heliotropes, tiger lilies, Scottish blue bonnet (which looked to me like *Campanula glomerata*), roses, rhubarb, and blueberries had all found their way from the old home to the Burrows farm. Some were about to continue their travels to P.E.I. where daughter Elaine also gardened — well, naturally! As always when we heard such stories of family continuity, Judy and I, immigrants ourselves, felt a little jealous, a little orphaned.

Mildred's interests weren't limited to heritage plants. Her collection of trees included pecan, butternut, and copper beech — all unusual in Atlantic Canada. She travelled to Corn Hill Nursery in New Brunswick to buy shrub roses from our friend Bob Osborne, and she shopped around for flower seed. Her 'Pacific Hybrids' delphinium seed came from Butchart Gardens in British Columbia. I promised to send her a seed list from VanDusen Botanical Garden in Vancouver.

While she was showing us around her perennial garden, Mildred's hands were never idle. It made me smile to see how quickly she accumulated an armload of weeds and spent blossoms. The habit was a trademark of real gardeners.

The perennial garden was beautiful and the family history enviable. They alone would have made our visit worthwhile, but I knew there was more to come. It was the wild splash of colour on the *other* side of the house that had first attracted my attention; it had been so totally unexpected in the midst of these peaceful Nova Scotian fields. I found it hard to believe that Mildred, retired school teacher and sensible, motherly woman, was responsible for such an outrageously showy piece of planting, and I was beginning to think my eyes had deceived me. If not, we were in for a treat.

Mildred deposited her weeds and led us round the back of the house to the other side — and there it was!

Set well out in the field, a long thin vegetable plot lay at right angles to the road. A row of sunflowers divided it across the middle and the back half contained the expected vegetables. The front half, however, was packed with flowers: lobelias, snapdragons, asters, salvias, zinnias, marigolds, petunias, ageratum, nicotiana …

Mildred's hands were never idle – it was difficult to get her to stop for a photograph.

The colours were as gaudy as a seed catalogue, and the layout was a real show-stopper. The flowers were in rows, Prince Edward Island-style, but the rows zigzagged and criss-crossed in a design so jazzy, so brilliantly zany, it made me laugh aloud. I took colour photographs — there was no point in using black and white film for *this* planting.

Mildred obviously got as big a kick out of her flower patch as I did. Tourists and neighbours apparently enjoyed it too; she told us people often stopped for a closer look. She had been creating a new pattern every year. For Canada's one hundred and twenty-fifth birthday, for instance, she'd made a design of maple leaves complete with the dates, 1867 and 1992, all done in flowers.

And why not? With the family grown up, she told us, she didn't need the space for vegetables, the ground was already in good shape and the flowers were inexpensive because she saved seed from year to year and started her own plants. She kept deer and raccoons at bay by leaving old boots and coats around and by changing them from time to time to ensure an adequately deterrent whiff of humanity. I couldn't help thinking it would take a very stinky boot — or a flying one — to deter the cheeky suburban raccoons who terrorize my goldfish in British Columbia.

After Wolfville we came upon even more rows — a high roadside bank was emblazoned with colourful horizontal stripes. The explanation was on a small sign: *Hennigar's U-Pick Flowers. Please cut from the top 7 rows. 20¢ per stem.*

Coming hot on the heels of the floral/vegetable patches we'd seen on Prince Edward Island, I found Mildred's annual garden fascinating. She'd taken the simple rows-of-flowers theme one step further, had reinvented the Victorian fashion of carpet bedding, and had done it with such refreshing verve, it gave the style a whole new look. This was the kind of garden I loved — a garden direct from the heart. It was good to know that in the thick of our responsible adult lives, a piece of land could still afford us a place to play, and I couldn't help thinking that an adult who played so brilliantly must have been a fine teacher.

Judy's Journal

On the road to Wolfville we get stuck behind an ancient farm truck piled high with rolls of hay. They look precarious. We keep our distance. When the farmer turns into his gate, the hay bounces right off, and Elspeth tells me I can't take it home for mulch, though I am very tempted. Queen Anne's Lace and white sweet clover decorate the side of the road, and look better than any garden. Sometimes I wonder why we bother.

In Wolfville, we give a reading at a small theatre with red plush seats. It's attended by four women. I don't know how

Globe thistles make the perfect setting for this garden sculpture.

we come to be here. The stage is cluttered with bric-a-brac and the manager tells me the chair I'm sitting on is plugged into the electricity. We thoroughly enjoy ourselves and I try not to think about the electric chair.

From Wolfville we travel to Aylesford, where we visit Grunt's Art Glass, run by Janis Cobb and Gary Grant. Janis was transferred to this area from Toronto, but quit her job after two years, realizing there is more to life than making money. Their business combines gardening with garden art.

It is a wild rambling garden, full of phlox, Queen Anne's Lace, and globe thistles. Each area is separated by wooden fences draped with vines. Throughout the garden we come across pieces of Gary's work: a concrete bench inset with pieces of stained glass; a scarab beetle made of glass and placed on a bird bath; Oriental concrete lanterns enriched with pieces of stained glass. Further along, we come face to face with a large sun constructed of wood. "Heaven is under our feet" is spelled out in pieces of glass set in concrete.

The garden is really the display room and is a beautiful way to present art. Elspeth covets a concrete bench, but I say, "Think of the car!"

By the side of the road we eat our usual fare — sardines and crackers — and look out across the fields. I remind Elspeth that my maiden name was Salmon and that quite soon, after all these sardines, I shall be reverting back to the fish family.

In Bridgetown we stay with friends who have recently moved here, and we sleep magnificently. For breakfast we feast on homemade preserves featuring zuchini-and-ginger jam, quite delicious and so different from our usual food.

We are scheduled to do a reading in the Secret Garden Restaurant of the Historic Gardens in Annapolis Royal. Our audience at the reading is responsive. We read, laugh, and talk. The Historic Gardens cover more than ten acres of garden, with different areas expressing different themes — an Acadian garden, a Victorian garden which uses strong colours and looks as smooth as velvet, and a rose garden with a rose maze and over two thousand roses in historic sequence.

From there, we visit the Mad Hatter's Book store in Annapolis Royal. Patrice, the owner, offers to show us her garden, which stretches out onto the waterfront of the Annapolis Basin. A bed of blue hydrangeas wraps around the deck and the white flower of a 'Henry Hudson' rose sprawls along the edge. To sit on the deck in the shade of the large maple and listen to the water is close to heaven.

In this garden, as in others in the area, we notice structures made of alder saplings. Patrice informs us they were made by Kevin Hanson, a man who lives in the woods and does odd jobs. She tells us that if we hang around, we will most certainly see him.

Another garden next to Patrice's intrigues us, so we go for a quick visit. This one is also on the beach, a small fenced area bursting with vegetables and flowers. Across from it we spot a restaurant called Newman's, and stop for a bite to eat. At the back of the restaurant is a garden enclosed by pink fencing; we sit there, at a table shaded by an umbrella. We've become used to eating outdoors — usually leaning against the car, swallowing sardines like seals — but there is something lighthearted about eating *al fresco* at a restaurant surrounded by flowers and trees, especially one as pretty as this. Groups of large terra-cotta pots from Portugal spill over with geraniums, and perennials thrive in this sheltered spot.

After eating, we explore the town, keeping an eye

Kevin Hanson's astonishing alder architecture. Kevin and the owner of this house eluded us.

open for Kevin Hanson as we go. The entrance to one small shop is decorated with a heart-shaped alder archway, and another has a tiny garden enclosed by an elaborate alder gate and fence. On the beach, directly opposite the door of a house, we find an amazing set of arches and fences. There is no reply at the house and we return many times until a neighbour tells us the owner is away.

Small gardens seem to be the trademark of Annapolis Royal: patterned paths made of pebbles; trellis work along a wall, supporting roses; and around a corner, splashes of cosmos and daisies. Then more arches, covered with honeysuckle and made by the elusive Kevin, whom, alas, we never meet.

Elspeth's Travelogue

The day was young and fresh as we set out from Annapolis Royal through Paradise, heading for Bridgewater. *"Morning has broken,"* carolled Judy, *"like the first morning."* Villages hereabouts seemed well named. In New Germany, most of the mailboxes bore names like Slauenwhite and Zwicker. We stopped to admire a particularly tidy garden there, but the owners weren't at home. At Pinehurst I took a photo of a pine garden.

We refueled in Bridgewater at our favourite doughnut shop, then called ahead to Bayport Plant Farm, our next port of call. When we walked back to the car, we found, tucked under the wiper blade, a leaflet telling us: "How to Get to Heaven."

"We just *left* Paradise," groaned Judy. "Why couldn't they tell us how to get to Bayport instead?"

The south shore of Nova Scotia had a jolly air about it. We passed a garden full of whirligigs: cartoon characters, seagulls, and planes, all for sale and whirling madly. Rectangular ponds were popular, most of them decorated with water lilies, fishing boys or wooden ducks. One garden was decked out entirely in pink annuals and another in purple liatris to match the

Cows beside the road to Granville Ferry. Cut-out animals are popular garden ornaments in the Maritimes.

painted foundation of its house. Other houses were red or green or blue.

At one point, the houses looked newer and the gardening style changed from jolly to tidy. Trim lawns, pots of flowers, and immaculate beds of impatiens were the order of the day. I asked Judy whether she'd noticed the name of the village.

"Neatsville," she said, and I believed her. For about five seconds.

The land and sea began to interlock like pieces in a jigsaw puzzle and we never knew on which side the water would appear next. It was a lovely area — the kind of place one dreams of retiring to — but seemed a strange location for a nursery. The land sloped up steeply from the shore into woodland, the soil was obviously thin, and a salty wind blew in off the Atlantic.

We came upon the Bayport Plant Farm suddenly; it was an unpretentious set-up directly across the road from the beach.

The founder, Captain Richard (Dick) Steele, had specialized in growing and breeding rhododendrons since 1973, and had become something of a legend in Maritime gardening circles. He was in Halifax when we arrived, but his daughter, Diana Cooper, greeted us and showed us around. She'd worked at the Plant Farm since 1978 as her father's lieutenant.

In the sales area, rhododendrons were packed in with primulas, heathers, and other plants which, in Atlantic Canada, were considered hard-to-find. The seedling heathers selected by the nursery had names like 'Indian Maid' and 'Indian Summer'. When Judy saw them, her eyes lit up, her pace slowed down, and I knew we wouldn't be leaving empty-handed.

Diana offered to show us the trial rhododendrons and stock plants, and we clambered into the battered nursery truck for a short drive up a bumpy track into the woods. Here, an astounding number of rhododendrons formed an understorey to a canopy of pines and other native trees. I wished we could have seen them blooming in early June. We plunged on foot into this extraordinary shrubbery. Without our guide, we'd soon have been lost. It was hard to imagine how anyone — even Dick himself — could keep track of all those precious species and hybrids that seemed, to us at any rate, planted randomly among acres of trees.

Just after we returned to the sales area, Dick arrived. He was an octogenarian who showed no signs of slowing up. We all sat in the shed that served as an office, and he told us a little of his history.

He'd been a rhododendron fancier since he was ten years old. Walking to school one day in Rothesay, New Brunswick, he'd noticed a shrub with gorgeous red flowers. From then on he was hooked on rhododendrons. He began to grow and breed them in 1947, but his plans were often interrupted over the next twenty years while he served with the navy and travelled the world. His interest in horticulture, however, never waned.

During the Korean war, while his ship was in a Japanese port, he walked into his cabin one day, looked round in disgust, and said to his steward, "McGoran, this place is damned dull — I want flowers!" Next thing he knew, the cabin was full of enormous bouquets, flowers from floor to ceiling.

"McGoran," he said, "I'm going to be a pauper."

"Yes, sir," McGoran agreed. "It's going to cost you three dollars every time you come into port."

Dick never found out exactly how the deal was struck (McGoran, alas, went to prison around this time!), but whenever they were in port after that, a charming Japanese woman brought them bunches of flowers.

Whenever possible, Dick would go ashore botanizing. When they were behind enemy lines and couldn't leave the ship, he'd take himself off to a little sea cabin under the bridge, and study the plant life at a distance through binoculars. The crew thought he was crazy. When he was forty, he retired from the navy and started his real life as a rhododendron breeder.

As Dick reminisced about his professional contacts in the world of plant breeding, I felt privileged to be sitting in the friendly little shed, listening. He told us about his early mentor, Joseph Gable in Pennsylvania. Then the narrative moved on to Philmore and Hancock at Ontario Agricultural College, Swain and Craig at Kentville in Nova Scotia, Brueckner in Ontario, Cook in Vancouver, and our friend Frank Skinner in Manitoba. I lost track of all the names and places, but I do remember that we crossed the Atlantic to Stevenson at Tower Court, Knight at Wisley, and Findlay at Windsor Great Park. The names were like a *Who's Who* of horticulture, and they gave us insight into a tight-knit community, an inner circle of aficionados.

"I'd take bits of blotting paper," Dick said, "write down the names of the pollens I wanted, and mail them to Findlay. He'd put them in his pocket and he wouldn't even shake the dew off the stuff when he collected it. Then he'd mail it to me. I'd dry it and put it in a capsule with silica gel and freeze it and I could use it for years — all viable."

The heather garden at Bayport Plant Farm.

These were the grand old men of plant breeding and, as Dick talked, it became obvious that they *were* all men. As hands-on gardeners, both Judy and I had shifted as much muck and rubble around as most of the men we knew. On our journey, we weren't a bit surprised to find that male and female gardeners tackled equally ambitious projects. We did, however, find that male enthusiasts were more likely to spend large sums of money on their gardens, and to zero in on narrow areas of interest. Our rose grower in Calgary, Don Heimbecker, had disagreed with our theory of male specialists and female generalists, but on the whole we had found it held true.

We remarked on this to Dick. He couldn't offer an explanation, but added that medical doctors were particularly inclined to join the rhododendron and alpine elites. At this point, as if on cue, Dr. Fazal Rahman and his wife, Pat, walked into the office. They had come to see if Dick could identify a small silver-leafed alpine plant. The Rahmans, like many of the nursery's visitors, were friends as well as customers. To our delight, they joined the group and Dr. Rahman told us he was becoming interested in rhododendrons as well as alpines. No surprise there!

We had to tear ourselves away from the conversation. We thanked Dick and Diana, accepted Pat and Fazal's generous invitation to see their alpine garden in Bridgewater, and left bearing heathers.

I expressed doubts about lugging heathers through Nova Scotia, then all the way to Newfoundland, but Judy had a plan: she would wrap the small plants in moist tissue, and leave them in plastic boxes, in ice, in the cooler, in the trunk of the car. While we flew to Newfoundland, they would stay in the long-term parking lot in the Halifax airport.

We spent the night in Halifax, then backtracked to Dayspring in the morning. Dick had suggested we visit our next gardener, Mary Conrad. "She's a real goer and a shaker and a mover and a doer," he'd said. "Such a little woman and she works out in her garden all the time! She must have seventeen thousand bulbs planted between the house and the road."

A bantam rooster was crowing cheerily as we pulled into Mary's driveway. More crowing and flurries of proud clucking punctuated our visit. I estimated a three-egg morning.

A jumble of planting surrounded the driveway and sprawled up the hill behind the house. This was definitely not Neatsville. It was more like a big, well-loved family room, full of interest, full of projects in progress, full of life. Mary's garden, we soon discovered, was made in her image. Her sense of fun was there, her wide-ranging interests, her largeness of spirit and bigness of heart. Mary may have looked small, but that was an illusion.

The day was already hot and Judy and I were happy to sit in Mary's kitchen sipping iced water while we heard about her childhood. Her mother had died when Mary was nine, and Mary was expected to do an adult's share of the chores on her father's small holding. Times were tough. It was the kind of grind that would have put most children off gardening, but Mary had thrived on hard work. Working in her garden, she told us, kept her alive. In winter, confined to the house, she "sagged down," but spring brought her out of the slump. The way she talked about the growing season reminded me of Mildred Burrows, another of the world's workers,

Mary Conrad performs with Bessie, her square-dancing scarecrow.

who had said with feeling, "Do I *ever* look forward to spring!"

There was no slump in evidence as Mary showed us around outside. In spite of the heat she was bouncier than either of us. Judy commented on the difference between her height and Mary's. "I tower over you like a wooden stork," Judy said. "If genes from both of us were put in a test tube and shaken up, a perfectly sized human being would come forth."

At the side of the driveway, bittersweet and clematis scrambled through precious trees and shrubs. (One fifteen-year-old magnolia from Dick Steele was doing especially well.) There were perennials and herbs, roses and orchids. Bessie, a square-dancing scarecrow, do-si-doed among the vegetables. Frogs swam in the pond. A variety of recycled containers served as rainwater tanks. The rare and the commonplace, the practical and the pretty — all received the same attention. A wilting alyssum caused as much concern as an expensive hybrid daylily.

Among this collection of plants, there was no trace of Dick Steele's lifelong focus. Every plant was grist to Mary's mill, and her enthusiasm literally knew no bounds. Her son had attempted to keep her territorial expansions in check by building a fence across the hillside, but his mother had already mounted a rearguard action and was planning to naturalize flowers on the slope beyond.

As she showed us around the front garden, I noticed that much of the foliage belonged to spring flowering plants — lungworts, violets, hellebores — and I remembered that Mary's spring bulbs had made a big impression on Dick. I asked her if she specialized in spring flowers. It was a silly question. I should have known by then that Mary specialized in everything. Still, if there was one time of year I'd have chosen to visit Dayspring again — a time when Mary and her garden would truly have been in their element — I'd certainly have picked a bright morning in May.

Judy's Journal

After Dayspring, we visit Fazal and Pat Rahman, the couple whom we met briefly at Dick Steele's. They live in Bridgewater in a marvellous house, large and old with bevelled glass in many of the windows. The house sits surrounded by trees and flower beds.

They show us their alpine garden. It's on a difficult site, sloping down from the house. At one time, it was covered with phlox and lupines. Pat tells us the site was bulldozed and graded, and then topsoil and bark were tilled in. Truckloads of gravel were dumped and arranged into hills and slopes. I walk across the paths and admire the delicate flowering alpines. Not only alpines, but patches of glowing portulaca enhance the slopes. Whenever I'm in a garden such as this one, one that is different, and has been planned, I always imagine that mine could be like it.

I ask Elspeth if she thinks I could do this to mine. Right away she says, "No," though quite kindly, adding that I don't have the resources and would never be ruthless enough in pulling out volunteers.

We talk about Elga's garden in Saint John, Sheila Paulson's garden in Calgary, and the garden belonging to Andrée, Alain, and Alfred in Rivière-Ouelle — all rock gardens, but each one completely different from the others.

Pat thinks the trees are a garden, but Fazal doesn't agree and wants some of them gone. In fact, he says that for his birthday he'd like some branches cut from an acacia tree — which doesn't seem much to ask. He does mention also that Pat's vinca has killed his hosta, adding that only God and vinca can kill a hosta.

After a cup of tea in Pat and Fazal's elegant drawing room, we make a quick visit to Manley Bennett, whom Pat has told us about.

Manley lives in Hubbard, just outside Halifax, and is a paraplegic. He tells us he looked a long time for a flat piece of land on which to build a house. He has only recently become interested in gardening, after being a school teacher and principal for many years, and has been trying to find manageable ways to gar-

Raised beds help Manley Bennett work in his garden.

den from a wheelchair. A ramp leads from the front door to a concrete path that has been made to look like attractive stone. The path goes down the side of the house, with beds on either side. A narrow bed borders the house and there is a wider one on the other side, both beds workable with long-handled tools. An accessible deck is bordered by dahlias and a pair of rose bushes — 'Henry Kelsey' and 'Henry Hudson'. Both roses are supported by lattice. Manley shows us an area he has set aside for a Zen garden, a space filled with small pebbles and large rocks where one can linger and even meditate.

On the way back to Halifax, we stop and walk along the edge of the sea. I hold up my skirt, take off my sandals, and splash through the water. If this weren't enough, afterwards we stop at a canteen and feast on raspberry-cheesecake ice cream. It tastes divine.

We arrive in Halifax quite late, and stay in a women's residence at the university. With two sons having gone to Dalhousie, I feel I should have free room and board at least.

The next morning is hot and muggy and we have a CBC interview and reading in the Public Gardens. I remind Elspeth of the reading we did at a restored house and garden on Vancouver Island. We swore we would never do another reading outdoors. The competition was too great. As soon as we started, a string quartet struck up. They were quelled by the management. Then planes roared overhead, and I knew Air Canada wouldn't take kindly to re-routing. Trucks changed gear, boats hooted, and crows sqawked in a tree overhead. We discovered that the sound of a croquet mallet against a ball can be quite distracting — especially if the hoop is right at your feet.

Halifax Public Gardens is no different! Ducks and pigeons go wild; a tour guide speaks loudly to his flock; an ambulance screams by; but it is the kilted bagpiper who finally finishes us off.

At noon we have another interview with CBC for Maritime News — indoors, I hope — and then a visit to a Halifax gardener, Roy Fall.

A few minutes from Spring Garden Road in Halifax, we turn down an alley and come across what looks like a small city garden at the back of a house.

We walk slowly across a painted blue deck connecting two houses and knock on the back door. No one comes, so we look around. Signs of work in progress are in evidence — earth piled on plastic bags and daylilies dug up.

"It is hot," I say. "Maybe he's just gone inside for a drink, or gone for a nap. I could do with one myself."

"I don't like to just wander around. D'you think we should?" Elspeth asks.

"Well, we're not breaking and entering, and we're not going to make off with plants, though I must say I am tempted. How about that arbour covered with kiwi vine?"

"No, I think he'd notice that," Elspeth says.

It is a relief to see no vast expanse of lawn but small areas separated by curved groupings of shrubs and trees such as honeysuckle, lilac, and buddleia, and beds planted in impatiens, chrysanthemums, heliotrope, and chenille plant. Each area has a quality of its own, such as shade, water, sun, sand, grass, or gravel.

Roy Fall appears at the back door and greets us. He is wearing a white T-shirt and jeans, and around his waist is a belt decorated with silver whales, elephants, and zebras. He ebulliently describes his garden. He and his partner, Frank Letourneau, now own the house next to theirs, and even before the sale of the second house was final, he had torn down the dividing fence and had plans for a deck.

"How d'you like the deck?" he asks.

"I love the blue," I say.

"A pilot lived next door," he says, "and told us that from the air the deck looks like a swimming pool. I always liked that."

When I ask him who built the deck, he says that he

Roy Fall and his niece Dawn Marie in the expanding garden.

Roy's passion for gardening has exploded into his neighbour's yard. Their car, just visible, drowns in flowers.

Roy Fall's garage door in disguise.

loves to do that sort of thing and can turn his hand to most things. We walk across a slate stone path, ducking under trees to the garage that Roy has revamped to look like a cottage, with small doors and windows painted on the large garage doors.

A small girl follows us around clinging onto Roy's legs. She hangs not just on his legs, but on his every word. "This is my niece, Dawn Marie. She came over to the house with my mother, who's in there watching *Priscilla, Queen of the Desert*, isn't she, Dawn?"

Roy continues with his tour. The slate stepping-stones across the grass lead from the deck to a goldfish pond. At the side of the pond, fastened to a shed, is a mirror which reflects the pond, making it hard to figure which is real, and which is reflection. He saw that done in a magazine and thought he'd give it a try. "I like it," he says.

At the side of the driveway is a bed of gravel planted with cactus. "What about all these cactus?" I ask.

"Well," Roy says, "I wanted a cactus garden. So I thought up against that fence might just be the place. Gets sun all day there. Put bags and bags of play sand over garden fabric and

Work in progress – sign of a real garden.

bought cactus from Zellers for $7.99 and planted them out on June twelfth, when the lilacs come out and it's my brother Fred's birthday. The clematis from next door looks nice coming over the fence, doesn't it?"

We walk down to the back of the garden with Roy and Dawn Marie, who is still clinging to his legs, and admire the tall hollyhocks.

"Feed them beer and wine. When we have parties here I pour what's left in the glasses over them. That's why they look so good."

He indicates an elderly woman sitting outside in the shade. "I help Margaret Bennett," he says. He is trying to persuade Margaret to take down her fence because the neighbours on the other side — Barney and Elizabeth — want him to do their garden, too. Then he'll have all four gardens to do. He adds that his mother throws up her hands:"She says, 'Oh, my God, Roy.' She thinks it's work. But it's my life. I love it." He and Frank rent out the first house to various tenants. Rhonda Crosby, one of the tenants, is already infected by Roy's enthusiasm and helps in the garden most days. Roy says, "All I want is for them to enjoy the garden. Use it. Entertain in it."

What a lovely thought!

Elspeth's Travelogue

Halifax has a substantial black population, and the only thing I knew about its history was the distressing story of Africville, a black community that in the name of progress was razed to the ground in the 1960s. Life in Nova Scotia hadn't been easy for black people, and I thought it likely that gardening ambitions had suffered along the way. By now, however, I knew a lot about the strength of real gardeners, and I wasn't surprised to find that Edith Chandler had a good share of that strength.

Edith was seventy-seven years old and said she'd "enjoyed every year of it." She lived above the docks on a street where most of the houses opened directly onto the sidewalk. When we arrived, road crews were stripping and relaying the asphalt pavement. It was hot, noisy, and smelly, and the gritty ribbing of the street surface added nothing to the ambiance. It was hardly necessary to check the number of Edith's house, though: tucked against the wall by the door was a painted trough standing on wooden legs and overflowing with nasturtiums. They were the only flowers in sight.

Edith met us at the door. Another visitor was just leaving, and Edith was obviously taking time off from a busy schedule but, having seated us in her living room, she gave us her whole attention. After the grimy atmosphere outside, it was a treat to sit in the cool, wall-papered room and listen quietly to her story.

She was raised one of fourteen children on a farm on the old Guysborough Road outside Halifax. "It was such a pleasure growing up," she said. "We were so blessed to have two beautiful parents. They worked hand in hand together and they were just *it* for gardening. People would stop their cars to admire the garden. My father went all out for his family; he would see them want for nothing. He stopped smoking just to make ends meet. He worked up at the Bedford Rifle Range and he'd come home for two weeks and put in huge gardens, then he'd have to leave again, and it was our job to look after them. I remember those lovely lazy days — well, you're right, maybe they weren't so lazy, but it was healthy work. We were tomboys, roaming round with our friends, the little ones climbing in the trees. We'd play baseball so late we couldn't see the ball. Days were longer then."

Eventually Edith married, moved to the city, had five children of her own and adopted another. When school was finished for the year, her mother would say, "Send the children out!" and another generation of youngsters benefited from those long summer days on the farm. Edith thought that every child should have contact with animals. Chickens, dogs, and ducks — they'd had it all.

The family was moved off the property when the Halifax airport was built. The Baptist church they'd attended was still there, however, and Edith was still going to it regularly. "The church — that's me," she said. "That's what I'm all about. The garden is part of it. Those two things are worth living for — the garden and the church."

She'd lived in her present house for thirty-three years. The place was "like the city dumps" when they first moved in and her late husband, Avery, hauled away truckloads of coal and wood ash left by the people who'd lived here.

Edith took us through to the back of the house. The garden layout was simple: mixed beds down each side, a wider bed for vegetables at the back (runner beans and cucumbers) and, in the middle, grass with a picnic table and some lawn chairs.

In summer, she read out there. She loved the peace and quiet. The grandchildren also enjoyed the garden, and when visitors came they usually sat outside as well. I suspected visitors came in a constant stream to Edith's place. Her garden seemed to be a kind of neighbourhood retreat, and I guessed that a little quiet counselling and a few prayers went on around that picnic table from time to time.

"This has to be heaven!" says Edith Chandler, who brings memories of her country childhood to her city backyard.

Edith told us she loved snow and cold weather but like most of the gardeners we talked to, longed for spring to come. While she waited, she looked at books with pictures of flowers. "It isn't a large garden," she said, "but the size doesn't matter as long as I have something to dig in. In spring, I'm out there in the morning, planting my flowers, and the birds are singing their hearts out, and I say, 'Father, this has to be heaven.' I'm the wealthiest person in the word — not with money but with blessings."

Apart from the calm of Edith's garden, it was the beauty of individual flowers that gave her most pleasure. Her clematis was "just precious!" and the weigela had "so many blooms you couldn't put a pin between them. It was gorgeous!" She told us she loved every kind of flower but nasturtiums were her favourite.

I remembered the nasturtiums we'd seen in the trough at the front door, and it occurred to me that they were the perfect choice. Like Edith, they were forthright and energetic. They spread their brightness around unstintingly, and if their ground was less than rich — no matter! They were surely the happiest of flowers.

Judy's Journal

At our reading at Frog Hollow Books in Halifax, we meet Susan Kerslake, whose name I recognize as the author of a book of short stories I've read. She invites us to her apartment to see her balcony garden, a five-by-twelve foot space.

Susan has lived here for twenty-two years. From the apartment, we step into a lush green space. Scarlet runners and morning glory climb to the balcony above. Sweet peas cling to an old tree branch. Small orange flowers of *Thunbergia alata* cover a metal frame. There is a surprise of colour from geraniums. Small fat tomatoes hang in abundance.

"See the chickweed growing over the buckets?" Susan points out. "I feed that to the budgies."

I mention the maple and elms — not usual for balconies — doing so well in their containers.

"Where I grew up in Illinois, there were a lot of elms," Susan says.

"So *that's* why you want them here then," Elspeth suggests. "But what about overwintering them?"

Susan tells us that in the fall she puts the smaller pots in

Susan Kerslake's garden from the outside (top) and the inside.

plastic bags, smothers everything with oak leaves, then places pots and bags of leaves close together around the elms. It seems to work.

As we are leaving, I remind Elspeth of the container garden we'd seen in Saskatoon. The one hundred and eighty buckets of runner beans growing up over the fence. And the one hundred and fifty white buckets of marigolds, to say nothing of the milk crates and oil drums full of marigolds. A sight to behold!

"It would be worth nipping back to see them," I say hopefully.

"No," says Elspeth firmly. "We're going to Newfoundland."

Walking along Argyle Street later that day, we glance up at the front of a restaurant called the Economy Shoe Shop and see acorn squash, pumpkins, and cucumbers dangling down from window boxes. We also see a woman hanging precariously out of a window. We rush into the restaurant and talk to the girl behind the counter.

Susan's plants, which include maples, elms, raspberries, and chickweed, are unusual choices for a balcony garden.

The Economy Shoe Shop in Halifax.

"The vegetables we use in the restaurant. A couple of artists live on the second level. The third level is just a façade, and the woman you see hanging out the window is a dummy."

"Oh," we say, quite deflated.

We leave the car in the long-term parking lot at the Halifax airport. I check the icebox in the trunk to make sure the heather plants are moist enough. I feel like I'm abandoning small children when I leave the little things alone in the hot car, and I feel guilty as I get on the plane.

From Halifax we fly to St. John's and wait at the luggage carousel for our box of books, which we're going to take to a local bookstore. I spot a box on the carousel among other luggage that looks as though its been going around and around for years. I haul the box off, only to find *The Book of Mormon* stamped all over it. I put *The Book of Mormon* back and wait for *The Garden Letters*.

As we head for the rental car area,

Elspeth asks me about the last time I was in Newfoundland. Tom and I had travelled to the west coast of the island. It had been this time of year — toward the middle of August. We had climbed Gros-Morne and stayed at Gros-Morne National Park. To keep our food cool in the ice-box, we'd collected pieces of iceberg that had washed ashore in a cove.

Elspeth and I pick up our rental car, find our B&B, then go in search of Janet Story, our first contact in Newfoundland. After a couple of attempts, which include going the wrong way down a freeway with drivers and passengers laughing and cheering us on, we find Janet's tall dark house. It has black railings and is surrounded by maples and sycamores.

Janet invites us into a high-ceilinged living room chock-full of paintings, records, and books, one of which is the *Dictionary of Newfoundland English*, written by Janet's brother. We want to find out about

Judy making notes about the splendid alpine garden at the Memorial University Botanical Gardens.

gardens in the area, and something of Janet's own history. At first she is a little reticent, but relaxes when Elspeth mentions her time on the Shetland Islands, a place Janet too has visited and liked. Her great-grandfather was a swiling captain, Janet says.

"Swiling?" I ask.

"Sealing," she explains. She tells us he built houses for his sons, and imported clergymen for his six daughters to marry. He built the house we are in now in 1870; it is a mirror image of the one next door, where her brother's family live. Janet says her brother terraced the steep hill at the back of the house, using quarried, dressed granite from demolished buildings, making areas more easily accessible for plantings of oxalis, candy tuft, and foxgloves, along with campanula and pots of primula that grow along a brick path. Alpines are planted in a special area beside the barn. Janet tells us that gardening has become popular in this area in the last fifteen to twenty years.

Outside the back door a sign stuck in the earth says: "This House is Protected by Attack Cats." It

Elspeth botanizing. Xeriphytes such as toad-flax and pearly everlasting grow in the road-side gravel close to moisture-lovers like the pitcher plant, Newfoundland's floral emblem.

doesn't surprise me. I saw the cats riding up the dumb waiter from the basement to the living room.

After Janet suggests gardeners in the area whom we may find interesting, we say goodbye and go looking for food.

"I'd love some fish and chips," Elspeth says. "After all, this should be the place for them."

I agree. I'd love some too, and what better place than St. John's? We amble down Water Street, looking in shop windows. There are some boarded-up businesses and few people around, and there are no fish-and-chip shops in this end of town. But we find a restaurant that uses cloth napkins and a linen table cloth, which is something we've not had in a long while. We enjoy the best clam chowder I've ever eaten.

The next day, we visit the Memorial University Botanical Gardens, which occupy a hundred-and-ten acre lot. Opened in 1977, the Gardens are made up of trails, natural areas, cultivated areas, and a magnificent rock garden. The rock garden is the part that fascinates me. It is designed to make the most use of the rocky terrain, with alpines and succulents snuggled into the rocks along with campanula, edelweiss, fritillaria, and ferns. Many of the plants growing here are ones I thought would not survive in this part of the country, but they look so comfortable, sheltered from the wind and in good drainage, I want to pat them on the head and tell them how well they are doing.

Halfway through our visit, a man in a tweed jacket walks up to me and says: "You are so beautifully dressed, my dear." I look around

This magnificent "Quiggley" fence encloses a garden of Newfoundland heritage plants at the Botanical Gardens.

to see who he means. After that, he seems to pop up everywhere. We see him talking to plants. *Well, that's OK, I do that myself*, I think. Then he seems to be addressing a tree and later on staring down a geranium. When it is time to leave, he is the only other person in the Gardens. When we realize he has followed us out to the car park, our steps become quicker and quicker. We leap in and lock the doors tight. A moment later, to our horror, he rushes up and bangs on the window. He points frantically to the bottom of the car and mouths the words: "Your skirt is caught in the door!"

Elspeth's Travelogue

As soon as we arrived in Newfoundland, I noticed that the past felt closer than it had in the rest of Canada.

Janet Story's house was so little changed from the days of her grandfather, I half expected the old man to put in an appearance. He'd have been perfectly at home there, sitting in a favourite armchair or straightening a familiar painting, leafing through his grandson's book or nodding in approval at Janet's efforts in the garden. The only surprises for him would have been the growth of his trees and the expansion of St. John's around his once rural property. The old sealing captain was such a real presence in the house, I wondered if Janet had ever dared introduce a newspaper headlining the campaigns of Greenpeace.

Our next brush with the past came the following day. We'd been invited to give a reading at the Botanical Gardens, and when it was over, we chatted with our audience of gardeners.

"The deeper I dig, the happier I get," said one woman.

"The deeper I dig, the more distracted I get," said another. This puzzling comment came from Mary Barry, a lively, middle-aged woman who introduced herself as a patriotic Newfoundlander. We wanted to hear more about Mary's distracted digging as well as her patriotism, and she kindly arranged for us to visit her garden.

Mary's ancestry was apparent in her thoroughly Irish gift for storytelling, and we weren't surprised to hear that she was a teacher of English literature at Memorial University. As she showed us round her garden-in-the-making, she kept us spellbound with stories of her family. They included tales of hardship, survival, second sight, and superstition, and they had a familiar ring to them. For some years, I had lived in the Shetland Islands — a tight-knit seafaring community much like Newfoundland's — and I understood what Mary meant when she

A rail fence and scarecrow protect this root garden on the road to Cape Broyle. A variety of ingenious fences shelter fragile gardens in rural Newfoundland.

said, "There are not many people here, but there are more than the ones you see. You carry your ancestors on your back."

She told us about her uncle, Captain Tom Dower, who built a number of small sail boats. He crossed the Atlantic in two of them (but not at the same time!), navigating with only an Elizabethan-style sextant and compass. She described him as a fearless fatalist who felt closest to God when alone at sea.

An earlier ancestor, John Dower, was a respected North Shore skipper. In 1873 when he was sealing at the ice, he began to dream that his wife had come to him on the boat. The dreams were so troubling he became convinced she was dead, and he returned home early, entering the harbour with his flag at half-mast. On shore meanwhile, John's wife had been in a coma for two days and had indeed just died. As skipper John approached the wharf, however, she began to stir. "I've been far," she said. "I've been with John." The skipper never went out to the ice again, but he loved to boast that his wife could get there and back faster than the *Eleanor*, the boat named after her.

The Real Garden Road Trip

The stories I liked best were about the womenfolk. At the beginning of World War I, Mary's grandmother had moved from Trinity to Conche, her husband's family home on Newfoundland's Northern Peninsula. She hadn't wanted to make the move, but her husband threatened to go to the war if she didn't. Conche was a tiny, remote settlement and the young mother was afraid it was too far north to grow fresh vegetables for her children. When the second child sickened and died, she took it as a sign, and this time it was she who laid down the law. Her husband could do as he pleased. She was going back to Trinity where the soil, like everything else, was blessed.

Eventually the family moved again from Trinity to Grand Falls, a place Mary's grandmother felt was *truly* blessed. Grand Falls was a paper-mill town and, apart from cash-pay jobs, there was fertile soil and even a farm to provide daily milk and cream. The town was founded by English families who brought a tradition of flower gardening which proved infectious. Soon many of the townspeople were interested in gardening and Mary's grandmother began to grow flowers. In time, Mary's mother grew flowers as well, and Mary herself grew up thinking that a pretty garden was just as important to a house as the front room furniture.

Mary's own garden was roughly laid out in curves and mounded beds. Her mother's garden, she told us, had been more formal, with flowers growing in rows. Mary had tried to soften things but the plants had been loyal to her mother, and had always done best in military formations.

Mary had married a politician. She hadn't faced the same hard times as the earlier women in her family, but her first garden had been a response to life's pressures nonetheless. As she put it, laughing, "There were more politicians buried there than will ever know they're dead." If Mary had put any political issues to rest in her present garden on Prince William Place, she didn't mention them to us. Maybe the ground was already too crowded. The garden was small, but only in a physical sense. In time, it went back a long way. I'd have called it a *deep* garden. It was impregnated with layers of history and myth, and as we heard more about them, we began to understand why digging there was such a distracting occupation.

Even before Mary moved into the house, she realized she'd taken on a long-term project with the garden. The first job was to haul away truckloads of debris. In one area, she turned up rusted horseshoes, straight-sided nails, and a quantity of broken china. Next door to Mary's stood an apartment building which had once been a kind of hostelry — a supper house. Prince William, Queen Victoria's uncle, was stationed in Newfoundland before he came to the throne in 1830. According to a newspaper clipping Mary found in her house, the Prince visited the supper house to dance and enjoy the sunsets. He also enjoyed the company of women, and rumour had it that one of his ten illegitimate children came from the Placentia area about an hour from St. John's.

Behind Mary's property lay a historic cemetery. Among the burials, she told us, were priests and nuns from the early days of St. John's. It was part of her garden — a borrowed landscape — because Mary made sure that her shelter belt of shrubs didn't obstruct the view. One summer, while Mary was away, she had loaned her house to the author Jane Urquhart, who found the atmosphere conducive to writing. Little wonder! One of Jane Urquhart's books, *Changing Heaven,* told of ghosts crossing the centuries.

After Mary had cleared the overgrowth from her back yard, she brought in topsoil. In the following years, she was astonished to find a variety of garden plants growing up through thick layers of new earth. Phlox and roses appeared, and one morning she noticed the purple shoots of a peony breaking through the surface. Then four more peonies emerged — all in a perfectly straight row (shades of Mary's mother). There were no blooms the first year, but Mary had a chat with them.

"I told them they must flourish again," she said, "and now they flower regularly. It seemed a miracle. A friend told me peonies are healing plants and I needed that at the time."

"Is that why you garden — for therapy?" we asked.

"My grandmother might have said it's just a different kind of survival," she explained. "My daughter gardens in a city — that's a kind of survival, too. In the garden, the world pushes back and it's only as large as whatever you hold in your hand."

I had the impression that Mary had always been sensitive to layers of history. She told us that as a youngster out on the blueberry barrens, she used to pretend that a group of Beothuk Indians joined her, or the child of early French settlers, or an English girl her own age. Mary's grandmother had believed in fairies and had

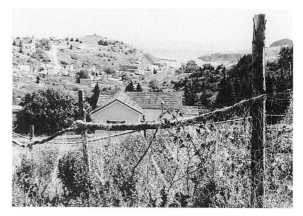

A fishing-net fence at Tors Cove. We picked blueberries and service berries here — the juiciest we'd ever tasted.

told Mary never to pick blueberries without taking bread in her pockets for the little people. "I wasn't sure what to do with the bread," Mary mused, "but I always took some — just in case." I asked Mary if she thought there were fairies as well as ghosts in her garden. She hesitated and then became aware of her hesitation. "Notice I didn't say 'of course not!'" she laughed. "Well, if there *are* fairies, I suspect they live under the peonies." And she laughed again when Judy pointed out that the potting shed was strung with fairy lights.

Mary talked so vividly about her family and the past, I felt she almost *wore* her history. I could see it like a train stretching from her shoulders into the diaphanous past, and embroidered all over it were swirling designs of blueberry barrens and stormy seas, Beothuks and Basques, nuns and raunchy royals, salty men and lonely women. It lent her dignity, but at times, she told us, it could also drag her down, so real was the weight of kinship and the turmoil of spirits caught up in it. Now and then, she'd even wondered if she might tear it off and walk away. Then she'd thought of those who'd tried to leave — the thousands of Newfoundlanders who'd fled to the Canadian mainland. "It's like transplanting a flower into a climate that's totally foreign," she said. "They become shadows of themselves." So she stayed on.

Most of the time, it was obvious, Mary wore her identity with pride and gratitude.

It was overcast the next morning as we set off to visit Betty Hall, another gardener who had been recommended to us. By the time we arrived at her house, the rain was coming down in torrents, and the roads of St. John's were awash.

We had phoned ahead and Betty met us at the door. "Please don't bother to come out," we said. "We'll just take a quick look around, then come in and talk to you." Did we really think that an ardent gardener — especially one with an English accent — would be put off by a mere deluge? Brushing our protests aside, Betty launched herself into a tour of the garden while Judy and I, umbrellas hoisted, splashed happily in her wake.

It wasn't only the accent and the drenched foliage that gave the garden a distinctly English feeling. It was the wide range of shrubs and perennials, the way they were mixed in appropriate areas of shade or sun, and the way the borders curved within the rectangular confines of a city lot. The choice of plants struck me

as intensely personal — a reflection of the owner's caring and thoughtful character.

Betty was having a hard year. Her husband, John, suffered from Alzheimer's disease and needed constant attention. She had arranged to have help first thing in the morning — "to get us on the road" — but from then on she was tied. She had given up her work, a study of preventive health, but obviously hadn't given up her garden. There were new steps, a new fence, and everything was well maintained. "I don't know how I managed to do it all this year," she said, shaking her head. We didn't know, either, although we did know by now that dedicated gardeners regularly manage the unmanageable.

We wondered how Betty had joined the ranks of the dedicated. As we dried off in the house, she told us it all began in England when she was no more than three or four years old. An aunt in the suburbs of London showed her how to collect snapdragon seed and she still remembered pouring the small brown seeds from their cases and making little packets of them. And yes — she still grew snapdragons. She also remembered asking people if she could weed their gardens. Afraid that such a young child would pull up the wrong things, they hadn't let her help. In my opinion, they had made a big mistake — Betty would *never* have pulled up the wrong things!

In 1961, she and John took their family to Central America where John worked as a hospital administrator. "After London, the flame trees and orchids were like paradise," Betty said. They had lived on the edge of a swamp but had immediately started to make a

Jonathan Hayward of the Evening Telegram

Betty Hall amongst the intensely personal selection of plants in her garden.

Jonathan Hayward of the Evening Telegram

It was raining too hard to take photographs, so Betty sent these later. Her note said that the heads of hydrangea 'Annabelle' had become as large as footballs.

garden. She smiled as she described their efforts. "There we were, scrabbling around in the mangrove and instead of growing the gorgeous native plants, we tried to grow things that reminded us of home: delphiniums and lilies. It was stupid, but orchids were easy to grow; the challenge was to grow rhubarb."

They lost everything they possessed in a devastating hurricane and eventually left Central America because of their three small children. By way of Hong Kong, they ended up in Carbonear, Newfoundland, "in a big old house that was just heaven." Betty obviously had a knack for finding (or making?) bits of heaven wherever she ended up on earth. In Carbonear she started a compost heap, studied wild flowers, and tended a garden outside the public library. "What are you doing?" her neighbours wanted to know. Flower gardening, known as "ladies' gardening," wasn't big in Carbonear in those days.

Although Betty was a relative newcomer, even *she* became entangled in Newfoundland's history. She found it growing in neglected gardens around Carbonear — lilies, veronicas, phlox — the good old standbys of many a British garden that had found their way to the new world as cuttings, bulbs, divisions, and seeds. They were simple, nostalgic flowers, and must have given much comfort to the immigrant women who had grown them and handed them on.

When Betty and John had moved to St. John's, she took some of her plants with her. The house in St. John's was new and a garden didn't exist. Because it was October when they moved, Betty was keen to get her transplants into the ground right away. She didn't have a spade so she asked some workmen, who were digging up the road, if she could borrow a shovel.

"I worked like a demon," she said. "They leaned on their own shovels and watched, and at the end of the day they said they'd never seen anyone work so hard. They told me to keep the shovel. I still have it, but the point is worn flat."

Steeped in the history of Newfoundland, Betty's plants continued to give comfort and they were still being handed on. A few of their offspring had even found their way into the heritage section of Memorial University Botanical Gardens.

Judy's Journal

It is a cold, windy, late-August evening when we meet up with Todd Boland, a young man Janet Story suggested we visit. Todd's house, originally owned by his grandfather, is in an old area of town, and is one of the few places that actually has soil, rather than rock.

"As you can see," he says, looking around and smiling, "the neighbours are not heavily into gardening. The house next door was torn down, so my garden was exposed to fierce winds. So the business that tore down the house put this fence in for me, and now I can grow delphiniums that don't break off in the wind."

He tells us that this is his parents' house and he has always lived here. He says the land where the Botanical Garden is now located belonged to his family and he works up there

Todd Boland shows us his well-rooted alpines. He'd raised the bed and dug gravel into the soil to improve drainage.

when he has the time. He started gardening when he was about thirteen and had a small garden under a maple tree — all slips. The maple blew over in a windstorm in 1992.

"We have terrible cold winds here from the northeast and northwest," Todd says, "and the greenhouse blew away as well. So with the greenhouse gone and the maple gone, there was plenty of sun. So I thought, heck, I'll put in a rock garden and grow alpines, which are the plants for this area."

He says that alpines need plenty of grit and he's dug a lot of it into the soil. They need sharp drainage, too, he says, because the wet conditions during winter are so detrimental. Cow manure was added to the soil when the old greenhouse was here, so it's almost too rich for alpines now. He has gentians, lewisias, *Dianthus deltoides*, *Campanula pilosa*, and dryas, which is a native Newfoundland plant he collected himself. Native Newfoundland plants are still being discovered by alpine enthusiasts, as we heard in Nova Scotia when Dick Steele mentioned plant-hunting expeditions to Newfoundland.

Todd's dream is to go plant-hunting in Argentina; "Oh my God, I'd love to do it," he says with great passion. "I work in a nursery from May to October, but if I had a job that paid enough money, I'd love to travel to these places." Instead, he has to be content for now with growing seventy-five orchids on his window sill and belonging to the orchid, alpine, rock garden, and bonsai societies.

He mentions he'd like a larger spot, but appreciates that with his small garden, once plants are in, and closely planted, maintenance is minimal. Elspeth says she finds she goes off gardening at this time of year, in the August heat.

"You don't have to worry about heat out here," he laughs.

There is little tradition of ornamental gardening in the province, but Todd tells us it's coming on fast. For the last ten years he's grown perennials from seed. Many haven't been grown in Newfoundland be-

Judy Maddocks

Todd's lobelia barrel sports shades of blue.

fore. He starts them under lights in the basement and keeps them potted up and protected through the first winter.

"The first winter is the telling winter," he says.

In the centre of the lawn is a barrel full of earth. Growing from the top are chrysanthemums, with lobelia in every shade, from the deepest indigo to the palest blue, sprouting from openings in the sides. "Never be able to move it," he laughs, as we admire the different blues.

When Elspeth asks him if he feels that horticulture is his career, he says he has a degree in botany and plant ecology, then adds, "I must say I do enjoy and love to grow this stuff, but there are no jobs in the field and I hate to leave this place." He does admit to feeling depressed at this time of the year, because he knows what's to come — though if it's a mild fall, his snapdragons and calendulas will still be blooming in November.

As we leave, Todd says he gardens because he finds it relaxing. "It's my vice," he adds, "and it could be worse."

In the evening, eating supper, Elspeth and I talk about how unusual it is to find a young man so passionate about plants. Elspeth says that how Todd took advantage of the disaster with the maple and greenhouse reminded her of Reg Porter on P.E.I., who said: "In life there are no catastrophes — only events, and all events can be useful."

The next morning, a Sunday, we go to Calvert in search of a folk garden that turns out to be a commercial operation charging $2.50 to go in. We decide against it. On the way we see a garden edged by a row of golden elders, rabbits, and swans filled with artificial flowers, and a rose bush overflowing with life. We stop and enquire.

A man comes to the door and tells us his wife is the gardener. She's making dinner, but he'll show us around. Mr. Howlett has lived in the house for seventy-four years and says his wife saw the garden fifty years ago and moved in.

"So that's why she married you? For the garden, was it?" I ask.

"Y'right. Y'right. Yes. Yes," he says. "She just took to gardening. Roots all these elders herself."

Elspeth comments that the house doesn't look that old.

"I moved this house on a Sunday morning," he says,

Bernard Howlett's fine tomatoes. With his wife, Dorothy, he also grew parsnips, broccoli, turnips, cabbage, cauliflower, and potatoes in the vegetable garden.

"and had to build onto it twice. Lived all my life in it. Yes. Yes. Eight miles from St. John's and two miles from the Wal-Mart."

We ask whether his parents gardened. Mr. Howlett says that his parents had a farm with cattle, pigs, and hens. Things have changed since then.

"Sure you won't see a hen around here now," he says. "Look ... look ... Joey killed it all. Gave them something for nothing. Didn't have to work, wouldn't set a garden out. No, no." Joey Smallwood, former premier of Newfoundland, who left politics over twenty years ago, still held up to censure.

We admire a bush heavy with roses. He tells us his wife gave it to her mother, and when the mother died, his wife got it back. It has thirty roses on one stem, he says, and when people come by, they can't get over it. He points to a bed of marigolds.

"There were poppies in those beds earlier," he says. "I'll tell you where they came from. They came from Flanders Field, that's where those poppies came from. Grand, grand, grand."

"Your wife does all these

flower beds?" Elspeth asks.

"Yes, yes," he says. "She does the flowers and I do the vegetables. She loves it. She loves it. Will stay out in the garden day and night. Only thing wrong with her is arthritis. Pain. Pain. But still she keeps at it. She doesn't care, keeps at it the whole time."

"Seventy-four years in the same house," I say to Elspeth as we drive away, "is something I envy."

Elspeth's Travelogue

History as a school subject was lost on me. I never did manage to remember the dates of Henry VIII and I couldn't see the point of dredging up catalogues of spurious glories and "man's inhumanity to man," as Robert Burns called it. As far as I was concerned, the past was dead and gone, and good riddance. But here in Newfoundland, history was as much a part of today as politics and the weather. History and politics were, in fact, inseparable. But it wasn't politics that finally brought the past to life for me. It was potatoes.

Several people had mentioned Ross Traverse to us. He was obviously *someone* in the local gardening world, he had qualifications, and along with his wife, Marcie, he ran a nursery at Torbay, north of St. John's. On our last day in Newfoundland, we set off to track him down. We headed south, determined, as usual, to do things the hard way. Our roundabout route took us through the muddle of Mount Pearl and west to Paradise. It was our second visit to a Paradise in two weeks — the first had been in Nova Scotia — and it inspired Judy to embark on a concert of Christmas carols.

The road twisted around the edge of Conception Bay where a neat little island lay offshore. Bell Island, according to the map, was served by frequent ferries and I had a sudden urge to forget about gardens and go island-hopping instead. But Judy was well into "Good King Wenceslas" by this time and we sped on regardless, "through the rude wind's wild lament" — and through Portugal Cove as well.

We had taken a chance on finding the Traverse nursery open, and we were in luck. Although Marcie was away, Ross was home and was willing to show us around.

Ross was a professional nurseryman who ran a successful business. He was young enough to have ambitions, but old enough to keep them on a short leash. He'd decided that an enterprise like theirs had an optimum size from both financial and personal points of view, and it struck me that the Traverse family had an unusually sensible grasp of priorities.

Ross obviously enjoyed what he did. He liked to experiment with native plants, ground covers, shrub roses, even rhododendrons, and he was also inter-

Ross Traverse in his two-hundred-year-old root garden.

a gardening project," Ross remembered. "You had to grow these vegetables and they said if you did OK with them, you could win a trip to St. John's." Ross had never been to St. John's, the big glittering city on the other side of Newfoundland, so he "put a little effort into it," won his trip, and had been putting effort into it ever since.

These days he didn't limit himself to run-of-the-mill carrots and turnips; he grew beets and leeks, chard and cilantro, pumpkins and the beautiful deep purple perilla. Fruit, too. Gooseberries, currants, and, of course, strawberries. Everyone in Newfoundland seemed to grow strawberries. He told us that English varieties of black currants did well in the cool climate, and asked us if we'd ever tried black currant liqueur — and would we like to? "No, we haven't," we said, "and yes, we would!"

Ross described how he was challenging the Atlantic winds and the cool, short summers with beans, corn, peppers, and tomatoes, but he seemed most at home with traditional Newfoundland crops. I saw him as a straightforward meat-and-potatoes man at heart — or at least, a Jiggs dinner man. "No self-respecting Newfoundlander's going to go through the week without a Jiggs dinner," he told us. He couldn't explain the Jiggs, but he knew how to make the dinner. First, salt pork or brisket beef was soaked overnight and boiled. Then whole carrots, cabbage, and turnip were added, along with dried peas done in a bag. Finally, the parts were served separately, the peas mashed into a dish with butter and pepper. It sounded filling; it sounded like real home cooking.

ested in perennials, especially novelties which he imported from Holland. He didn't, however, take us immediately to see any of these. He took us straight to his vegetable garden. Ornamentals may have been his living, but vegetables were obviously his first love.

It had all begun when he was ten years old and a member of the 4H club in St. George's. "They had

After so long on the road, it sounded pretty good to us.

We admired the rich spongy soil of Ross' root garden. The land had probably been cultivated for two hundred years, but the previous owner had used only chemical fertilizer, and thought the ground was "runned out." Ross soon put that to rights with plenty of organic material.

"This is where the old people used to haul the capelin," he said.

"Haul the capelin?"

"The little fish that come in for a week at spawning time."

Ross explained that the old-timers netted the fish, hundreds of thousands of them, hauled them up onto the beaches, shovelled them into carts and took them to the root gardens to use as fertilizer. Apparently they shovelled up a fair bit of the shore along with the fish. "The soil is still full of little beach rocks," he told us.

He bent down, ran his fingers through the dark earth, produced a small black pebble, and handed it to me. Here we go again, I thought — history! It wasn't a question of dredging it up from remote depths; it was right there on the surface, constantly underfoot and now in my hand. I fingered the small stone stowaway and could almost smell the fertile odour of those ancient fish.

Ross used to truck a few capelin himself and compost them with peat, which he harvested from their own peat bog, but the fish were scarcer now and he didn't bother any more. In the old days, he told us, capelin were often added directly to the "lazy beds."

We heard more about lazy beds as we sat chatting in the comfortable Traverse kitchen, and we heard more about the old days too. This capelin kind of history was real to me. I loved it — couldn't get enough of it.

Or was that the black currant liqueur?

In the outports, Ross explained, everything revolved round the fishery. It was such a demanding way of life, there was little chance for fishermen to fiddle with gardens. Lazy beds were the answer to a chronic shortage of time and topsoil. Early in the season, before the fishing season started, the men used mattocks to loosen patches of the scanty soil while it was still cold and wet. They spread a layer of compost — peat, seaweed, household waste, whatever came to hand — on top, and laid their seed potatoes on top of that. They then used trenching shovels to cover the potatoes with a thin coating of soil from between the rows.

Ross brought a shovel to show us. It had a narrow blade and a sturdy wooden shaft which was bent. Deliberately? "Oh yes! The old fellows would spend a day, if necessary, looking for just the right handle; it was used like a lever across the knee and had to curve to fit." He stood up to show us, then passed me the shovel and I tried it over my own knee. It felt hopelessly heavy and cumbersome.

When the potato sprouts were a few inches high, they needed a second "hilling up." This work coincided conveniently with the capelin run, and fish were spread on the earth over the potatoes and covered with more soil. After that, the main fishery started in earnest and it was often the women, or the old folk, who took over the shovels for the final trenching. The whole process sounded far from lazy to me. Potatoes were the one crop considered essential for survival. Other root vegetables and cabbages were "small seeds" and women's work. Small seeds they may have been, but it can't have been a small task to grow them, and they must have made a vital contribution to the family diet. Mary Barry's grandmother sprang to my mind.

By this time I was so steeped in the old days, I could easily imagine myself as one of those women, worn out with chores and with wielding that hefty shovel. Briefly I knew how it felt; I really *knew* the weariness of it, and I wondered if I'd have had the strength left at the end of the day to tend a few hardy flowers, cherish a rose, and hang onto the hope that life could mean more than potatoes.

We spent our last evening in Newfoundland — and the last evening of our road trip — at Cape Spear,

At Cape Spear, we'd gone as far as we could go — even the gardens had disappeared.

the most easterly point in North America. It was fitting that our trip had begun at a lighthouse; now it would end at one, too.

Like the light at Point Atkinson on the west coast, the Cape Spear light was due to be automated. The station had been staffed for generations by the same family, the Cantwells, who had lived there until 1971. St. John's was five kilometres away by water, and seventeen kilometres by road. The Cantwells would have been able to see the lights of the city from their headland. However, the sea crossing was often impossible and the road impassable. For getting to the city, they might just as well have lived on the moon as on the cape. We knew that the Cantwells had planted root gardens, and we searched the windy headland for remnants of rock walls or telltale patches of green.

At this farthest point on our journey, our final search for a garden was in vain. We could find no trace of the little plots that had once sustained the isloated family. We knew then that the time had come to go home.

The following morning we were at the airport early. We sat in the airport coffee shop nursing mugs of coffee, not saying much, happy to be going home, steeling ourselves for another goodbye.

I flew out first, headed for Vancouver. Judy returned to Halifax, eager to rescue the heathers waiting in her car.

Judy's Epilogue

Shortly after arriving home, I was at an auction and was introduced to a woman who had heard our interviews on CBC while we were driving across the country. At the time, she and her husband were living in a trailer with cats, dogs, and belongings while they built a new house. Everything was going wrong. She heard us on the radio, laughing and talking, and said: "Well, I'm glad somebody is having a good time!" And we were. The best of times.

We soon got into a routine. Elspeth found the gardens and navigated. I drove and found the motels — though not all the motels were as satisfactory as the gardens.

The gardeners we met were generous with their time, all were optimistic, and not one was daunted by the amount of work they'd lined up for themselves. I feel a kinship with all of them.

Elspeth's Epilogue

Our trip has been over for almost a year now. Judy and I are back on our respective coasts, caught up in our separate lives, just as before. But not quite as before.

We'd hoped to see a few interesting gardens. We were astonished to find that fresh and fascinating aspects of gardening cropped up at *every* turn. I had been right in thinking that picture-book looks are a very small part of what real gardening is about.

We had also hoped to meet a few memorable people. Not just a few, but *all* of the people we met were fascinating and wonderful. We came across gardeners from an astonishing variety of cultural backgrounds. We talked to enthusiastic teenagers and equally enthusiastic octogenarians. We visited apartments, farms, and, relatively speaking, palaces. Men and women gardened with equal vigour; we found that gender parity is a horticultural fact. We met gardeners who considered their disabilities mere items on the list of gardening handicaps — some had aphids, some arthritis. All made us welcome.

Canadian gardeners are tough — they have to be — and they're full of fun. We shared many laughs. But real gardeners are also passionate, and where passion is involved, pain is never far away. Some of the stories we heard were tragic, but Canadian gardeners are, above all, optimists. Indeed, their optimism often verges on fantasy. I have a vivid memory of one tiny figure eyeing a stretch of crab grass wild enough to daunt a bulldozer, admonishing it with a trowel, and proclaiming confidently, "*Next* year, when I've cleared this lot out..."

Our trip began with a lighthouse garden in jeopardy and ended with another that had apparently vanished. The fleeting nature of gardens became a recurring theme as we poked and pried our way across the country, and sometimes we had moments of panic when we imagined the havoc spreading in our own gardens. Most of the gardeners we met, however, appeared unconcerned by the knowledge that their works would be short-lived.

Over and over we asked gardeners, "Why? Why do you put yourself through so much toil and trouble?" And over and over, they talked about a fleeting scent, a small sound, some brief gleam of glory they recalled from way back. It seemed that garden memories, like William Lord's octopus, had unbelievably long and cunning tentacles. They sneaked up from shadowy depths and stole away gardeners' caution, sometimes their common sense, and frequently their cash.

On the table beside me is a small black stone — the capelin stone Ross Traverse fished out of his root garden in Newfoundland. I kept it in my pocket and brought it back to Vancouver thinking if I held it now and then, the vivid reality of Canada's past, so strong in Torbay, might rub off on me again. I have other souvenirs: a butter dish from Mission, a candle holder from Brooks, maps from just about everywhere, seeds — plenty of seeds, mostly unidentified — and all the photographs, notes, and tapes.

But we came home from our trip with more than mementos. I can now put faces to names like Brandon, Penetanguishene, and Rivière-Ouelle. We have new friends all across the country. Our trip took us farther than either of us ever imagined at the start, not just across Canada's breathtakingly beautiful surface, but deep into its heart.

Postscripts

We have heard from many of the people we met on the real garden road trip, by mail, telephone, fax, in person, and by e-mail. Here are some updates on them and their gardens.

Atkinson Point lighthouse is now automated. The future of Don Graham's garden is still in doubt.

Elspeth paid another visit to Frieda Matthies in Sechelt and found her garden as peaceful and pretty as ever, with a pink lacecap hydrangea in its prime, the late summer sun slanting across the fading roses, and faintly, in the background, the sound of the creek running into the sea.

Barbara Samarin in Lantzville, whom we never met, but whose husband, Joe, showed us the garden, said she has been planting a new rockery along the shore with drought-tolerant shrubs, trees, and rugosa roses. She was looking forward to visiting the World Rose Convention in the Benelux, followed by three weeks in England looking at gardens. While she was away, Joe would look after the garden.

Larry and Peggy Wick now have twenty-four varieties of *Eucalyptus* on Keats Island. After our visit, more than sixty people from the Exotic Plant Society arrived by ferry, water taxi, and private boat to see the garden. Before their visit, Larry put in one set of temporary wooden steps; we were happy to hear that the art of shovel-vaulting is alive and well.

Shirley Thompson of Whistler said that a natural pruning job over the winter, plus her husband's propensity for pruning, has opened up the "forest" a little. The snows of 1997 completely dismembered what was left of her Japanese maple, leaving space for more loyal herbaceous perennials.

Dee Harvey, also of Whistler, said the roses (on either side of the arbour) that we inspected so meticulously were well and truly dead. In their place she has planted clematis. The bear has not been back.

Susan Giardin invited Elspeth to afternoon tea on the sidewalk in Vancouver and it rained again. Susan's garden has expanded to include a water lily in a tiny pond and a very large apple on a very small espaliered tree.

Gail Barwick in Aldergrove said that her son, Cameron, had a horrendous winter, but they have since had "an extraordinary three months of discovery, anxiety, panic, and joy." Lauren, Gail's daughter, fell off a mare and broke her neck, but despite headaches is riding again. Gail now has one-hundred-and-eighty rose bushes and a rose-covered pergola.

The seed package that Ayako Kanayama showed Elspeth in Hope was for a vegetable like a small turnip. *Yama-imo* means "mountain potato."

Sue Kobold's beautiful little pond in Penticton *did* inspire Judy to create one of her own.

Nina Koodrin is keeping well. In the spring, Elspeth planted the precious Doukhobor beans. Five days later — a miracle — two types germinated. Elspeth was over the moon. Ten days later a third type germinated but didn't develop. Twelve days later, slugs attacked. Elspeth is still hoping to harvest enough fresh seed in the fall to replant in the spring.

A few weeks after we visited Calgary, and while we were still on the road, a hail storm pounded the city with stones as big as golf balls. On the last day of September, another storm dumped the heaviest snowfall in eighty years. Watching newsreels of flattened crops, we felt sorry for Don Heimbecker and his roses, but only briefly. What's a bit of weather to the likes of him? He's seen it all before and come through smiling.

Sheila Paulson and the Calgary Rock and Alpine Garden Society are excited about hosting the 1999 Rock Garden Society annual meeting in Banff.

Joey Stewart spent time away from her amazing rock garden in Calgary to visit even more amazing rock gardens in the Andes. She then spent time in Vancouver where, missing her own garden and feeling, as she put it, "a desperate need for dirt," she offered to work in Elspeth's garden. Needless to say, her offer was accepted.

Rita Wildshut's latest project in Brooks is a rhubarb birdbath. Thirsty birds leave her strawberries alone if she keeps some water around. To make the birdbath, she shaped a hill the size of the bath she wanted, placed rhubarb leaves face down over the hill, spread cement about four centimeters thick over the leaves, covered the whole thing and kept it moist for four days, then turned it over and cleaned out the residue.

Tutok the orphan musk ox is thriving in Saskatoon.

Bob Hinitt's latest Christmas display was "A Walt Disney Cavalcade." Fifty-six figures (including some of the 101 Dalmatians) descended a long ramp from a golden castle with eighteen turrets.

Bob wrote: "It was great fun to do and brought back many pleasant memories from over the years since 1947 when I first started doing Christmas displays."

In May 1997, when parts of Manitoba suffered disastrous floods, Hugh Skinner wrote: "We've had a much more favourable spring here than the last two — there are advantages to being on high ground in certain years."

Joy and Keith Smith wintered in Vancouver, where Elspeth and her husband Ray enjoyed their company and sampled more of Joy's great cooking.

Joe Tsukamoto has been away from Brandon again, working as a volunteer in Russia.

Michelle Showalter has been collecting glass blocks and headboards to make partitions in her Dryden garden. By the end of the summer, she hopes to have it fenced and joined to their existing back yard.

Marie David and her sister Anne Hicks, of Wawa, have planted rhododendrons as a result of our visit and look forward to spring with even more trepidation than usual.

Jean Marr near Mallorytown had foot surgery during the winter and had to sit with her foot up for long spells, which gave her even more time to peruse catalogues and spend more money on plants.

Diane Greenfield is still helping to organize garden tours and other fundraising events for the library in Penetanguishene, including a presentation by Judy and Elspeth.

Barbara and Chris have been planting quite a few perennials around their patio and they say that the tangerine marigolds are now a fading memory. Too bad!

Martha Burka's four children are off to universities in Nova Scotia, Ontario, Alberta, and New Zealand. She's glad the heavy muscle-work in the garden was done before they left.

Judy was horrified to hear that Betty Lou Frizell-Abbott of P.E.I. has increased the size of her beautiful gazebo and her already large perennial beds.

Mildred Burrows wrote from Nova Scotia: "Next time you come, you won't have to wait for the P.E.I. ferry. The fixed link is done. Since the opening came smack in the middle of the gardening season, I did not dare risk overdoing it, so I did not venture to cross the whole way, but I did walk three kilometres from the N.B. side before I turned back."

The Real Garden Road Trip

A one-hundred-and-six-year-old willow tree in Roy Fall's Halifax garden fell over in a wind storm, narrowly missing the neighbours' parked vehicles. Roy quickly recovered from the shock and planted the vacant areas with a tulip tree, a lilac, and three poplars. The unexpected event provided Roy and Frank with inspiration to name the property Willowfalls.

Susan Kerslake moved to another apartment in Halifax and gave her maple-in-a-bucket to a neighbour, whereupon it was eaten by a puppy. Susan has taken to carrying buckets of water for newly planted street trees. The day Judy heard from her, Susan had made thirty trips!

Betty Hall, with a little extra nursing help, is still managing to care for John at home in St. John's. She writes: "It would be difficult to emphasize how much I depend on the garden for relaxation, exercise, outlet for creativity, and sheer delight."

Little wonder Judy and Elspeth couldn't find remnants of the garden at Cape Spear! Gerry Cantwell, the last keeper to work the light, explained in a phone call to Vancouver that the plot lay more than a kilometre away from the station in a slightly more sheltered spot at the edge of the woods. Stone walls can still be seen there, but nature has rapidly reclaimed the abandoned ground.

Sophia Bella

Elspeth Bradbury (right) is a Landscape Architect and Master Gardener. Her garden writing and her poetry have been published in numerous newpapers, magazines and literary journals. She lives in West Vancouver, British Columbia.

Judy Maddocks is a writer and avid gardener who has published in a number of gardening and literary magazines. She lives in Hampton, New Brunswick.

Elspeth and Judy's bestselling first book, *The Garden Letters,* was widely praised for its lively, humorous and evocative writing. It has been excerpted in *Reader's Digest*, *Western Living* and *Canadian Living*.

Polestar Book Publishers takes pride in creating books that enrich our understanding of the world and introduce discriminating readers to exciting writers. These independent voices illuminate our history and stretch the imagination.

FICTION

BROKEN WINDOWS by *Patricia Nolan*
"When I think of successful literary portrayals of devastated lives, I think of Raymond Carver, Dorothy Allison...After reading *Broken Windows*, I will also think of Patricia Nolan" — *Quill & Quire*
1-896095-20-8 • $16.95 CAN / $14.95 USA

COMFORT ZONES by *Pamela Donoghue*
"Donoghue establishes herself as a masterful observer of humanity...she is bursting with knowledge about the shades of dark and light in human hearts." — *Vancouver Sun*
1-896095-24-0 • $16.95 CAN / $13.95 USA

CRAZY SORROW by *Susan Bowes*
"...an astonishingly vivid portrait of small-town childhood. Everyday scenes are so detailed that anyone with an ounce of Maritime history will wax nostalgic." — *Vancouver Sun*
1-896095-19-4 • $16.95 CAN / $14.95 USA

RAPID TRANSITS AND OTHER STORIES by *Holley Rubinsky*
"[These stories] will return to haunt the reader in the middle of the night. Forceful and beautifully evocative...these finely crafted stories grab the reader about the throat."
— Sandra Birdsell
0-919591-56-6 • $12.95 CAN / $10.95 USA

SITTING IN THE CLUB CAR DRINKING RUM AND KARMA-KOLA
A Manual of Etiquette for Ladies Crossing Canada by Train
by *Paulette Jiles*
All Aboard for this quirky, elegant work of detective travel fiction, now a cult classic.
0-919591-13-2 • $12.95 CAN / $10.95 USA

POETRY

LOVE MEDICINE AND ONE SONG by *Gregory Scofield*
"[Scofield's] lyricism is stunning; gets within the skin. Be careful. These songs are so beautiful they are dangerous."
— Joy Harjo
1-896095-27-5 • $16.95 CAN / $13.95 USA

TIME CAPSULE by *Pat Lowther*
Acclaimed poet Pat Lowther died tragically; her husband was convicted of her murder. *Time Capsule* consists of excerpts from a manuscript Lowther had prepared for publication at the time of her death and selected poems from previously published works.
1-896095-25-9 • $24.95 CAN / $19.95 USA

WHYLAH FALLS by *George Elliott Clarke*
Clarke writes from the heart of Nova Scotia's Black community. Winner of the Archibald Lampman Award.
0-919591-57-4 • $14.95 CAN / $12.95 USA

NON-FICTION

FLAPJACKS & PHOTOGRAPHS: *A History of Mattie Gunterman, Camp Cook and Photographer* by *Henri Robideau*
Mattie Gunterman purchased her first camera in 1897, at the age of 25. She spent the rest of her live chronicling life in the mining and forestry communities of eastern B.C. and northern Washington.
1-896095-03-8 • $24.95 CAN / $19.95 USA • photographs throughout

THE GARDEN LETTERS by *Elspeth Bradbury & Judy Maddocks*
"...lively anecdotes and humorous writings of the labours of life and gardening." — *The Guardian Weekend*
1-896095-35-6 • $19.95 CAN / $15.95 USA • illustrations throughout

SURVIVAL GEAR by *Rita Moir*
In the fishing community of Freeport, Nova Scotia, Moir comes to understand that survival can take many forms and rescue has many guises.
0-919591-81-7 • $14.95 CAN / $12.95 USA

Polestar titles are available from your local bookseller.
For a copy of our catalogue, contact:
POLESTAR BOOK PUBLISHERS, publicity office
103 – 1014 Homer Street
Vancouver, British Columbia
Canada V6B 2W9
http://mypage.direct.ca/p/polestar/